HUGH MCMILLAN was born in 1955 and lives in Penpont in Dumfries and Galloway. He is a poet and writer. He was the winner of the Smith Doorstep Poetry Competition in 2005, the Callum Macdonald Memorial Award in 2008, a winner in the Cardiff International Poetry Competition and was shortlisted for the Bridport Prize, the Michael Marks Award and the Basil Bunting Poetry Award in 2015. He is the recipient of five Arts Council or Creative Scotland Bursaries and been published, anthologised and broadcast widely in Scotland and abroad and translated into a variety of languages. An excellent reader of his own work, in recent years he has read to sell-out audiences in the Poetry Festivals of Wigtown, StAnza and Edmonton, Alberta.

McMillan's Galloway

A Creative Guide by an Unreliable Local

HUGH McMILLAN

Luath Press Limited
EDINBURGH
www.luath.co.uk

First published 2016

ISBN: 978-1-910745-18-2

The paper used in this book is
recyclable. It is made from
low chlorine pulps produced in a low
energy, low emissions manner from
renewable forests.

Printed and bound by
CPI Antony Rowe, Chippenham

Typeset in 10 point Sabon by
3btype.com

Contents

C

D

E

K

L

M

Acknowledgements

I have included these excerpts of poems or poems by contemporary poets with their permission, that of their publishers, or the holders of their copyright.

'Sundaywell' by Donald Adamson (from *Both Feet off the Ground*, Dumfries Libraries, 1993), 'What's Human' by Jean Atkin (from *Not Lost Since Last Time*, Overstep Books, 2013), 'Curling' by Angus Calder (from *Waking in Waikito*, Diehard Publishers, 1997), 'Tall Poppies' by Kirkpatrick Dobie (from *Collected Poems*, Peterloo Poets, 2003), 'Spelling Galloway' and 'The Cottage Garden, Clatteringshaws' by Davie Douglas (from *Spelling Galloway*, Grey Granite Press, 2013), 'Epistle to Twa Editors' by Bill Herbert (from *Mr Burns for Supper*, Greit Bogill Publications, 1996), 'Seagulls' by Brian McCabe (From *Body Parts*, Canongate Press, 1998), 'Jarama Valley' by Alec McDaid (from *The Book of the XV International Brigade*, The Commissariat for War Madrid, 1938), 'Mr Burns for Supper' and 'A Knell for Mr Burns' Willie Neill (from *Mr Burns for Supper*, Greit Bogill Publications, 1996), 'Dundrennan, Greyness, Lockerbie, The Marksman and Peel Tower' by Willie Neill (from *Selected Poems*, Canongate, 1992), 'From Criffel to Merrick' by Liz Niven (From *Cree Lines*, Watergaw, 2006), 'In Memoriam Solway Harvester' and 'Devorgilla's Legacy' by Liz Niven (from *Stravaigin*, Canongate, 2001), 'Douglas Hall' and 'No Summer Yet' by Stuart Paterson, 'Memorial and The Promised Land' by JB Pick (from *Being Here*, Markings, 2010), 'Pilgrim' by Tom Pow (from *Landscape and Legacies*, Lynx, 2003), 'Shopping Trolley River Nith, Mennock and Tom Pow on a Bike' by Rab Wilson (from *Life Sentence*, Luath Press 2009)

Foreword

WHEN HUGH MCMILLAN asked Luath to consider re-publishing his *Gallovidian Encyclopedia*, commissioned by the Wigtown Book Festival, I knew we were in trouble. The publisher, assuming I had read it along with the 'new and selected' anthology of his poetry I was currently chortling over, suddenly asked whether it was an Encyclopedia or a Gazetteer? I said 'pass'. Curiousity aroused, he asked, what's it about? I said 'Hugh McMillan', and he said 'pass'. Just joking, at least regarding that last bit. When I asked Hugh McMillan whether it was an Encyclopaedia or a Gazetteer, he of course said 'yes', which confirmed my strong suspicions that it was neither.

It was, in fact, something much more important: a writer's tour – incorporating occasional intemperate rants – round this rather off-the-beaten-track corner of south-west Scotland, with its colourful Covenanting and witch-drowning past, hopefully all behind it now, its huge skies and long coastline, its rural, still-working landscape, its Wigtown Book Town, its Kircudbright Artist's Colony, its Dumfries Pubs and their denizens (lovingly detailed by Hugh), its only Tory Westminster MP still left in Scotland, and Hugh McMillan, its indigenous award-winning poet and anarcho-syndicalist Yes-campaigner, former Dumfries Academy history teacher, and someone you should not approach after six-o'clock mid-week, or any time over the weekend, or you might well end up in a book like this or, worse, a poem.

One could say that *McMillan's Galloway* is an Encyclopaedia in the same way that the *Hitchhiker's Guide to the Galaxy* is a travel book. His Galloway is less a geographic than an imaginary space, an imagined place more like, built on and in dialogue with perspectives borrowed from those who have written, drawn, filmed or simply visited it in the past, including the recent past (see Anthony Hopkins' Bench) and including those who have lived and survived here over the centuries, its extremists and its ordinary people, who were often both – all of whom McMillan savours and argues with, or about, in ebullient and informative style as befits his literary and historical background and local cultural pursuits and interests.

In this fashion, he draws on writers, artists and film-makers associated with the place – religious fanatics, heretics, British fascists, Levellers – and the ordinary working population from tree-fellers to dykers – as witnesses to 'people's history' and so to their own epic survival and existence, revealed through their own language, inner thoughts, epic grudges and fluent expletives undeleted. Into the latter category, under the letter 'C' – alphabetical arrangement being one of the few resemblances Mr McMillan's book actually shares with normal Encyclopaediae, along with richly detailed subject matter – comes the entry titled 'Clatteringshaws Hydro Electric System as described by Keith Downes in the King's Hotel Dalbeattie 21 January 2014' – whose title alone probably qualifies as 'found poetry':

It's f ...... incredible, see the loch we ca Loch Ken, it's an artificial loch, ye ken? On an old tidal system, 6 dams, a third o the power o the whole Stewartry comes fae that, ken, it's a f..... great system, I'm proud as f.... of it. Built in the 1930s ken. It's incredible. I'd like you to see it. You'd be f...... dancing for joy when you see it, mukker, f...... dancing. Feenished in 1937, yon Tongland, what a great wee power station. See I'm a Stewartry man, born and bred. F.....Dumfries, C'mon now Dumfries has stolen New Abbey frae us, f........ Southerness, f....... Creeton's awa. It's a f.... land-grab by Dumfries, it's a f...... disgrace. A f...... conspiracy pure and simple. I'm makin too much noise am I? Should be shoutin it frae the rooftops. F...... disgrace. Pure and simple.

At one and the same time, this extract passes as oral history, cultural history, literary history, industrial history and social history – 'people's history' – rubbing shoulders with the real, the written, the imagined, the rumoured, the unprovable, the uncertain and the downright vexatious and funny. The same mix informs the bulk of the book. Our scribe, being a Latin scholar, and as shrewd as a mole-catcher, is of course wise enough to have guarded against any possible defamation suits by quoting Tacitus and David Malouf – 'Maybe, in the end, even the lies we tell define us' – which just might be enough to keep him from litigation and the publisher out of the small-claims court.

Mr McMillan's book, as he explains in his Introduction, initially set out in his own mind to be a kind of sequel to John Mactaggart's 1824 *Galloway Encyclopedia*, in some ways seeking to 'follow in the footsteps of one of the region's great self-taught and quirky geniuses'. He certainly manages that, scholarship rubbing shoulders with quirkiness verging on genius on many occasions, but I think there are more profound parallels to be drawn with Dr Johnson's great Dictionary, as described in this extract from the British Library: 'Thus the quotations reflect his literary taste and rightwing political views... Johnson was criticised for imposing his personality on to the book.' Of course, this is exactly what modern readers value most in literature, subjectivity and partiality, so long as the personality is strong enough to bear the scrutiny. What Hugh McMillan and Dr Johnson share, therefore, is not their politics, extreme though both are in forwarding their own opinions, but their extreme love of their native and also regional languages, especially as regards what Dr Johnson calls their 'energetic unruliness', matched by their own willingness to go to wherever that leads, and taking their readers with them. And like Dr Johnson in his epic work, Hugh McMillan is right bang in the centre of his book, whatever one wishes to call it, which for me is one of its chief delights.

This said, it was not until the letter 'D' was crested in what follows, specifically 'Dalbeattie Civic Week and Lawrence of Arabia' (please don't ask, just read), that another source of Mr McMillan's inspiration was allowed to escape, and which readers should perhaps be aware of from the outset, the American writer, Hunter S Thompson, author of *Fear and Loathing in Las Vegas* and many other titles. As Mr McMillan describes the influence: 'Hunter S Thompson invented the term gonzo journalism which is reporting that makes no claims to objectivity at all and which often includes the writer himself as part of the story'. Indeed, and I would say, thank goodness for that. And so, dear reader, you have now been amply warned, for this once hidden part of Scotland now stands revealed through the less than impartial eyes of one of its own, who also happens to be in my opinion one of our ablest and most entertaining writers – pure and simple – as Mr Keith Downes himself might have put it, down in the Stewartry.

Alistair Findlay

Introduction

Ubi solitudinem faciunt, pacem appellant.
They created a desert, and called it peace.

TACITUS ON CALGACUS

The Galloway landscape with its bleak mists and mudflats, glens and mountains, empty moors and ancient moss-covered stones has been the backcloth for countless poems, novels and films. It's a place where people have left and ghosts and whispers fill the gap: the crack of a shotgun, the fields of white turbines in the hazy distance, the ruined castles, the stars at night. It is a land made for dreams and nightmares. It is where the fairies last bade farewell to Scotland. A battlefield across a thousand years of history, its scattered people are still suggested by place names in Gaelic, Welsh, Norse, English. It was a land cleared of people, no less ruthlessly than in the highlands, a lawless land, a void filled by anarchic smugglers and reivers and levellers. It was a land of walkers, poets, geniuses. And now what is it? Traditional industries are dead. There are tourists of art, of history, of poetry. There are shooters, a book town, dark skies: Galloway is a blank page for people's fantasies. People come here, and they still work here, live and die, but overall, as it has ever been, the rhythm to life is the steady bleed of Galloway's young, taking their individualism and talent somewhere else.

Dumfries and Galloway has always been my home, my stomping ground. It is where I met my friends, my loves, it is where my kids were born, where I worked, where I found my sense of history, where I became a poet. All that would disqualify me from writing anything objective or scientific about the place but luckily I am required to do neither of these.

Instead I am required to follow the footsteps of one of the region's great self-taught and quirky geniuses, John Mactaggart.

Mactaggart was born of a poor family in Borgue. He did not have much patience for school but somehow, as it worked sometimes in the 19th century, the fact he had no qualifications at all did not stop him becoming a respected engineer, poet and writer. He published his *Scottish Gallovidian Encyclopedia* in 1824 and it was withdrawn from publication the year after following complaints by relatives of some of the people in it. He went to Canada to work and returned to die at the tragically young age of 38. At the time of his death a huge narrative poem called the *Engineer* was unfinished and unpublished. Cut forward 89 years and I am having a telephone interview for a commission to write a sequel to the *Gallovidian Encyclopedia*. I have just emerged from the Black Sea, covered with mud and full of rakiya. I envy other countries their independence, their certainties, but it can be boring knowing who you are and where you're going. Did I say that in the interview? The phone line wasn't very good and neither is my memory. Rakiya is tasteless but extremely powerful. After drinking it in Plovdiv once, I'm sure I saw the Kaiser on a surfboard. In the interview my voice has wings. I promise that it will be funny, and that it will be eccentric. I get the job. This was never going to be a work of ethnography, though it has drawn in the most part from the things people have said to me over the last several months or in the past. The stories here have not been scientifically collected but trawled at all times of the night and day. Some I have checked, but not all. What is truth after all? As a broken-down old history teacher I know the slipperiness of facts. This book unashamedly builds a shooglie layer of tales on those that have come before. Sometimes I have looked for resonances, echoes from Mactaggart or further back to posit a continuity or a coincidental link. It was fun doing that. Resonances remain as clearly as if they were caught still echoing in stone, and I have worked on ripples from the past as well as the testimony of living people. I have also injected myself, gonzo like, into proceedings throughout, and in this I am following the example of Mactaggart whose Encyclopaedia was very much Galloway through one very individual set of eyes.

Mactaggart's book was rich in Scots, a language that has been very much driven underground in the last hundred years, when so-called Standard English, a completely artificial construct, was thought of as the way to speak if you wanted to get on in life. Many of the people I spoke with recall being forbidden to, and even beaten for, speaking Scots in school. It has led to a loss of identity, a kind of linguistic disenfranchising which I feel very keenly myself. My mother was a native Gaelic speaker and my father's family, all miners from South Ayrshire, were Scots speakers, but ideally placed at the crossroads of two ancient tongues, I was left doing my version of the BBC because 'English was the language for scholars'. Scots as a commonly spoken language exists now, it seems to me, only in pockets in rural Wigtownshire and, most proudly, in the Upper Nith Valley where the schools take a keen interest in it. Scots words and phrases still exist everywhere, however, and I have included them here, or at least the ones I heard on my travels.

Also, like Mactaggart, I have filled the book with both poetry; mine and that of others I admire. We are lucky to be having a literary renaissance in Dumfries and Galloway, not that the rest of the country pays a blind bit of heed, and we have an excellent crop of poets with local, national and sometimes international reputations. I have used their work, though knowing only too well what a tricky bunch they are, I have been keen to seek their permission. If I missed anybody, I apologise.

Like the original Encyclopaedia, I hope this volume is unique, full of fun and good poetry. Although Mactaggart would recognise some things in here, the same feudal arrangements seem partly in place for instance, other things would be utterly foreign to him: Mactaggart's Galloway is not my Galloway. We are both in perfect agreement, however, that it is a weird and magical place.

And so I would launch this volume with a final toast – a Bladnoch 12-year-old, not a rakiya – to three recipients. First Mactaggart himself. Then Adrian Turpin and the Wigtown Book Festival without whose imagination and support this work would never have been written. Lastly the young people of Dumfries and Galloway, whose love for the place is, as ever it was, constantly in conflict with the need to make a living beyond it. Slainthe. Good Health to all.

A

Anthony Hopkins' Bench

An isolated bench in Douglas Hall overlooking the Solway Firth occupied at various instances by the Hollywood film stars Brian Cox and Anthony Hopkins. The bench is representative of a syndrome whereby people in the region believe that celebrities are living secretly in their midst, as in, when on one of these wee buses that circle the region relentlessly, some auld heid jerks a nicotined thumb in the direction of a farm track and says something like 'yon Claudia Schiffer lives doon there'.

Anthony Hopkins' Bench syndrome emanates from wishful thinking, as well as a kind of pride in Dumfries and Galloway's insular and highly remote landscape, as though folk with all the world to choose from couldn't see past sitting in the drizzle at the top of Auchengibbert Hill when they weren't partying in Monte Carlo or Cannes. Perhaps it's a folk memory of past glories too, from when the area was a frontier, strategically, economically and culturally important, when everybody who was anybody from Agricola to Walter Scott did indeed walk there.

Although some celebrities do stay in the area – Joanna Lumley has a house in Tynron, Alex Kapranos does yoga in Moniaive (though he's Scottish so that maybe doesn't count) – Anthony Hopkins' Bench syndrome is largely speaking a delusion unsupported by many facts. For every 'A-lister' who has lived here there are plenty who have visited and hated the place. Britt Ekland, while filming *The Wicker Man*, described Newton Stewart as 'The most dismal place in creation... one of the bleakest places I've been to in my life. Gloom and misery oozed out of the furniture.' Scarlett Johansson's feelings about being filmed in the moors round Wanlockhead in the middle of November pretending to be an alien harvesting hitchhikers' body parts are not recorded, but might also be imagined.

Nevertheless the legend and lure of Anthony Hopkins' Bench continues. Did Brian Cox really stride ashore from a boat and sit on it while taking a break during the filming of *The Master of Ballantrae*? Did another local spot a holidaying Anthony Hopkins on the same seat? I'm told so, and I'd like to think so too. For every superstar who thinks karaoke in Creetown is not her cup of tea, there must be many a soulful one drawn to the lonely, mythic land and seascape.

See Anwoth, Douglas Fairbanks Junior, Village of the Damned

Anwoth

A small parish near Gatehouse containing a highly atmospheric ruined church which featured in the cult film *The Wicker Man*. The church itself was that of a very Presbyterian minister, Samuel Rutherford, who in the early 17th century was a highly articulate and well-regarded scholar, though a non-conformist who, career wise, came to a bad end. A very large and rather penile monument dedicated to him is on the hillside above. This place, according to one account a century ago, 'suggests a humility and reticence that are in keeping with its finest associations'. What an irony therefore that its best known association now is with *The Wicker Man*, variously described as 'a barbarous joke, too horrible for pleasure' (*The Sunday Times*) and as 'a beautifully filmed story of primitive sex rituals' (the *Evening News*). Is it just one of a whole nest of ironies that the church of this very religious and dogmatic man was used in this most pagan and chaotic of enterprises? In history, mind you, Rutherford fell foul of the prevailing religious orthodoxy and was disgraced in the end. Fell from grace, so to speak. Like his church. Like the film.

I have a fair idea what he would have made of *The Wicker Man*, with its portable phalluses and its crew's anarchic occupation of the area for a suitably biblical span of 40 days and 40 nights in the spring of 1973. In the film, the church comprised part of the pagan island of Summerisle, where the failing apple crop called for the sacrifice of a virgin, namely the policeman called Howie, played by Edward Woodward who, while investigating the disappearance of a young girl, was really being set up for a ritualistic slaying. According to the script Howie was meant, for reasons I don't understand, to be an Episcopalian from the west of Scotland. I had always assumed he was a Wee Free, or certainly some form of extreme Protestant: it enhanced my enjoyment of the burning scene to imagine this.

This religious confusion is just one of the very many anachronisms and mysteries of *The Wicker Man* which, while portraying a mythic version of Galloway, created as many myths itself, some of which people are still trying to puzzle out. I have laced the film through various entries in this book because in so many ways it seems to sum up some important truths about the region, and its continuing association with the double-headed god of reality and myth, the difficult marriage between what you see and what you believe.

The church played an important and atmospheric part of the film, its ruinous condition being used to demonstrate how far Summerisle had rejected Christianity. In the churchyard Howie finds the missing girl Rowan's grave. Nearby, a gravestone, a prop specially made for the film, reads, 'Here lieth Beech Buchanan, protected by the ejaculation of serpents.' A woman inside the church sits, breastfeeding a new born baby. Rowan's grave contains only a joke; the body of a hare, the old symbol of death and rebirth. The actress who played the breastfeeding woman, Barbara Rafferty, describes the month on location as one of the most entertaining periods of her life; 'My daughter Amy and I had a wonderful paid holiday. It was marvellous.' She had a month's stay for a 30 second scene because her filming was always being delayed. She thought there was something hugely dodgy about the whole enterprise, 'everyone did', but she wasn't complaining. When her turn came she sat on the gravestone, holding an egg and breastfeeding her child. 'Edward came in,' she recalled, 'and said "Oh my God, what's happened?" and I had to look a bit witchy.' I think Edward Woodward could have been playing Samuel Rutherford at that point – or at least I thought that, until I came across a strange account describing Rutherford. 'His indulgence in erotic imagery when he is dealing with spiritual relations and affections offends modern minds,' said a minister of the early 20th century. How great. Rutherford as Lord Summerisle. Maybe the giant phallus on the hillside is not so misplaced.

The cottage opposite Anwoth Church, a holiday let, is much in demand for *Wicker Man* fans, needless to say. The area retains a timeless, unspoilt gloom, enhanced by the tall pine trees enclosing it. In Allan Brown's *Inside the Wicker Man*, Edward Woodward is described revisiting the area in 1998 and casually picking up the wooden cross he had made as Howie and discarded during filming, which was still lying in the grass 25 years after it was thrown down.

A suitably gothic postscript occurred when Craig McKay of Castle Douglas CID was called to Anwoth House a few years ago to investigate the finding of a human skull by one of the household's chocolate Labradors. When he got there, the lady of the house had the skull sitting on the sideboard. 'It was stained brown, shiny, just sitting there, quite the thing.' The forensic team was called in and the skull was found to be two centuries old. The labradors had been chasing rabbits, found the skull and came home pleased as punch. A wee investigation revealed a gravedigger had been tidying up some of the graves. 'I gave it to him,' said Craig, 'I think he just poked it back in. I never asked.'

We ask in vain for volunteers
to leave this world of doubt and
 dreams
and enter that teetotal land
where everything is what it seems
('The Promised Land', JB PICK)

*See **Anthony Hopkins' Bench,
Village of the Damned***

Art

When I worked at Dumfries Academy we used to have an old storeroom where we kept obscure books, piles of mouldering photies, bric-a-brac, all sorts. Very occasionally I used to go in search of some learned tome, *Percival's History of the Sassanid Empire* for instance, and tut with irritation at a dirty old canvas of obscure theme which lay underfoot, its glass cracked. Many people stood on this over a period of years, and no one bothered to pick it up. This painting turned out to be *Rose Window Cathedral* by Sir Robin Philipson RSA, donated to the school and later flogged for more than £35,000 once somebody realised what it was. This episode, which does me no credit at all, does however reveal that I know little about art, though I do later in this book extol the virtues of the magical Chrissie Fergusson. In any case, to overcome my shortcomings on this topic, I have chosen to take the famous Kirkcudbright painter EA Hornel out to the pub for a pint to ask him a series of questions on art rather than make it all up myself.

In the Selkirk Arms EA Hornel is dressed rather fetchingly in a lovat green knickerbocker suit with a long coat and drinking a whisky mac, equal measures of Grouse and Ginger Wine. He is a prepossessing looking man with a disarmingly intense gaze, maybe the result of chronic myopia. He refuses to wear spectacles and carries with him a large magnifying glass in case he needs to read anything more closely.

ME: Edward, let's cut to the chase. I've known lots of artists and a more bitchy crew I've never met, apart perhaps from writers. They can't agree on the colour of piss. They're pretty mixed about you. What's been your most important achievement in your working life would you say?

EA: I disagree with the premise. The circle of painters and kindred spirits fostered here in these historic and beautiful surroundings forged friendships that supported and nourished the gifts each one was given. I had friends like Jessie

King and Willie Robson and the Fergussons. Of course there are among creative people often tensions.

ME: I like the way Chrissie Fergusson makes Dumfries and Galloway look Mediterranean. It probably didn't rain as much in your day, did it?

EA: Summer here brought exquisite colours with no parallel in other parts, but when it rained, it rained.

ME: Why did you never marry?

EA: What's that got to do with the price of cheese? I thought you were going to ask about art?

ME: Okay then, why did you stop experimenting with the controversial but innovative use of patchworks of colour, such as in your work *Summer* for instance, where the figures seem organically joined with the background, and start instead painting twee pictures of wee lassies rolling about in grass?

EA: The artist wants most of all to present his ideal of vision without regard to tradition, but at the end of the day he also needs to buy the groceries. And people couldn't get enough of art that showed a romanticised view of the countryside.

ME: You sold out then? At the end were you not photographing wee girls and painting the results? Had it not become a lucrative formula?

EA (*exasperated*): I turned down a fellowship from the Royal Scottish Academy. I denounced my critics as incompetent to express an opinion about the weather never mind art like mine which celebrates the world in all its glorious garbs. I am a friend of poets, of barefoot travellers who know they will receive here a roof over their heads and the warmth of an open heart.

(*He stands up*)

ME (*also standing*): What's this obsession with wee girls anyway?

EA (*reaching for stick*): I suppose you think you're far more revolutionary you smart arse. I bet you're on expenses.

(*A small scuffle ensues*)

ME (*later, seated, breathing*

heavily): If you'd been alive what would you have made of the public art in the region, say Andy Goldsworthy's *Striding Arches* or Matt Baker's work in New Luce or the various installations done by, among others, the Stove initiative in Creetown?

EA (*perfectly composed*): Art above all is there to give a message in a unique and challenging way. But I also detect in these enterprises an attempt to contextualise, to present a work which speaks not just of the artist but of time and place and even community. I find it interesting. Last time my driver Sam Henderson took me to the villages round about here I found them sadly changed. My art set out to glorify the landscape. These pieces seem wistful, like a commemoration, and in some ways are carrying on a long tradition of trading on a lost landscape. But art carries on as an expression of the sublime, in many forms. Do you know that Pink Floyd's co-manager Andrew King lives here in Kirkcudbright and has all the Pink Floyd album covers on his wall? Now all that mystical LSD-inspired stuff remind me very much of some of my esoteric work, especially the *Druids, Bringing in the Mistletoe*? Do you know it? One of the druids looks like Syd Barrett.

Actually I think (*signalling to barmaid for another round*) that the crowning achievement of my later years was in fact my library, which in terms of its accumulation of the rich literature and lore of Dumfries and Galloway was second to none. No one loved Galloway and its inhabitants more than me. Do you need the receipt?

*See **Chrissie Fergusson, EA Hornel, Midnight in Stavanger, Villages of the Damned***

Away with the Fairies

A term, sometimes derogatory, used to describe someone with an unworldly aspect, or lacking in common sense, practicality or logic, as in 'Don't ask him, he's away with the fairies.'

Of course being away with the fairies was once a literal condition in Scotland, and especially in Galloway, one of Scotland's most fairy-infested parts, and the area of the country where, the legends agree, the fairies held their last strongholds. Infestation is rather a cruel term but it's certainly true that being away with the fairies was a mixed blessing. George Douglas in his *Scottish Fairy and Folk Tales* described Annandale as:

> the last Border refuge of those beautiful and capricious beings, the fairies. Many old people yet living... continue to tell that in the ancient of days the fairies danced on the hill... Their visits to the earth were periods of joy and mirth to mankind, rather than of sorrow and apprehension. They played on musical instruments of wonderful sweetness and variety of note,

spread unexpected feasts, the supernatural flavour of which overpowered on many occasions the religious scruples of the Presbyterian shepherds.

Powerful food indeed to do that. The Corriedale fairies described by Douglas interbred with the locals in a kind of mixed race Brigadoon-like harmony. There are many other stories too of the fairies' benevolence to humans, especially in return for kindness. When the Knight of Myrton, Sir Godfrey McCulloch, received a visit from the King of the Fairies complaining that a sewer he was having built was undermining the fairy kingdom, he immediately diverted it. This was a good move because the King of the Fairies turned up at Godfrey's execution in Edinburgh and spirited him away just before the axe.

Many other sources show the fairies' dark side, however. The beautiful fairy girl of Cairnywellan Head near Port Logan, for instance, was a rose-complexioned 12 year old who could be seen dancing and singing wildly when fugitives of the Irish rebellion of 1798 were found in the Rhinns and summarily shot or hung by the militia. She disappeared for 50 years but couldn't contain her glee when the Potato Famine broke out and was soon out in the hills, again, dancing to celebrate the mounting body count. The story of the fairy boy of Borgue can be found in the records of the Kirk Session there. This boy would disappear for days or weeks on end, saying he had been with his 'people'. His grandfather sought help from a priest who banished the fairies. Thereafter the boy was shunned in the community, not because he'd been away with the fairies but because he'd got the help of a Catholic. Trust Dumfries and Galloway to have the only anti-Catholic fairy stories.

Fairy abduction is a classic theme. It's only too easy to believe that the child who's just posted all your credit cards through the neighbours' letter boxes is not in fact yours at all, but a changeling, and that if only you could get your mild-mannered one back things would be okay. Changeling stories range all over the region.

Unattended cradles and neglectful nannies were opportunities for the fairies to abduct children and leave in their place spiteful and weird counterparts that you really wouldn't want to show off to your friends. Unlike your real children, however, you could get rid of changelings in a variety of ways, for instance riddling them with rowan smoke until they disappear up the chimney, as happened to Tammy McKendrick in Kirkinner. Rowan of course is a tree that wards off evil, the reason you see so many planted in sacred spots or churchyards. My mother used to make rowan jelly and feed it to people she didn't like but I'm not sure they went away any quicker.

Adults also disappeared, sometimes voluntarily, sometimes as a dare or punishment. Thomas the Rhymer, stories of whom are found right across the Scottish Borders, went partly out of curiosity and partly because he was asked by a very alluring woman:

A lady that was brisk and bold,
Come riding o'er the ferny brae.
Her skirt was of the grass-green silk,

Her mantle of the velvet fine;
At every lock of her horse's mane,
Hung fifty silver bells and nine.`

('The Ballad of Thomas the
Rhymer', 18th century Scots ballad)

At the Cove of the Grennan near
Luce Bay, sailors used to throw
bread ashore for the fairies to
ensure a good voyage round the
Mull of Galloway. There was a
fairy cave which led by a narrow
passage all the way through to
Clonyard Bay on the west coast.
Everyone avoided it but one day a
piper was dared to explore it. He
strode in with his dog. The sound
of the pipes echoed deeper and
deeper then stopped. The dog,
traumatised and completely bald,
finally emerged from the cave at
Clonyard Bay but the piper was
never seen again. It is said, of
course, that on windless nights
you can still hear the faint sound
of the pipes, which is not unlikely
really given the number of pipers
and pipe bands in the area. But
why just on windless nights? In
my experience a good piper can
cut through a gale.

As is explained elsewhere in
this book, Galloway was the last
stronghold of the ancient folk,
leaving from Burrowhead, though
their influence long remained. In
A Forgotten Heritage, Hannah
Aitken quotes Galloway roadmen
who in 1850 refused to cut down
an ancient thorn tree to widen the
road between Glenluce and
Newton Stewart because it was
'fairy property'. The tree stood
for a further 70 years. Nevertheless
the fairies were victims, no less
than other endemic species, of
agricultural improvements, their
green habitats ploughed over, the
land preached over by successions
of Calvinist ministers, no matter
how the fairies occasionally
subverted the message.

It's a sad world without fairies,
but are they really gone? Very
recently I was in a public house in
the centre of the region. I was
meeting and interviewing a man
who said he had been abducted
by aliens. I like the idea of beings
from outer space and really want
them to exist but am sceptical
about tales of abduction, which
can often be excuses for other
kinds of behaviour. A wee bit like
thinking your badly brought up
kids are changelings. I was struck,

for instance, when looking at the so-called 'Falkirk Triangle' tales of the 1990s how often the abductees are men coming home late from the pub:

Lorrayne
before you hit me with that object
shaped like a toblerone
let me explain.
We only went for a half pint and a
    whisky
then set off home but somehow
lost two hours on a thirty minute
    journey.
My mind's a blank
but Brian clearly saw
Aliens with black eyes and no lips
leading us onto a kind of craft.
I tried to lash out, explain that I
    was late,
but they used some kind of
    numbing ray on me:
it put me in this state.
Lorrayne, don't you see what it
    explains?
All the times I crawled home with
    odd abrasions.
Put that down Lorrayne,
don't you see I have to go again,
for the sake of future generations?

('The X-Files Bonnybridge')

As far as I know the man I was talking to is the only such abductee in Dumfries and Galloway although the area is an extremely fertile one for sightings of alien spacecraft or UFOs. He insisted on anonymity but told me he had been taken from his home and returned several days later after various procedures had been made under some form of painless anaesthetic. He seemed to have been away for days he said, but when he was returned home he found no time had passed at all. If it hadn't been for the painless anaesthetic, it all sounded very much to me like a visit to the dentists. However, the procedures were described in detail, though I am not allowed to annotate them here, and he seemed quite sincere, though nervous in the telling of his story. The aliens he said were 'small and big eyed'. Time, he said, 'seemed to be suspended'. He couldn't tell 'if they were good or bad'. He was returned 'unharmed'.

When he left, and I was finishing my pint, the bar owner beckoned me over and said, 'He's away wi the fairies, by the way.' Of course, he was. Small people, morally ambivalent, time standing still; the echoes are obvious. It's as though, having mastered our geography to such an extent that we can't believe the fairies could share the same physical space as us, we've had to re-invent them in outer space.

Having said that I've met several folk in my travels who'll swear to having seen fairies, though most are talking about many years ago. An exception is Scott Maxwell, dyker and travelling folk singer, who swears he was taken in the back of a van once to a fairy pool up in the hills near Moffat: 'It was two lassies, like. They wouldn't let me see where I was going, but when I got there it was like nothing I'd ever seen. Moving lights, like the sun in the water really bright, really brilliant but it was a dull day. There was something there, I cannae explain it, still cannae explain it.'

See Mull of Galloway, Myrton and Monreith Bay , Unrequited Love and Guilt, Pine Martens, Things that Go Blink in the Night

B

Badges

The palm trees of Whithorn are bending in the wind. Debbie Mcclymont, curator of the Whithorn Priory like her father before her, and part-time barmaid of the Railway Inn, has just been on the phone to Historic Scotland. 'That big oak was making some noise last night. There were two trees once, a beech and an oak. They said the beech would never come down and it did. That oak's right over the house, could kill us all.' She seems relatively cheerful about it, and loves living in the old 16th century schoolhouse that overlooks the ancient site. 'When I was young my friends would wait for me in the street, they were scared to come through the dark. It never bothered me, it's a privilege living there.'

The priory is closed in the winter, hence the bar job. 'Whole town runs on tourism, really. We get a lot of folk here on pilgrimage. Not this time of year, of course, so it's all shut up. Ninian's Cave brings a lot of people, some walk from Mochrum or from further in

easy stages.' Ninian, our native saint but not our patron saint, has been a magnet for a lot of people here over the ages; Scottish royals in need of forgiveness like Bruce and James IV and plenty more humble people too.

Later at the Isle of Whithorn I'm overhearing a group of young folk, visitors like myself, but not so very humble. They're talking about the forthcoming referendum on Scottish independence, a subject close to my heart. They've seen the large blue badge on my bag and are loudly predicting that they'll need passports to cross the border soon. I bury myself in a pint of Guinness. This part of Galloway has always played host to waves of immigrants and invaders and only one set has ever been required to produce passports. In 1427 James I issued a safe conduct for English pilgrims to Whithorn and the religious sites round about on the condition that they talk about absolutely nothing except devotional topics, wear one badge on their way to Whithorn and one on the way back to the boat and leave no later than 15 days after they arrive. James hated the English and loved badges in equal measure actually: he personally spent 13 shillings on religious badges between the years 1504–5.

I inadvertently catch an eye.

'Will we need a passport?'

'How long have you been visiting?' I ask, pleasantly.

'A fortnight', a gentleman in plus fours says.

'Tomorrow would be your last day then', I say, adding hurriedly, 'if this was the time of James I'.

See **Ritual Roads**

Bank Managers, SR Crockett and the British Union of Fascist Lifeguards

If you don't count the intelligence services, I have only been in trouble with the authorities twice. Once when I was a boy and my next door neighbour shot an elderly woman in the bottom from my skylight window as she was weeding her flower bed, and another time when I wrote a rather intemperate letter to my bank manager accusing him of being 'rat faced' and a 'Nazi' when he refused me an extension to my overdraft facility. He did not object to being called rat faced – how could he? The evidence was there for everyone to see – but he did take exception to being called a Nazi. He was in fact a pillar of the village near

Dalbeattie where he lived, a Rotarian, active in his local Conservative Party, a member of the golf club and not a Nazi at all. Of course, I apologised.

It is a fact, however, that the biggest branch in Scotland of the British Union of Fascists was in Dalbeattie and was led by the son of a local bank manager, James Little, who was Town Clerk. They had more than 400 members in the town and the countryside round about. Dumfries had 120 members and the area was described in the BUF's newspaper as the 'cradle of fascism in Scotland'.

The *Galloway News* of 14 April 1934 describes a meeting held in Dumfries by Oswald Mosley:

Great interest was taken in the visit to Dumfries last Friday night of Sir Oswald Mosley, the leader of the British Union of Fascists and a brilliant orator. The demonstration held in the Drill Hall was attended by over three thousand people and although efforts were made by Communists to hold up the meeting by organised interruptions they were effectively dealt with by the large body of Blackshirts who attended as stewards. There were several lively melees when interrupters were forcibly ejected and two of the stewards received injuries.

Why did fascism catch on in Dumfries and Galloway? Almost certainly because the area was, still is, deeply conservative.

Conservatism doesn't equate with fascism of course but it provided fertile ground for the highly patriotic and romantic delusions of early British fascism. Alistair Livingston, a political blogger and analyst who lives in Castle Douglas notes:

> From 1931 until 1997, when the SNP won in Galloway and Labour in Dumfriesshire, the region was solidly Conservative – apart from a narrow SNP win in Galloway in October 1974 which was reversed by the Tories in the next election.

In his blog, Livingstone describes a dinner given on 28 September 1906 in SR Crockett's honour in Dalbeattie:

> Amongst those attending was 'Councillor Jack' of Dalbeattie whose son was later to become a BUF member and James Little, whose son was to become leader of the local fascists.

After toasts to 'The King' and 'The Imperial Forces', Major Gilbert McMicking, Liberal MP for Kirkcudbrightshire and then Galloway from 1906–1922, made a long speech in which he emphasised that:

> the health and vitality of the Empire would increasingly rely on the health and vitality of Britain's rural rather than urban population. Mosley's meeting in Dumfries was likewise peppered with references to agriculture and the land. This mystical attachment, symbiosis, between society and the rural is evident in Nazi theories. Only through a re-integration of humanity into the whole of nature

can our people be made stronger. That is the fundamental point of the biological tasks of our age... this striving toward connectedness with the totality of life, with nature itself, a nature into which we are born, this is the deepest meaning and the true essence of National Socialist thought.

(Ernst Lehmann. Lehmann was a professor of botany who characterised National Socialism in Germany as 'politically applied biology'.)

What has this to do with SR Crockett, whose harmless stories have been entertaining people for generations and whose popularity at the time of the banquet described above was at its height?

After the savage economic reorganisation which followed enclosures, emigration and depopulation become the key motifs of Galloway. Where Burns' poetry is pithy, connected, grounded in real life, the writers that come after are dealing with an emptying landscape. Their work is often a whimsical invocation of life as it once was, or, in fact, as it never was. Art of the period too portrays bronzed country folk in a variety of idealised rural settings.

Crockett was a perfect makar for the ghost landscape, the same one artists and writers in the area struggle to interpret and interact with today. This is the second verse of a poem Robert Louis Stevenson dedicated to Crockett:

Grey recumbent tombs of the dead
    in desert places,
Standing Stones on the vacant
    wine-red moor,
Hills of sheep, and the howes of the
    silent vanished races,
And winds, austere and pure!

('To S.R. Crockett', Robert Louis Stevenson)

As the region became a playground for the rich, as it now becomes a playground for the tourist to indulge his or her fantasies about landscape and history, is it a wonder that Galloway was for a while the focus for one of history's great romantic delusions, fascism? Of course, as in all interpretations of history, there might be a far simpler reason. It was just plain good fun being a fascist. These are extracts from the magazine *The Blackshirt*:

Scottish Blackshirts are well to the fore in sports, and inter-branch tug of-war contests are being arranged. It is hoped also that there will be a contest between an English and a Scottish team.

Next winter there will be at least six Blackshirt football teams in South of Scotland, and negotiations for a Blackshirt Football League are being made.

The Dumfries Life-Saving Team have been greatly augmented, and now patrols a 80-mile stretch along the Solway coast.

Blackshirts Life-Saving patrols upon the shores of the Solway Firth are much appreciated and their ambulance men have already handled 12 minor cases.

So great was the attendance at a Whist Drive and Dance held in the Queensberry Hotel, Dumfries that a larger hall is being taken for the next one.

*See **Ghost Landscape, Jarama, Makar***

Barbados House

Just back from the film *Belle* which was not to my taste but was based upon the true story of Dido Elizabeth Belle, the illegitimate mixed race daughter of the nephew of William Murray, first Earl of Mansfield and later Lord Chief Justice of England.

The film deals with her imaginary love affair with a lawyer and a court case which prefigures the abolition of slavery in Britain. It also deals much with social attitudes of the time. The inspiration for the film is actually

a painting of Dido by Johann Zoffany, a German artist with a highly interesting past, including a shipwreck in the Andaman Islands in the course of which the survivors ate one of their number in order to stay alive, thus making Zoffany, in the words of the writer William Dalrymple, 'the only member of the Royal Academy who was also a cannibal'. This painting is currently in Scone Palace and shows Dido with her white cousin, the two portrayed as equals.

Apart from the cannibal artist, and a much more interesting story if you ask me – so interesting that author Donna Brewster wrote about it recently – is that of Margaret McGuffie, daughter of Wigtownshire merchant John McGuffie who had made a mint trading in Barbados. While there he had a love affair with a mulatto, Mary Ann Stenhouse, and fathered two illegitimate children whom at the time he did not officially acknowledge. He returned to Wigtown, became Provost and constructed a sumptuous mansion, Barbados House. Six years later his daughter Margaret tracked him down and instead of rejecting her he welcomed her in as his heir.

After his death on a trip to Liverpool, she inherited the house and lived there for another 35 years, 'The Black Lady', waited on by white servants. On her death, the fortune was left to her brother's children in the West Indies who used it to relocate to North America. Margaret seemed to be respected in the community, her immense wealth, I'm sure, enabling the locals to temporarily overcome their prejudices.

Unfortunately, the same cannot be said regarding the treatment allegedly shown to another black and illegitimate offspring a century or so later, Jerry Rawlings.

See Jerry Rawlings

Barrie, JM

Perhaps because I trod the same ground as him for so many years, in Dumfries Academy, and saw his name on the prize boards at the school, his photographs on the wall and even the section of desk he carved his name on, I've always been interested in JM Barrie; all four foot ten inches of

him. He has a huge literary reputation, soon to be fostered further, I hope, when the newly restored Moat Brae House in Dumfries becomes a museum and children's literature centre. He was, however, a very strange man.

Johnny Depp's film portrayal of Jimmy with Kate Winslet as Sylvia

Llewelyn Davies in *Finding Neverland* presents the view of Barrie as a kindly uncle who, after their parents' tragic and early death (both the Llewelyn Davies parents died of cancer aged 44) adopted their five sons, Jack, Peter, Michael, Nicholas and George Barry, having met the family while walking his St Bernard in Kensington Gardens. The truth is perhaps more complicated. I do not believe that Barrie was a sexual predator or paedophile, though some passages in his stories, especially *The White Bird*, an early version of Peter Pan, are pretty peculiar:

> David and I had a tremendous adventure. It was this – he passed the night with me… I took [his boots] off with all the coolness of an old hand, and then I placed him on my knee, and removed his blouse. This was a delightful experience, but I think I remained wonderfully calm until I came somewhat too suddenly to his little braces, which agitated me profoundly… I cannot proceed in public with the disrobing of David.

In fact Barrie seems curiously asexual. His marriage, from 1894–1909, appears to have been unconsummated. His interest in children seemed born less out of a desire to corrupt them and more from his own obsession to return to a childlike state of innocence. He probably felt he had a lot to escape from. Barrie was damaged goods by his early teens. He was ignored by his father and the victim of psychological abuse from his mother, who never recovered from the death of Barrie's older brother, and who possibly blamed the younger boy in some way for the skating accident that led to the death. After it, his mother addressed James constantly as David, the name of his dead brother and to appease her he often wore his dead brother's clothes.

The case against Barrie, most recently stated in a brilliant if speculative new biography by Piers Dudgeon, is that he was fascinated by the power of manipulation and set out to control the lives of a regiment of young children – not just the Llewelyn Davies – with invariably tragic results. The ghosts of dead or damaged children stalk Barrie's work. He befriended, for instance, a little girl called Margaret Henley, who used to call him 'my friendy', lisped as 'my fwendy'. The girl died aged six but lived on in Barrie's world as Wendy in Peter Pan.

Barrie was fascinated by the writer George Du Maurier, author of the Victorian sensation *Trilby* in which an innocent girl is controlled by hypnosis by the evil Svengali. Barrie was so obsessed with the book and the man that he followed Du Maurier about but never dared meet him, once reportedly running away when the man approached him. He called the St Bernard dog that he and his wife adored Porthos, after the St Bernard in one of Du Maurier's other novels, *Peter Ibbetson*. This St Bernard was to make an appearance in Peter Pan but more immediately significant is that George Du Maurier's daughter was Sylvia who married Arthur Llewelyn Davies and had five boys, the children Barrie 'accidentally met' and befriended in Kensington Gardens. Sylvia's brother was the famous actor Gerald Du Maurier (who met his future wife rehearsing in the Barrie play *The Admirable Crichton*). Barrie also befriended this family, especially Gerald's young daughters, one of whom was to ascribe many of her later problems to the early part of her life and her strange relationship with both her father and her 'Uncle Jimmy'. The name of this young girl? Daphne Du Maurier, who was to go on and write another classic of psychological manipulation and control, *Rebecca*.

While Sylvia Llewelyn Davies was on her deathbed Barrie, then divorced, said that she had agreed to marry him, a story that her sons never believed. He also forged his name on Sylvia's will to make it appear that her wish was for Barrie to become guardian of her children. In reality, Sylvia had left a handwritten document, which said:

> What I wd like wd be if Jenny wd come to Mary & that the two together wd be looking after the boys & the house.

Mary was the boys' longstanding and faithful nanny, and Jenny was Mary's sister. Barrie changed Jenny to Jimmy. The 'error' in transcribing was never challenged, unbelievably, by the Llewelyn Davies boys' many other relatives.

Perhaps all this is overstated. It's a fact that few people that knew him closely had a bad word to say about him. Perhaps also the era he lived in with the grim shadow of the Great War and its slaughter of the innocents casts a gloomy light on everything he wrote and the events that surrounded it.

DH Lawrence said that 'JM Barrie has a fatal touch for those he loves'. The Llewelyn Davies boys felt that touch most keenly. George was killed in the trenches in 1915, Michael drowned in a suicide pact with another young man in 1921, Jack died from lung disease and Peter waited until 1960 to throw himself in front of a train. Only Nicholas escaped, his attitude to Barrie unsoured.

*See **Minerva***

Berthing the Big Boats

Sitting on the rocks outside Corsewall Lighthouse I watch the P&O and Stena Ferries carefully nudging out into the open sea, passing each other as they sail between Cairnryan and Larne. These are pretty big ships and it is a pretty big operation, so it was a surprise when a Stranraer man told me:

> of course whaun they used tae cam in here, the man wha was in charge o docking them used to da it by walkie talkie fram the pub. You used tae hear tham asking 'everything clear, ok?' and he used ta say 'aye fine' while ordering anather pint. You'd think they'd ha chosen a pub whar they could at least ha watched out the windae.

Needless to say I told him I didn't believe a word of it.

Bobby Dalrymple, Winston Churchill and the Science of Coincidence

Bobby Dalrymple of Newton Stewart, having just shown an approving gaggle of spectators the mark of an adder bite he'd got as a boy on Cairnsmore, moves effortlessly onto a discourse on the science of coincidence.

'Is it not bloody strange,' he asks us, rhetorically, 'My Grandfather Bobby was in the KOSB, and was killed in Cape Hellas in Gallipoli on the 4 June 1915, his body was never found, though he's on the memorial there. My youngest brother is going in October to see it, by the way. Anyway, do you know the Turkish man who's got the cafe across the road?' Everybody nods. 'Aye, a really good man. Anyway I was telling him all this and – this is completely kosher now, he showed me the proof – his grandfather was killed in exactly the same place on exactly the same day, except fighting on the other side. Is that no incredible now?' Everybody agrees.

Bobby doesn't like Winston Churchill, the architect of the disaster at Gallipoli, and not only does he blame him for his grandfather's death but also his grannie's sister's death. 'He was that desperate to get the Americans in the war that he set up the sinking of the Lusitania in 1915, just off County Cork in Ireland, and my great aunt was on board coming back from New York and was drowned. Two women from Gatehouse were on deck and survived, you know. They're born lucky in Gatehouse, no even Winston Churchill could get them.' Everybody nods. 'Born lucky', they mutter.

*See **Dalbeattie Civic Week and Lawrence of Arabia***

Bodkin

One of my doctors years ago was clearly more ill than me. He was, in fact, mad and often referred to himself as Doctor Bodkin, the personal physician of Tsar Nicholas II. I knew this to be impossible as he would have had to be at least 123 years old. Bodkin's preferred diagnostic method was to give you pills that were completely useless then, when your symptoms persisted, advise you to give the pills up because they were obviously making you ill. Bizarrely this treatment occasionally worked. Bodkin disappeared from the profession some years ago under mysterious circumstances and was replaced by someone very efficient from Somalia, and illness, though less hazardous, was never as much fun again. The rumour was that Bodkin had finally poisoned someone.

Strangely enough a doctor from Skipmyre near Lochmaben, Dr James Mounsey, was in real life the personal physician of, first, the Empress Elizabeth of Russia, and then her successor Tsar Peter III in 1761–2. They both died shortly after his appointment, Peter from poisoning followed by strangulation. His widow Catherine, possibly fearing for her own life, pensioned Mounsey off five days later. He is still celebrated in Russia for the medical reforms he introduced, if not the survival rate of his patients. Bodkin would have been proud.

Talking of dead emperors, Archibald Arnott from Eccelfechan, a near contemporary of Mounsey, was the Emperor Napoleon's physician in his exile on St Helena. There is a deal of historical debate about Napoleon's death, and many have said that he did not die of stomach cancer, as his father had and as the official report stated, but rather liver failure due to poisoning. Archibald Arnott was at the autopsy and at the funeral where, like a Russian doll, Napoleon was sealed in four coffins, two of mahogany, two of lead. Of course this is all speculation.

Ecclefechan was also the birthplace of a doctor who wasn't associated with the slaughter of major historical figures but had another celebrity patient, Emmeline Pankhurst. Dr Flora Murray was a lieutenant colonel, making her the highest ranking woman in the British army in World War One, and ran a military hospital in London from 1915–19. She was a radical feminist, and had been, prior to the war, the official doctor of the WSPU, the Women's Social and Political Union, treating many hunger-striking Suffragettes after their release from Holloway Prison.

*See **Burns, his Murder***

Book Town

Fitting perfectly into the new dawn of cultural tourism and explorations of different types of landscape comes Wigtown, a decrepit rural town rescued, after the death of its dairy industry, by books. The idea that people might want to travel to a place simply to experience the joy of books is not a new one but it has become, in an age where speed and instant gratification is the norm, a way in which people can entertain ideas of slowness, nostalgia and alternative living usually in a rural or peripheral location. Booktowns such as Wigtown are for people who yearn for:

> space for new ways of thinking, communing with others, and pleasurable intellectual immersion... aesthetic values and ethical practices... a locale with an ambience of heritage, scenic beauty and nostalgia, perfect as the setting for book-based leisure.

(*Slow Books: A Meeting of Landscape and Literature.* Article by Jane Frank in the Queensland Review 2016)

Booktowns also provide a much needed catalyst for rural regeneration. The creation of book towns as a way of reviving local communities is a new and world-wide phenomenon, inspired hugely by the experience of Richard Booth in Hay-on-Wye, the first book town, who was on the expert panel entrusted with the job of choosing the site for Scotland's first book town in 1998. Interestingly, he did not opt for Wigtown due to its extreme remoteness and:

> his view that it would be unable to service a mobile economy, despite being a picturesque location with a rich history. He preferred the town of Dalmellington at the foot of the Galloway mountains on the road

north to Ayrshire where 'the community spirit was as strong as the liquor,' the main street containing three large ruined factories and warehouses. He considered this a site of grittier realism that had practical advantages, being geographically closer to Glasgow and Edinburgh and nearer to Prestwick Airport.

(*Making Something out of Nothing*, PhD Thesis by Jane Frank)

When I went to Dalmellington I found no unusual distilling activities. The contrast between the two wee towns is obvious however, and in spite of what one Wigtown resident told me in his cups – 'This used to be a dump, now it's a dump with a book festival'. – it's clear that the book town status has brought a confident gloss to Wigtown and certainly brings in much needed income. Its peripheral location may be problematic, but can also be seen as an attraction in itself. Adrian Turpin, the Director, claims it to be an advantage, saying the town thrives:

because of, not in spite of, its edge-of-the-map location. Visitors,

including writers, have time to talk, to drink, to spark unusual friendships, while the town's size – 980 people – makes visiting an intimate experience.

(quoted in *Making Something out of Nothing*, PhD Thesis by Jane Frank)

I've been a regular visitor to Wigtown since the very first Festival and one thing that strikes me is that the town at other times of the year fails the McMillan vibrant Scottish community test in that, outside festival time – when the town is creatively vibrant and full of visitors – its pubs have no or restricted opening hours during the week, showing that there are not enough drinkers, ie ordinary Scottish people, to sustain them. This is a bad sign, though it may merely mean that a new population of book-selling coffee grinders has arisen to take the place of the original inhabitants which is not a bad thing, is it? And alcohol is an evil, after all.

It makes me wonder though, who or what regeneration is for and whether the town is run by cultural tourists who have set up camp for other cultural tourists who arrive once a year when the town, Brigadoon like, blossoms with books and writers are shipped in from the airts to entertain them. My bitter and cynical inhabitant told me the town has been saved 'by and for outsiders'. In a politically and economically marginalised place is it economic regeneration or colonisation? Or both? If you accept that the more jaundiced view that it's the latter then Wigtown fits perfectly into the ghost landscape, a gigantic theme park for history, mystery, myth, star gazing and culture, visited annually by a shifting crowd of tourists, staffed by folk just like themselves.

Michel Foucault invented the concept of Heterotopia to describe places and spaces of otherness, 'which are neither here nor there, that are simultaneously physical and mental, such as the space of a phone call or the moment when you see yourself in the mirror.' Or come to Galloway.

See Darkness and Light, Dumfries, Emigration, Frontiers, Geophanta-sapsychiatry, Ghost Landscape

Books: Existing, Lost, Made up, Vanished, Made of Wood

There is a lot in print about the region, especially its glamorous and mysterious past. At my elbow throughout the writing of this book have been Temperley, Mactaggart and MacDowall, a trio of tough literary bruisers. There has also been a raft of modern authoritative or anecdotal interpretations of our history and geography in Galloway. I even co-wrote one in exchange for a couple of hundred quid. My attempt to have it named *Dumfries: A Plagiarised History* was rebuffed by the publishers, I remember. All this can be found in the bibliography, however, if I, and you, make it to the end of this book, and if there is a bibliography.

Don't you think that in a way, though, books that don't exist are more interesting than ones that do? Take the following titles:

Black Art and Necromancy; *Philosophy of the Devil*; *Satan's Almanacks*; *The Fire Spangs of*

Faustus; The Soothsayer's Creed; The Witch Chronicle and The Black Cluds Wyme Laid Open.

These comprise the lost library of the wizard Michael Scott, buried in Glenluce, interred deep in a vault along with this priceless and dangerous reading material. There's a story that someone dug the wizard up just before the First World War, found him sitting reading, and went completely mad as a result. I can't find a record of these books having existed at all, so I'm pleased to think John Mactaggart made them all up. Correct me if I'm wrong, anyone currently ploughing through *Satan's Almanacks*.

Then we have books that nearly existed but didn't, like Thomas Carlyle's huge *History of the French Revolution*, the first manuscript of which, having been sent to his friend John Stuart Mill's house, was the subject of ad hoc lit crit by a maid who thought it was rubbish and threw it on the fire. In a huge effort Carlyle rewrote it, 'direct and flamingly from the heart', but was it the same book? I doubt it. At this point I think of Dumfries and Galloway's successor to the makar Willie Neill, Tom Pow, who had a suitcase of poetry stolen from him in Peru, the fruits of months of work. The regret at losing this can only have been matched by the despair of the thief, opening the suitcase in some wretched pueblo, expecting expensive camera equipment and not part of the literary heritage of Dumfries and Galloway. Of course some books do and don't exist. When I was in my late teens I had the ideal summer job in Dumfries, sitting in a sunlit garden in George Street doing nothing. I read voraciously, one book led to another, and I found my way to Laurence Durrell and then to Henry Miller. I went to the Ewart Library to find his *Rosy Crucifixion Trilogy, Sexus, Nexus* and *Plexus*. The titles were there all right, pasted on to book-size bits of wood with the notice 'If you want to read this type of book, apply to the Librarian'. That was a good 12 years after the *Lady Chatterley's Lover* obscenity trial but Dumfries Library was still holding firm. I didn't apply.

*See **Michael Scott Superhero, Makar***

One of the most famous incidents recorded on what is often called Britain's most haunted road occurred in 1962, when Derek and Norman Ferguson were driving along the A75 around midnight and were on the stretch of road between Annan and Kinmount when a large hen flew towards their windscreen and vanished. The hen was followed by an old lady who ran towards the car waving her outstretched arms then a man with long hair and further animals, including 'great cats, wild dogs, goats, more hens and other fowl, and stranger creatures', which all disappeared. When the brothers stopped the car, it began to sway violently back and forth. Derek got out of the car and the movement stopped. He climbed back in and then, finally, a vision of a furniture van came towards them before disappearing. Other sightings include lovers arm-in-arm in the middle of the road and a man with a rag in his hand. A local group of ghost hunters, Mostly Ghostly, run tours now along this famous stretch of highway. One of them told me 'The Ferguson Brothers sighting wasn't a conventional haunting, what they saw was like mad scenes from a film.'

'The run to the outskirts of Dumfries where the traffic increased was another wild rush.' It's a little known fact that Bram Stoker set one of his last novels on the road between Dumfries and Gretna. In *Lady Athlyne*, the central characters crash their car and have a passionate night of love somewhere near Annan. It's a disjointed romantic novel and Stoker, ill at the time, was clearly not in good form. His last book, the gothic *The Lair of The White Worm*, was similarly criticised for being confused and incomplete. In *The Lair of the White Worm*, Australian Adam Salton moves to his great uncle's house, falls for a beautiful girl and dynamites a giant white worm which lives in a neighbour's garden.

It is clear to me, only me, that the spectacular apparitions on the A75 are not ghosts but scenes from the book Stoker should have written about the A75, or perhaps filmed, as the *White Worm* eventually was, by the maverick and brilliant director Ken Russell. Stoker's worm itself, after all, is said to be based on the famous Galloway white worm recorded in ancient stories as having lived near Castle Douglas, further up the A75. Look at the elements: the lovers; the farmyard animals the couple swerved to avoid; the furniture van carrying the possessions of Adam Salton. As for the man with the rag, he is clearly wiping the camera lens on a difficult shoot during a particularly damp Dumfriesshire evening.

*See **The Poetry Highway***

Burns

No one can talk about Dumfries and Galloway and not talk about Burns. He frenetically covered the whole region, scraping feverish on windows and impregnating barmaids. And what's more he's dead and buried here, so in a sense, he's ours. And don't we know it! As I write this it's nearly supper time again, Rabbie's Birthday. The kilt sweat shops are in full swing, the malt is flowing and craggy nosed Burns hacks are boarding their planes to Western Samoa, Uzbekistan and all points in between, exporting once again our most successful cultural trademark, Rabbie Burns. Love it or loathe it, if you're a Scot you can't avoid addressing, sooner or later, the pulling power of Robert Burns. If you're a poet, moreover, you can't avoid Burns fallout, which can be more deadly than radiation.

When Robert Burns died he was already famous and his posthumous reputation was built on an existing estimation of his genius in his own lifetime. Few poets, in fact few literary figures at all, have established such a large reputation in such a short working life. An Edinburgh obituary spoke of Burns' 'tenderness and sublimity'. To be accounted sublime is almost something worth dying for.

Of course it goes without saying that Scottish poets today

are treated differently and it's strange that the nation which more than any other reveres a poet as a national figure and national symbol should, in general, hold contemporary poetry in so much ignorance and contempt.

As William Neill, said in a poem addressed to Burns:

> Now poets write books that
>   Scotland does not buy,
> shrink in their eyes to the status of
>   eccentric.
> Poetry's drowned out by every
>   parrot cry
> feeding the multitude the latest
>   cantrip.
> They value verses less than a
>   clownish trick;
> once a year within a phantom nation
> they shrink your head to fit a social
>   occasion.

('Mr Burns for Supper', William Neill)

Of course Burns was a star. He was certainly regarded as matchless in his own time by people and poets who were in a position to know.

> Burns! With honour due
> I have oft honoured thee. Great
>   shadow, hide

thy face! I sin against thy native
    skies.

('On visiting the Tomb of Burns', Keats)

Why did poets like Keats and Byron, mainstays of English Romanticism, so much admire the Scots-writing Burns? The answer is that these poets, like Burns, were radicals, espousing radical causes, which in the 18th century was no pose but a dangerous course of action which could lead to charges of treason, transportation, or even worse. Burns himself recognised this when in 1784 he wrote:

> They banished him beyond the sea
> but ere the bud was on the tree
> adown my cheeks the pearls run,
> embracing my John Highlandman

('John Highlandman', Burns)

Transportation was the sentence. Being Scottish was the crime.

When Burns visited Edinburgh he visited a city where only a fraction of people had the right to vote for a member of parliament, where to suggest even basic democratic change was a treasonable offence punishable by death. He also lived in a Scotland which, after the Treaty of Union, was about to be absorbed big time into the Anglo-Imperial ethic, with the massive anglicisation of language and literature which that entailed. Burns' heroism in championing the cause of the common man, of themes resonant of an independent Scottish history and in utilising a vibrant but soon-to-expire Scottish language is something that struck an immediate chord at the time, and afterwards.

Contemporary Scottish poets like Willie Neill and many others who use or used Scots language as a form of cultural identity take their cue from Burns, though the language they use is more synthetic: few writers in Scots stray very far from their dictionaries these days. Other poets clearly identify Burns' humanity as an ever-present and relevant theme in today's society, quite right too.

However, it always seemed odd that Burns seems more honestly admired in other countries. By honestly I mean that his political stance, his socialism if you like, his republicanism, his nationalism, the stuff that his contemporaries, even Keats and Byron found indivisible from his work, in fact part of his genius, is and was acknowledged more in other countries than our own. Yes, here we seemed to revere Burns but through the thick filter of two hundred years of Scottish History we have consistently turned our backs on most things he stood for. How can we, living in a Unionist, industrialised, anglicised and free-market society still purport to admire the man so much?

This leads us on to why many contemporary Scottish writers see the impact of Burns, as opposed to his ideas, as negative and destructive. An ex-writer in residence for Dumfries and Galloway, Bill Herbert, takes the mick in Burns' own favoured stanza form:

> His morals werenae aa that PC,
> his sentiment a wee thing cheesy,
> his hairstyle wiz a quiffy greasy,
> auld Elvis Burns –
> but still, he goat me on BBC
> that's a stunt that earns.
> His politics were kina muddy
> a tory when tipped the noddy
> syne nationalist and unca bloody

fevh meenuts later –
Whit're we daein cheerin a shoddy
auld fornicator?

('Epistle to Twa Editors', Bill
Herbert)

This backlash stems less from the poetry and more from the creation of the cult of Burns, which Keats identified as early as 1818 when, after visiting Jean Armour he travelled to Alloway to visit the poet's birthplace. Already there was a curator, whom Keats described as:

> A great bore with his many anecdotes. He is a mahogany faced old jackass who knew Burns and ought to have been kicked for having spoken to him.

The adoption of Burns by his countrymen in a celebration that somehow ignores his radical genius is a recurring theme with today's poets in the region and beyond. They are trying to explore what is actually meant by contemporary Scottish identity, not the synthetic version bandied around once a year.

> Once a year, Robin, they will
>   remember you

in a word or two beyond your
    actual name.
The fatuous speeches will scarcely
    encumber you
the maudlin tear, the exaggerated
    claim.
Who love what you love measure
    your true fame
in a kind of silence the foolish find
    too great.
They take your measure by their
    own puffed state.

('Mr Burns for Supper', William
Neill)

Another writer, Ian Ferguson, says:

> Robert Burns has become a national icon more tarnished than the most garish phony tartan. The marketing of Burns has everything to do with tourism and nothing to do with literature. Burns is the quintessential symbol of the commodification of a writer. Only a fool... would not lament this state of affairs.

The reaction found its true exponent in Hugh MacDiarmid, a poet as concerned as Burns with Scottish nationality, with republicanism. MacDiarmid was a Communist Scottish Nationalist and claimed Burns would, in the modern context, have been the same, but he despised the use that was made of Burns by the establishment:

> The Burns Cult must be killed stone dead- and would be instantly if a single flash of the spirit of Burns were alive in Scotland... the whole raison d'etre of the Burns Club is to deny that Burns was Burns- and to make him instead acceptable to conventional standards that would have found in him their most powerful and persistent enemy.

The Burns cult, MacDiarmid says, has:

> denied his spirit to honour his name. It has denied his poetry to laud his amours. It has preserved his furniture and repelled his message.
>
> ('The Conspiracy of Silence', Hugh MacDiarmid)

It has preserved his furniture and repelled his message. It's a good line and one that's difficult not to believe if you're at a Burns Fest packed with Rotarians who toast the Queen and don't allow any women anywhere near the establishment unless they're replying for the poor old lassies, or serving up the haggis.

One of the things that has happened is that Scotland, its culture and its literature, has been marginalised and romanticised, a process fully encouraged by Scots themselves who saw aping the manners and attitudes and prejudices of the English as much more important than defining their own country's potential.

In the words of Ian Gilchrist:

> It is Scotland's fate to become a Romantic object or commodity: glamorous scenery, a series of fake, kitsch, sentimental inventions of tradition, from Ossian and Waverley to Brigadoon and Braveheart.

The ghost landscape, again. This would explain how Burns can somehow be peeled away from his essential ideas, to become a kind of tabloid celebrity, a glamorous tragic hero and womaniser or, even better, a massive tourist attraction. We can visit his house, see the Tam O Shanter Experience, buy a range of products, then go home and vote for our favourite centre unionist party. Shouldn't happen, should it?

The lack of political courage in Scotland, our own studied

ignorance of our history, and the history of our ideas, has also led to perverted ideas of what being Scottish actually means. Burns Night has become a kind of way for people to express their nationality once a year, to flirt with their country's past without doing anything too dangerous like think about its future, and to think about concepts like humanity in their most gaseous form, before going home and forgetting all about them. It also enables us to pretend we've got one up on everybody else – we may be crap at football and have a balsa wood parliament but well they don't have a Pushkin Day or a Rimbaud Day, so we must be cleverer than the French and Russians. We can also pretend we care or know about culture and literature.

Burns remains a potent symbol. Of what we were, of what we are, but most of all of what we might be. His talent is mesmeric, his message is universal. Kofi Annan paid tribute to him at the Inaugural Burns Address at the UN speaking of 'his poetry of peace'. As Maya Angelou said, 'He was the first white man I read who seemed to understand that a human being was a human being and that we are more alike than unlike.' 'A Man's a Man For A' That' rang out at the resumption of the Scottish parliament. When the universal meets the parochial, however, it's a tough contest especially if you're talking about Scotland, where we naturally despise our geniuses or try and cut them down to manageable shape, say about the size of a shortbread tin. Burns should not become a tradition. Part of the reason that young people reject the man's poetry is because it comes wrapped up in tradition and, as Andrew Borthwick said, 'for the young finding tradition boring is a tradition in itself'.

Let's hope that one day we get a land worthy of the man. A land that's independent, humane, fair and artistic, and that the makar Willie Neill, in his poem, 'A Knell for Mr Burns' didn't have the last word.

> I think of you, Mr Burns
> lying in your death bed;
> sweating and sick by turns,
> desperate dreams in your head.

In articulo mortis beset;
lacking a tailor's fee:
seven guineas in debt
for a worldly vanity...

Strange that the living face
should suffer so much rage,
while birth-and-burial place
grew to a pilgrimage.

('A Knell for Mr Burns', William
Neill'

See Big Shuggie MacDiarmid,
Ghost Landscape, Makar, Pie

Burns, his murder

I once spent an entire evening with a man who argued, utterly convincingly, that Burns was murdered by Dr Maxwell, his personal physician. If this is true, Maxwell was but the first in a long line of dodgy regional doctors. The motive, this man argued, was that Maxwell was a rabid republican who believed Burns, with his acceptance of government pay as an exciseman and his antics in the Dumfries Volunteers, had betrayed his principles. Maxwell, allegedly, had attended the execution of King Louis XVI, dipped his handkerchief in the blood, and kept this grisly artefact in his pocket to stiffen resolve. Suspecting, I think, that this story might make a great film script my confidant also told me that the child born posthumously to Burns and named after Maxwell was actually the doctor's child, as 'Burns could no longer manage the act of love.' Words fail.

See Bodkin, Burns

C

Carsethorne

I am standing at Carsethorne early on a rainy Thursday morning in January. Last week a high tide driven by gales covered the road into the village and the strand is even more desolate than usual today, with the flotsam of the Solway and beyond – driftwood, wrack, plastic bottles – strewn high on the shoreline. Across the estuary to the left I can guess is Annan, directly ahead Silloth. It's hard to imagine that this spot was once a busy port, one of the busiest on the west coast, trading manufactured goods especially from the late years of the 18th century. Mostly this would have been Dumfries and Galloway's, and Scotland's, most prodigious and heart-breaking export, its own people.

A triangular trade developed: emigrants to New Brunswick and Prince Edward Island, embarking at Richibucto, Miramichi and the Baie de Chaleur, with timber returning in ships built in Canada by Solway shipwrights to Liverpool then back, with some timber and other goods, to the Solway. The

reason for such a trade in people? Pure poverty, caused by rural depopulation and price rises. In 1775 the *Lovely Nelly*, Captained by William Sheridan, took 82 emigrants to Lot 59 on Prince Edward Island. The reason given on the manifest for the families going? 'To get more bread'.

In 1850, 10,000 people migrated to America, 7,000 to Australia and 4,000 to Otago Province in New Zealand, leaving from a jetty built by the Nith Navigation Commission and used by the Liverpool Steam Packet Company.

In 1872, an entire village, Busy Bit near Dunscore, inhabitants; school teacher, blacksmith, plough horses and all, took ship to New South Wales.

As I stand here I can see the jetty, the stumps filing down into the deep water channel and I'm trying to imagine the mixture of excitement, misery and fear of the families waiting to board, reckoning that even a voyage on rough seas into the unknown was a better bet than staying in their own inhospitable land. It seems a miserable enough day to contemplate all this and also to realise its place in the continuum. According to the Oxford Migration Observatory, more than 3,500 people left Dumfries and Galloway for abroad in the years 2006 to 2012, the vast majority between 18 and 34, our prime working population.

I'm phoning one of them, an emigrant, to conduct an interview as I stand here. It's not just a worker I'm phoning it's a poet, so I'm expecting a witty or arty interchange. I've also prearranged this so she's not sitting in some office in Brisbane but hopefully standing on Dicky Beach on Queensland's Sunshine Coast in midsummer. Pause while I take my gloves off to try and work the phone. Dropped it. Trying again:

What do you see? I see stumps of wood in water flat against a sunless sky.

I see silver she-oaks and pandanus frame the sea like stained glass and cornflower blue sky.

What do you hear? I hear sea birds, a curlew's cry, nothing.

I hear crashing waves, washing machine foam, a strong rip pulling south.

What do you feel? I am chilled to the bone by a hard wind and stinging rain.

I feel water round my ankles, tepid velvet, a breeze blowing, the smell of salt air, seaweed and tea-tree.

What do you really feel? I'm miserable as fuck.

I'm glad to be alive.

Well I make that 4–0 for Australia in every sense. Numb with jealousy I make my way to the Steampacket Inn, Isle of Whithorn.

*See **Crossmichael, Emigration, Ghost Landscape, Palnackie***

Carsphairn

Carsphairn is a current model of regeneration, in that its entire population has left and it has been reborn via immigration largely if not exclusively from beyond the region, if not the country. A poet, who wishes to remain anonymous, sent me this verse which seems to sum up the issue very well:

> Carsphairn was the last wurd in colonisation a wis telt,
> 'a mean they advertised doon south fir settlers,
> like the Wild West, ken, here's a slice o land fir ye
> dinna fash aboot the savages they're a extinct.'
> Am no sure. Nationality's a queer construct,
> an being 'local' has aye seemed as real here.
> I tak nae pleesure in stanes turning green,
> an these weans may hae accents flat as fens
> but they fill the air wi joy nonetheless.
> Isn't it like a change, a over?
> Somethin gained for a while,
> mair lost forever.

Cats or Bawdrons

While working on some Scots language poems with school-children I was struck by one written by a very demure girl which read:

> The bawdron jouked abut the hoose wi skrieghs an we were feart.

This is more than just an insight into home life in Amisfield but rather a poem tapping into the great reservoir of Galloway cat lore and in particular areas haunted by the spirit of the Gibb Cat.

Mactaggart talks about Barr's Cat, 'a monster of a bawdrons', that was known around Penningham in the mid 18th century, the 'size of which was proverbial all over the country', but most importantly he also wrote a poem about 'Crumwhull's Gibb', or 'The Gibb Cat', a ferocious super-cat with a keen sense of injustice, quite capable of making mincemeat of any human that got in his way.

> When in calm spanging tae the cheese
> the hule and wha was that,
> Lord save our souls they yelloch'd a',
> it is Crumwhull's Gibb Cat...
>
> By the chulders he seised on the gudewife,
> an soon wud hae stap'd her breath,

had na her man, her sons and
   daughters,
barried him to death –

A wee thing didnae kill the chiel,
he fuff'd, he bit and spat,
sae merry Scotsmen now ye'll ken
about Crumwhull's Gibb Cat.

('Crumwhull's Gibb Cat', John
Mactaggart)

It's clear the Gibb Cat still roams
Dumfries and Galloway, righting
ancient wrongs, and settling
troublesome vendettas. There
have been many sightings.

In 2013, Craig Johnstone and
his girlfriend Gillian Kennedy from
Paisley were staying in a hotel in
Nithsdale when they found a
'large, black cat' lying down
staring at them. As Craig said, 'It
was around 50 metres away from
us and its head measured
approximately one and a half feet
from the ground… it was jet black
with small rounded ears… It
stared at us for 30 seconds.'

On July 2013, 22-year-old
Samantha Garden was on her way
to work in Lockerbie when she
noticed a 'strange looking cat'
standing in the middle of the road
near Hoddom Bridge.

In January, 2012 Aaron
Halliday and Nathan Crosbie
spotted a cat as big as a panther
in a field near Dalbeattie.

In 2011, Dan Alexander claimed
to have seen a huge creature on
the A75 near Newton Stewart.

Before that, lorry driver John
Spence saw two big cats run in
front of his vehicle near Creetown.
On the same day, Janet Davies
spotted an animal near Tynron
which she said was a panther.

Police confirm there are many
sightings but 'no verifiable
evidence'. The Gibb Cat is too fly.

I too seem to have had the
same strange urge as Mactaggart
to write about Cats.

The Street of the Cat unrolls
to the water's edge.
Follow its trajectory past
the lighthouse's pulse
you'd end in Africa.
In the dark I hear the sea
rubbing holes in stone
but no sound from the cats
I know are there.
The same cats we saw
this afternoon liquefied,
condensed by night,
flying on rags of shadow
or cool midnight air.

While I retrace a path
through the dark,
the cats are coiled round the street
like one cat;
I see the full moon
in its mad yellow eyes.

('The Street of the Cats')

*See **Bram Stoker and the** A75*

Cavalry & the Role of the Oatcake in Medieval Warfare

At Port William they're renovating the old corn mill and hoping to make it more than a museum. When it is completed the mill will be a centre for traditional farming and craft activities, bringing the tourists in when the rain is not quite as horizontal as it is today. I am eavesdropping on the conversation of a visiting family who are watching a pair of heavy horses. The father is patiently explaining that these are the kind of horses which in history not only worked the land but fought in battle as warhorses since these skittery wee things you see in the movies couldn't possibly have borne the weight of a fully armoured knight. This is very true, fair play to the man, but it must be said that warhorses in Dumfries and Galloway have

always been skittery wee things. The Scots in the Middle Ages favoured not the *destrier* which took too much feeding and money but the *hobelar*, descended from the Connemara pony which was a hardy wee beast used to rough conditions and travelling big distances and perfect for the fast-moving type of skirmishing the Scots usually resorted to when faced by superior firepower.

Sir James Douglas, Robert the Bruce's right hand man, was a great proponent of this type of warfare and his descendants, based in Threave Castle, took their ponies with them to France to fight the English there during the Hundred Years War. With them they won a notable victory at the Battle of Bauge in 1421, killing the Duke of Clarence, the

English King's brother, news of which caused the Pope reportedly to clap his hands with glee and announce that the 'Scots are the perfect antidote to the English.' Archibald Douglas was rewarded by being appointed the Count of Longueville. Jean Froissart the French chronicler was amazed at the resilience of the Scots Light Horse and put it down to the fact that in the evenings they griddled and ate their own oatcakes:

> The Scots are able to make longer marches than other men because they carry and make cakes of oats to eat and comfort their stomachs.

Inspired, I've also written of the historical role of the oatcake.

> It's a fact:
> These oatcake crumbs in your
>   pocket
> are scions of a noble race,
> the mighty oatcake,
> paste of the Gods.
> The English gave them to their
>   horses
> but it was oatcakes won freedom
> for the Scots and French,
> not Wallace, Bruce or Joan of Arc.
> What did Archibald Douglas have
>   in his bloody mitt

> when he stove in the Duke of
>   Clarence's head at Bauge?
> A rough oatcake.
> 'What think ye of the mutton
>   guzzlers and winos now?'
> asked the Dauphin of his effete
>   courtiers
> when the Scots had swept the field.
> He saw the power of the oatcake.
> The Maid entering Orleans
>   victorious in 1429 was
> flanked, they say, by Scottish
>   guardsmen,
> warrior giants with twice fired
>   oatcakes,
> their banner three oatcakes rampant
> on a sable field.

('The Role of the Oatcake in Medieval Warfare')

Famous exploits on horseback weren't just restricted to the Middle Ages. Later on in history Colonel Alexander Clark-Kennedy of Kirkcudbright led the charge of the Royal Dragoons at Waterloo, capturing with his own hands the Imperial Eagle of the French 105th Regiment.

No need for cavalry now, though, unless you want to hire the tanks at Garlieston for that very special birthday treat. At Galloway Tanks you can get your very own Abbot Self Propelled Gun or Armoured Personnel Carrier and pretend to be Big Arnie for the day. 'See the loonies you get in there,' said a local, somewhat uncharitably. Better to pretend though, isn't it? And why shouldn't Galloway be the place for sociopathic fantasies. Fruitcakes, in a sense, replacing the oatcakes. War by other means? *See War*

Chrissie Fergusson

Christine Fergusson is the best artist to come out of Dumfries and Galloway in the last hundred years, and would be much better known, no doubt, had she been a man and had she been painting elsewhere. As it is, she has a fine reputation.

Chrissie was the daughter of a Dumfries solicitor and after attending Dumfries Academy she studied at Crystal Palace School of Art in London and then Glasgow School of Art. She was Principal teacher of Art at Glasgow High School before marrying and moving back to Dumfries, where she and her husband founded the Dumfries Fine Arts Society. She painted in Brittany and other parts of Europe but was particularly fond of her local area and produced beautiful work based on her travels around the Galloway coast. She was a friend of Jessie King and EA Hornel in Kirkcudbright. She also captured on canvas a number of the places described by Dorothy L Sayers in her 1931 novel *The Five Red Herrings* and we know that the well-known author visited the Fergussons at their home in Dumfries.

Her dreamy representations of the closes and wynds of Dumfries, often reflected in riverlight, transform the town into a kind of Venice of the imagination.

Take the painting *On the Nith*, looking from just past Devorgilla Bridge across the river to the buildings there, including the balcony of what is now the Salutation Inn. Golden honey coloured stone in sunlight with tall trees and their mirror images shimmering on the river's surface, it could easily be Montmartre. In fact the painting has that magical effect particular to great art; it transforms your view of the scene itself, so that next time you look across the river, you see less the moss and the damp and the decay and more that vision of sunlit and stone hovering on water.

Of course there will be always folk who stubbornly refuse such visions when offered them and prefer a pragmatic and logical way of considering things. This strikes me as understandable though it is a highly tedious way in which to conduct your short existence on the planet. It is better to sometimes try and be 'away with the fairies', even if only for a wee while.

I was once jabbering at a friend of mine, a girl who affects a prosaic outlook on life as a disguise for a truly poetic soul, about that very scene and Christine Fergusson's interpretation of it. Later, I wrote a poem.

There's a balcony in Dumfries,
between cypresses,
above the black wall of river,
and when the sun's hung above it,
no doubt at all it's Venice,
and from Venice isn't it just a step,
when the light falls on water
like shining pieces of a mirror,
to happiness?
It's nothing like Venice, you say,
when you're up there it's freezing
and unsafe,
but so is dreaming
and there are rats,
rats too, in Venice and in dreaming.
The thing is, you're thinking
of the Venice in that lagoon,
at the top of the Adriatic,
not the one in my brain where,
lit by electrical impulses
like the Lido at night from Sant'
  Elena,
we will have love and poetry all
  year long.

('The Salutation Balcony')

See Art, EA Hornel

The Clatteringshaws Hydro Electric System as described by Keith Downes in the King's Hotel Dalbeattie 21 January 2014

It's f...... incredible, see the loch we ca Loch Ken, it's an artificial loch, ye ken? On an old tidal system, 6 dams, a third o the power o the whole Stewartry comes fae that, ken, it's a f...... great system, I'm proud as f... of it. Built in the 1930s ken. It's incredible. I'd like you to see it. You'd be f...... dancing for joy when you see it, mukker. F...... dancing. Feenished in 1937, yon Tongland, what a great wee power station. See I'm a Stewartry man, born an bred. F...... Dumfries. C'mon now Dumfries has stolen New Abbey frae us, f...... Southerness, f...... Creeton's awa. It's a f...... land grab by Dumfries, it's a f...... disgrace. A f...... conspiracy pure and simple. I'm makin too much noise am I? Should be shoutin it frae the rooftops. F...... disgrace. Pure and simple.

Colin's Father on the Moon

Recently I was in Castle Douglas and talked to a teacher called Colin Fisher, who told me about his dad, a tortured man who never knew his own father. He had been invalided out of the navy, taught himself electronics and, working for a company called *Varian* in Dalgety Bay, designed a gas chromatograph that measured the amounts of elements that a star, or any light-giving body, gives out. The chromatograph was put on Apollo 17 and deposited by the Lunar Module *Challenger* in the Taurus Littrow Valley on the moon on the 11 December 1972. It broadcast until September 1977, 'testament to your father's great skills', as an expert told Colin, when it was switched off because NASA needed the control space to monitor Skylab. 'He was a dark man,' said Colin, 'we witnessed him do a lot. The family's divided about him, but I think, what a legacy, such a complex man ended up measuring light, in the all darkness of space.'

Conversation about Davie Coulthard the butcher in Dalbeattie

'Davie Coulthard gave us a lift up the road.'

'Davie Coulthard that drives?'

'Aye, he gave us a lift up the road.'

'Aye he's good at driving.'

'Aye.'

'I saw him driving in what's it called, Monaco.'

'Never knew he'd been there.'

'Oh aye, no just there, Singapore.'

'Singapore?'

'Aye.'

'Davie Coulthard?'

'Aye.'

'You sure?'

'Aye.'

'Davie Coulthard the butcher?'

Covenanters

Extreme Presbyterians, named after the two religious covenants to which they adhered, characters of whom Dumfries and Galloway has historically been inordinately proud. Many of them gave their lives for their beliefs, their beliefs being that they should worship the same God slightly differently from the Episcopalians. Sanquhar saw the formation of the most extreme Presbyterians, the Cameronians, who some historians have represented as left-wing revolutionaries rather than the cheerless fanatical troupe that they undoubtedly were. It is true that the covenanters were prosecuted horribly during the Killing Times but it was less for their religious beliefs and more for the fact they incited civil unrest and armed insurrection. Anyway it's hard to escape the impression that they rather enjoyed it. Certainly I would have become an Episcopalian rather than be put in a barrel of burning tar and rolled down a hill but that perhaps shows my moral bankruptcy. Covenanters' memorials and stones are romantic locations of course, but no substitute for the beautiful buildings, tombs and memorials that the Presbyterians gleefully smashed and pulled down all over Scotland whenever they got the chance. Imagine how Whithorn, Sweetheart Abbey and Dundrennan would look, how their surrounding towns would be enriched, if they had not been pillaged and burned down by these vandals. It would be like walking in an Andalucia on the Solway.

Here was a Queen's last rest before the ferry
took her to exile in the final prison;
far from the iron kirk, she sought to bury
too many sins below an alien heaven.

Unhappy widowed and unhappy wed,
south to scant mercy made her pilgrimage
from a rough country to a rougher bed,
intrigue and counter and the axe's edge.

While time and prejudice knocked down the walls,
burned the poor land to fuel sectarian fires,

turned to another purpose choir and stalls
and used the scattered stone to build new byres.

('Dundrennan', William Neill)

After the succession of William of Orange whom the Covenanters rather liked even though he didn't accept either of the Covenants, the Presbyterians got their own back for the Killing Times by a full and hearty involvement suppressing the Jacobite Rebellion and in the long campaign of rape, murder and theft in the Highlands that followed. The arguably malign influence of the Presbyterian Church was long seen in Scotland in its legacy of glum Sundays and a reluctance among people to engage joyfully with life. The historian Tom Nairn said Scotland would only be free when 'the last minister is strangled with the last copy of the Sunday Post'.

There are Covenanters Trails around Dumfries and Galloway. Although they were usually buried in unmarked graves, great care has been taken to mark where they were killed. The south west of Scotland and Ayrshire was the centre of their activity and therefore the scenes of the most famous killings, such as the Wigtown Martyrs. James Kirko of Sundaywell, allegedly the last martyr, was shot on the Whitesands from Devorgilla Bridge. Donald Adamson gives a less splenetic interpretation of his motives:

> ... the source surely
> did not spring from tributaries
> of bible text, nor flood from any bull-
> throated preacher at conventicler

but rather, trickled
from childish things put away, the moor's
bare Pentecost, its wind and fire-

water that seeped through
peat-hags till it filled
a first communion cup among the hills
of Sundaywell.

('Clearer Water', Donald Adamson)

See **Ritual Roads**

Crossmichael

Locals call it the Mickle, a village north of Castle Douglas, an ancient place with no less than 16 different sites – forts and stone circles – scattered round about. The church tower is 17th century but the site is far older. When I visited in November, the village was rain swept and deserted. Like all these communities – I know, I live in one – it must flare episodically into life but not that afternoon. Maybe flare is the wrong word because Crossmichael recently became fleetingly famous for its 'fireball', a strange meteorological phenomenon which

burned out everyone's routers and flat screen TVs. Reports say that telephones and Sky boxes exploded and some were blown across the room. Jim McLellan of the Thistle Inn reported, 'There was huge clap of thunder along with the lightning. It was absolutely horrendous and must have been right above us. The sky just went black at the time and there were hailstones which covered the whole village.' It was a kind of Sky Box Apocalypse.

Crossmichael will also be famous, sooner or later, for the tin hut that is the headquarters of the

Crossmichael Drama Club where the 'rude mechanicals' scene from *A Midsummer Night's Dream*, translated into Scots by poet John Burns, was filmed one rainy afternoon on a mobile phone. It won them through to the finals of the Nation's Best Am Dram Competition, filmed for Sky TV. Then they won the entire competition, the prize being a performance of Moliere's *The Hypochondriac* at the Lyric Theatre, London.

No signs of thespian activity when I was there, though, or any activity. Emptiness is not a new experience in Crossmichael. In fact it could be said to have invented it. Sir Robert Gordon who donated the bell in the Church Tower in the 1620s was one of the very first to obtain a charter to establish a colony of emigrants in Nova Scotia and thus to begin, as I've said previously, Scotland's most consistently successful export to date, its own people. He and his son called the colony Galloway.

A couple from Hull recently told me that it was the emptiness that attracted them here, but like the Highlands, the south west was once busier, until economic changes forced ordinary folk out and saw the emptiness repopulated by hippies, reiki therapists, holiday homers and geofantasists. No matter what changes occur, Crossmichael will always be known to me as the home and burial place of the poet Willie Neill. Willie lived in a house adjoining the pub then later in another at the entrance to the village. He wrote in all the languages of Scotland, and was a terrific poet who, while not neglected in Scotland, didn't get accorded the status he deserved, the status he would probably have been given if he'd lived and worked elsewhere:

> Forget the poet; he has gone;
> His seeing work is done.
> Birds don't brood in sorrow:
> They sing while they can.

('Memorial', JB Pick)

See Emigration, Geofantasapsychiatry, Ghost Landscape, Makar

Curling

Recent headlines from Dumfries concerning the disappearance of curling champion Rhona Martin's Olympic gold medal from an exhibition are confirmation of the vitality of two ancient Scottish pursuits, curling and theft. However, of the two, curling is uniquely Scottish and uniquely entrenched in the lore of Dumfries and Galloway. Local papers have rightly been full of the exploits of the Lockerbie curlers who came home from the 2014 Sochi Olympics with medals but this is just the latest in a long line of national and international honours to come the way of local enthusiasts who have been practising this art since the Middle Ages.

Curling is an odd game to have evolved when it did, in the period between 1500 and 1700, in that other sports, archery for instance, had a clear military application. Curling, unless you can drop the stones onto the heads of your enemies, clearly has none. The implication is that this was a popular pursuit organised from the bottom up; a true people's game, born also, mind you, of the many terrible winters when work on the land was impossible. Early references to the game were a wee bit shamefaced, testimony to its populist nature as well as the fact that it was a true working class game. The prevalence in the early 19th century of women curlers, predictably evoking the criticism of the ministers, is another example of the rich egalitarian aspect of the sport:

> On Tuesday last, 28 blooming damsels met on Dalpeddar loch, in the parish of Sanquhar, to play a friendly bonspiel. They formed themselves into two rinks, and although wading up to the ancles in water, seemed to enter into the spirit of the game, and to contest it with as much intense anxiety as if the question that the losing party should all die old maids had depended upon the issue... and as the ladies, like true curlers, had resolved to adjourn to the toll-house, where a het pint had been ordered... our heroines resorted to whisky toddy. It may be true that there is no good reason

why females should not have their hours of recreation as well as men, but it seems advisable that these recreations which they do engage in should be of a character befitting their sex.

(*Dumfries Weekly Journal*, 1826)

For most of the 19th century, until the growth and popularity of football, curling remained supreme as the sport of Scotland, and its empire-building practitioners took it to any country cold enough for it to catch on. Another Scottish invention, tarmacadam, meant curling pits could be built and frozen, forming regular surfaces across the region. As in all games someone had to come along and spoil it by making rules and in the 19th century the Royal Caledonian Curling Club began to regularise the game, standardise the weight and size of stones, length of rinks, organise matches or bonspiels, and under its auspices the game grew even more. The upper Nith Valley and Wigtownshire witnessed the formation of many curling clubs in that period, though clubs in Sanquhar and Wanlockhead dated from a

century earlier and Sanquhar was the last to abandon its own local version of the game.

John Mactaggart made great mentions of curling, typically championing his own native curlers of Borgue against Kirkcudbright and Twynholm's, a 'shilpit crew... pewtring bodies at bonspiels'. Thirty years before, the Kirkcudbright poet David Davidson had described a curling match in the bardic tradition:

> God prosper long the hearty friends
> Of honest pleasure all;
> A mighty curling match once did
> At Carlingwark befal.

> To hurl the channelstane wi' skill,
> Lanfloddan took his way;
> The child that's yet unborn will sing,
> The curling of that day.

('Thoughts on the Seasons', David Davidson)

In the modern game the pre-eminent clubs are from Lockerbie and Stranraer where the North West Castle Hotel has an indoor rink. Where are the modern poets of curling, though? An enthusiast told me there's nothing more 'graceful than a stane gliding

home one time in a million
exactly where ye meant it to gan.
It makes a the iher humiliation
worthwhile.' The poet and historian
Angus Calder wrote of these
passionate amateurs and their
search for perfection, the 'final
realities':

Time cannot stale
our pot bellied skittishness. Watch us
frisking like penguins who've guzzled
too many tunas
off Tristan da Cuhna. But who
dares lampoon us? Directed
by steely skips, we address
elementals with modest finesse.
Not 'bowls on the rocks' this, but
    stones
over ice: final realities…

('Curling')

Cut Off

People imagine that in the past,
before the internet and Amazon
and high speed trains, communities
were completely cut off and the
inhabitants spent their time making
clothes out of tree bark and so on.
The truth of course is that more
people make clothes out of tree
bark today, albeit mostly artists.
In actual fact in the previous
century not only was public
transport quicker and more
comprehensive but there were
postal deliveries on a Sunday too.
Requests for dresses or funeral
suits could be sent by telegram
and the finished product would be
back in three days. Or a postcard
could be sent on a Sunday, received

on Monday morning and sent
down on a train that very day.
Local contractors would pick
packages up from stations and
bring them back with great speed.
Having a station in virtually every
town of any size in the region
brought newspapers, letters, fresh
food in every day. An old gentleman
in Dalbeattie took out his wallet
and showed me with great pride a
return ticket between Dalbeattie
and Dublin. The decimation of
rail services 50 years ago –
decimation is a mild term in fact
– hugely contributed to the area's
marginalisation and the difficulties
faced by the inhabitants. It made
it a less attractive place for the

indigenous population while ironically making it a more attractive place, on account of its remoteness, for the retired or those from outside seeking alternative lifestyles.

Of course a thing that did cut people off, and does today, is snow. During these times communities were used to helping themselves. John Wallace told me of when people from Keir in the terrible snowfall of 1996 dug their way out up towards Penpont, opening up farm roads and delivering vital supplies to folk, and eventually after six or seven hours coming to the Volunteer Arms in Penpont. 'As they stormed in the door the landlord announced last orders. He wasnae very popular.'

I remember wandering about Dumfries during such weather, wondering at the snowscape. The school was shut and Minerva Hall in Dumfries Academy used for almost a week as an emergency centre for motorists stranded on the A74. Strangely though, the pubs remained open, mysteriously fully stocked with beer.

See Alcohol, Lauren in Snaw and Flood, Weather

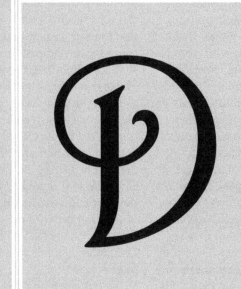

Dalbeattie Civic Week and Lawrence of Arabia

There are only two jokes centred on Dumfries and Galloway that I have ever laughed at. The first is one that the publisher thinks is not funny enough to include (about the kangaroo hopping down the Castle Douglas road who tells a motorist who stops to offer a lift, 'No thank you, I'm just going to Springholm') and the second is funny because it goes on for ages and involves two men crawling across a desert, dying of thirst. Eventually one says to the other, 'what date is it anyway?' To which the other replies, 'about the second week of August'. 'That's Dalbeattie Civic Week,' says the first. 'Aye, nice weather they're getting for it.' Hunter S Thompson invented the term gonzo journalism which is reporting that makes no claims on objectivity at all and which often includes the writer himself as part of the story. I've employed this technique quite a lot in this project, and love the spirals that come out of it, the coincidences and connections which are surprising in their own right but which also provide an odd, prismatic view of people, places and events. The Dalbeattie Civic Week joke provides a great working example of this. I am in the pub at Twynholm recalling this joke when someone tells me that the war memorial there contains the name of Trooper William P Smith, 1st Scottish Horse regiment, who died of thirst in the Sinai Desert in 1916. He was one of two men who had transferred to the Camel Corps, had lost their unit and died in the desert. On 16 August. Dalbeattie Civic Week, if there had been one then. Of course there's no connection between the joke and the sad story from World War One, though, mind you, I suppose there is now.

We talk for a bit more about the desert and I tell him of a picture I used to have of my father in the desert astride a great white horse. 'Lawrence of Dumfries, I used to call him,' I say. 'Of course,' says my companion to my great astonishment, 'Lawrence of Arabia used to live in Kirkcudbright.' And it transpires he did. Lawrence's father, Sir Thomas Chapman, had become involved in a romance with a Scottish governess called Sarah Lawrence, 15 years younger than him, and absconded with her to a series of quiet locations in England, Scotland and Wales. In the course of the next 20 years they had nine children, the second of whom was TE Lawrence, Lawrence of Arabia. One of the quiet locations was 89 St Mary's Street, Kirkcudbright where Lawrence of Arabia lived between 1889 and 1891 and where his brother William George was born. TE Lawrence was best known for his work in the Arab Revolt against the Ottomans in the Middle East which began in 1916, and in which Trooper Smith of Twynholm and the Camel Corps played a small part. One of Lawrence's great successes, and the greatest camel attack of the war, was the attack on Hejaz Railway Junction by the Imperial Camel Corps in August 1917. Dalbeattie Civic Week. If they'd had one then.

See Geofantasapsychiatry

Darkness and Light

When I was at the Wigtown Book Festival recently I got talking to some writers. The Festival's a favourite among many of them, I think, because of its location, close to the sea and some of the best unspoiled countryside in Europe. I agree with them; there's something about Galloway, a feeling that you're close to the past. More than that, close to some kind of raw truth that the worries of contemporary life have obscured which in places here, seems more tangible. Perhaps it's a sense of desolation, a sense of what once was, before the Galloway clearances.

A writer I know has recently returned to the area and speaks of moving here from the city in which he lived as being like travelling 'from dark to light'. He then went on to recall a story that showed the exact opposite was true.

He had been invited to attend a weekend writing event in the east of the region and arrived late by bus on the Thursday, met his contact to pick up a key, had a few drinks in Langholm and was delivered by a taxi, in driving rain, to his accommodation, a farm cottage some miles away. It was a very isolated place at the end of a long track surrounded on two sides by conifers. The taxi drove off. Without the headlights the place was in pitch darkness. By the light of his mobile he made his way to the door, inserted the key. It didn't work. He turned it harder and it snapped in the lock. He looked at the mobile. No signal. What should he do? He was rather overweight, it would have been tricky to break in, and he was a law abiding man. But what was the alternative? Walk for miles in the freezing rain? Go into the forest and look for shelter? In the space of two minutes this worldly person had all certainty stripped away and was faced with the stark requirements of historic man: shelter, heat, light. Now, as it turned out, he blundered about for ten minutes and eventually got a phone signal, but the story shows how desperate we are,

when it comes down to it, to get out of the dark. Nietzsche might say 'I am a forest, and a night of dark trees: but he who is not afraid of my darkness, will find banks full of roses under my cypresses,' but it clearly wasn't a dreich night near Hog Fell he was describing. By the way, 'dreich' is the ultimate Scots word, meaning miserable damp and grey, both a physical and a psychic description, so all-encompassing and terrifying in its power that a recent YouGov poll voted it as the nation's favourite Scots word.

'I was never so happy to see a pair of headlights,' the writer said. Lucky for him they were headlights and not dead lights. The incidence of strange lights prefiguring death is an old theme in tales across the region where the 'dead licht' prefigures sudden death, for instance in this example quoted in Maxwell Wood's *Witchcraft and Superstition in South West Scotland:*

> In Glencairn, a woman was going to lock her door one night, saw a light go past, carried, as she supposed, by a neighbour. There was nothing unusual in this, but

there was a high stone dyke with a flight of steps in it close to the foot of the garden, and she was surprised to see the light and supposed light-bearer pass right through the obstructing fence as if nothing of the kind had been there, and although the ground below the house was very uneven, the light itself was never lost sight of for a moment. The woman, rooted to the spot, watched the light go down through the fields, then along the public road until the churchyard was reached. When turning in that direction it passed through the locked gate with the same apparent ease that the other obstacles had been surmounted, and, entering the graveyard, became lost to sight among the tombstones. A week later the woman's daughter was carried a corpse by the same route to the same churchyard.

Joe Porter of Dalbeattie was describing to me recently, during an interview, the delight of his great uncle who had electricity installed at last in his cottage in 2004. No more traipsing around lighting paraffin lamps. Ironically though, as some people strive for more light, some look for less, or none. One of the benefits of having no population is the lack of light pollution. The dark becomes a tourist attraction. Galloway Forest Park was established as a Dark Sky Park on 16 November 2009, one of only a handful in the western world. It's a perfect spot for stargazing and is one of the few places where you can see the Milky Way without a telescope. Dark tourism is growing: Dumfries and Galloway leads the way in new 'dark lighting', new LED lights with a life span of 60,000 hours which give off a white glow rather than orange and face downwards, or if uphill are fitted with shields, so the light is not visible from a distance. In this way the region hopes to become the first official Dark Skies Community in Scotland and only the second in Europe.

All this is good isn't it, unless we snap our keys in the lock? We've always been looking at the sky trying to make sense of our lives in relation to the stars, though, perpetually trying to puzzle it out, as Jean Atkin says.

Outside under
this field of stars
in a frost   that slows
the blood

we are the dark.

We hold in a creel
of air
what's human

and stretch out
our fingertips
to the whorl   of galaxies

to feel what's not there.

('What's Human', Jean Atkin)

*See **Book Town***

Deafness, Oily Fish and Hugh MacDiarmid

I wake up just before the Dumfries and Galloway sign on the Dalveen Pass. I would like to say it is the pull of the region that stirs me from deep sleep but it is in fact the potholes. I am in the back of a car and in the front is John Manson, poet, academic and great expert on Hugh MacDiarmid. We have both been at the Saltire Society in Edinburgh talking about Scots language poetry, a subject of which I know virtually nothing, though this did not stop me haranguing the audience about it for a long time. We were also meant to be having a hugely intelligent conversation about this topic and I think this went well. John Manson is a gifted and charming man, though ever so slightly deaf. When I dozed off in the car I'm sure John Manson had been telling us about the Independent Labour Party's criticism of MacDiarmid's views on fascism in the 1920s.

'Rich in vitamin D of course,' he is saying now, 'and comes from Kirroughtree.' For a moment I wonder if he is describing James Maxton, the head of the Independent Labour Party who took such a dislike to MacDiarmid, and who often argued or 'flyted', as they say in Scots, with him but I have never before heard him described in these terms. There is no clear connection between MacDiarmid and oily fish, unlike Neil Gunn whose father was a herring boat captain. If there had been a connection between MacDiarmid and oily fish, however, I am certain that John Manson would have ruthlessly tracked it down. Having published the unpublished letters of MacDiarmid, he moved onto the unpublished poetry of MacDiarmid and now is working on the unpublished prose of MacDiarmid. If there was an oily fish in there, this most tenacious of scholars would have found it.

It soon becomes clear, however, that John Manson is talking about Ferry Fish, the company who sell oily fish in Castle Douglas and elsewhere. His doctors have recommended it to him to improve his general health. As I am still a bit argumentative, I ask John Manson if there is a reason why so much of MacDiarmid's work was unpublished, but unfortunately he has not taken enough oily fish to hear the question.

Disasters

It's strange that Dumfries and Galloway, a rural area on the periphery of international and national events over the last century and on the fringes of the transport network, should yet have witnessed three of the greatest disasters in British history, on rail, at sea and in the air.

The Gretna or Quintinshill rail disaster happened on 22 May 1915 near Gretna Green at Quintinshill, a signal box with tracks on each side on the Caledonian Railway Main Line linking Glasgow and Carlisle. The crash, involved five trains, killed approximately 226 and remains the worst rail disaster ever to occur in the United Kingdom. Those killed were mainly Territorial soldiers from the 1/7th (Leith) Battalion, the Royal Scots heading for Gallipoli.

The MV *Princess Victoria* was one of the earliest roll on/roll off car ferries. Built in 1947, she operated from Stranraer to Larne. During a savage storm on 31 January 1953, she sank in the North Channel with the loss of 133 lives, including all the women and children on board.

Pan Am Flight 103 was a Pan Am transatlantic flight from

Frankfurt to Detroit via London and New York City that was destroyed by a terrorist bomb on Wednesday 21 December 1988, killing all 243 passengers and 16 crew on board. Large wreckage fell on Lockerbie killing 11 more people on the ground.

Disasters often come accompanied by strange ironies The Gretna rail casualties were men on their way to war who were killed in their own country, by the negligence of their own countrymen, shot in some cases in their burning wooden carriages by their own officers. The *Princess Victoria* was a state-of-the-art ferry whose revolutionary stern doors were designed to stop the very swamping that was the cause of her sinking. Pan Am was brought down at Christmas, the season of good will.

Of these disasters the last is the most painful, perhaps because time has not added much perspective to the misery or maybe because its unexpected and gothic unreality is so stark.

...They are mingled now in death, the joyous hearts

that were bound homewords in festal time,
a unity with those who walked these streets.

And evil finds no yield in the clear souls
of those who yet remain; what man calls grace
triumphs at last over the setters of snares.

As dawn comes up and the mist fades on the hill.

('Lockerbie', William Neill)

Lockerbie, whether it likes it or not will forever be associated with the atrocity perpetrated on Pan Am Flight 103. It is perhaps too soon to properly interpret events. Certainly the whole back story has a yard or two to unravel yet. Much of it is too raw in the memory to digest beyond the stories that people construct, quite rightly, to see them through such times. Lasting relationships have been established between the people of different nations, friendships and marriages made. However people have also been scarred for life by what happened and by what they saw. Traditional Scots small town cynicism – or is it pragmatism? – sometimes meets and rubs against the desperate desire to see long term good.

A resident who didn't want to be named told me 'A lot of the people who spout about Lockerbie now, weren't even present at the disaster, some weren't even living here yet. There's a sick kudos in it. The people that were here were the people that don't speak, the folk who found the bodies in their gardens. They don't talk much about it. There's an industry to the Lockerbie disaster and that brings strength to some but most folk wish it had never happened, obviously, and want to forget it. No disrespect to anyone, but they want to forget it. The politicians like to be in the photographs though.'

Of course the personal takes precedence, raw statistics mean nothing, but there's an insatiable need for people to tell the side stories; why were there no women and children among the survivors of the Princess Victoria; why were so many people booked on Flight 103 who didn't go; why at Quintinshill were four children's bodies, unidentified to this day, found on the train? Reams of print have been produced about these issues, and more will come. The minutiae of disasters seem endlessly fascinating.

One last irony I've never seen in a book but I was told of very recently by a man from Eastriggs. One of the signalmen, James Meakin, who helped cause the disaster at Quintinshill spent the rest of the day after the crash ferrying food and supplies on his motorbike from the crash site to the village and back. People say he was genuinely horrified by the disaster and the part he played in it. No matter, in the process of his repeated journeys, he ran down and killed a child, the great uncle of Hugh Bryden, the man I was talking to. After being jailed for his part in the derailment, Meakin returned to the area, and could often be seen sitting outside his door, whittling at pieces of wood, and occasionally directing visitors to the scene of the disaster.

Domino Lingua

When I was just out of school, I occasionally went to the Newton Hotel to play dominos with the auld heids there. An 'auld heid' is a sage or bikku, one who has lived long and never fails to dispense the accumulated wisdom acquired during a difficult life. I think being in their company is the best modern equivalent I can imagine to meeting the Delphic Oracle or the priestesses of Vesta because these old men came accompanied not only by their own personal cloud of cigarette smoke but their own brand of magic. I could swear, I will swear, that when you laid the first domino down they knew with perfect accuracy the rest of your hand, who was going to win the game, and the next, and what age your father was when you were

conceived. How this was possible I have no idea beyond that they were possessed of genuinely supernatural powers. As befits magi, they also had their own ritual language and song. A double six was 'toffee teeth', a double blank a 'dooble baker'. The winner, placing the victorious double, would recite 'too late, too late, will be the cry when the man with the double passes you by'. They would taunt each other by chanting 'the mair you lose, the mair I booze.' Dominos remains an arcane science to me, I just lay down whatever tile comes to hand. I think, having mixed with Olympians, anything more presumptuous would be disrespect.

*See **The Old Tongue***

Dorothée Aurélie Marianne Pullinger

Dorothée was one of the 'feisty' women who advanced equality between the wars in Dumfries and Galloway, or took advantage of the times to make her mark.

Dorothée Pullinger was educated at Loughborough then began work as a draftsman in The Arrol-Johnston Motor Works in Dumfries which her father managed. During the First World War the Vickers company appointed her to manage a munitions factory in Barrow and Furness which employed 7,000 women. In 1916 a new munitions factory was established near Kirkcudbright which included an engineering college and apprenticeship scheme just for women. After the war, this munitions facility, in Tongland, was converted to the manufacture of automobiles and was renamed as Galloway Motors Ltd. The company employed a largely female workforce making cars 'built by ladies, for those of their own sex'. The factory had a swimming pool, a music room, and its own hockey team. The college provided 'educated women, to whom a life of independence from relations is necessary, a new career of brilliant prospects.' The company badge was the same colours as the Suffragette tricolour.

The factory produced the *Galloway*, a lightweight vehicle designed especially for female drivers. Dorothée herself was an enthusiastic race car driver and won the cup in the Scottish Six Day Car Trials in 1924. In 2012 she was inducted into the Scottish Engineering Hall of Fame.

See Feisty, Munitionettes

Douglas Fairbanks Junior

On one of the few regional bus journeys I wish had lasted longer I am talking to a gentleman in his eighties about being propositioned by Douglas Fairbanks Junior.

'Of course,' he is saying, 'my mother and father knew Douglas Fairbanks Junior quite well. He was often round for coffee. He was very fond of coffee, never tea. My mother used to bake for him. I used to look forward to it because he always brought things we couldn't get, it was wartime you see, and every time he went away he would give me two bob. He used to visit a lady – the Merry Widow we called her – in Tynron. My mum knew her quite well. She had a bright red sports car, very unusual, and they used to go about in it. He borrowed it one day and asked my folks if he could take me away for the day and they said no. I always wondered why, asked my mum years afterwards and she said "There was something not quite right about him." What a story that would have made. Of course, it was just the chocolate I was after.'

See Stagecoach – not the Company, the Mode of Transport

Drink & Accordions

There is a strange Scottish complaint in which your body resolves internal aesthetic conflicts by an uncontrollable spasmodic tapping of feet. The mind knows that the perfect pitch is the sound of an accordion hitting a skip but the body can't help itself responding to ancient genetic memories by keeping time. Accordions are the curse of Scotland according to some, the perfect music of the kailyard. The rasping and rhythmic gasping for air as well as continual fiddling with the fingers makes this a peculiarly appropriate instrument for Scots, however, and the piano accordion remains hugely popular in the region. One of its greatest exponents, Max Houliston in Dumfries, still plays to bus tour audiences in his pub the Hole in the Wa every week. Another accordionist, one who liked a tipple, also used to play in the Hole in the Wa. 'Max,' said a regular one day, 'that accordionist has a drink problem.' Max leaned closer. 'That drunk', he said, 'has an accordion problem.'

Athough I have played my part in keeping up the regional averages, it is not true that in Dumfries and Galloway more drink is taken than in any other part of Scotland because in truth we are a nation that likes its drink and Dumfries and Galloway just forms part of the great liquid heritage that is Scotland's history. However, as befits a frontier area, it has done more than its bit. After all wasn't it at the Mull of Galloway that the last Pict with the secret of heather ale jumped into the sea rather than give that secret to the Romans? And what resulted? Drinking heather ale, the Roman Legions would surely have been able to gub the Goths and the Vandals and all these other tribes over the Danube and perhaps we would all still be Romans, eating quail and rubbing our chins with pumice stones. Would that not be good? Let me have another pint and think about it.

Carting booze around the region, especially without paying duty, was a popular and life-threatening pastime for many years, and the proliferation of unlicensed drinking establishments gave a ready market. When Burns was an exciseman he visited my own village Penpont which now doesn't even have a single pub but then had nine. He was beaten up for his snooping, quite wrongly as didn't Burns, in 'Tam o' Shanter', write the greatest poem about being drunk in the history of the world?

Ae market night,
Tam had got planted unco right,
Fast by an ingle, bleezing finely,
Wi reaming saats, that drank
   divinely

In 1716 there were no less than 91 brewers in Dumfries. An early 19th century street plan of Dumfries shows more than 30 pubs or premises selling booze in Queensberry Street alone. Stranraer in 1869 had 51 licensed premises, described by the council as 'in far excess of the requirements'.

Though the number of pubs declined, the region's love affair with alcohol continued. Even after the Defence of the Realm Act in 1915 when pub opening hours were restricted to stop munitions workers falling steaming in the cordite, folk found a way round it. England's more relaxed licensing laws, at least until the 1970s, meant that people in some parts of the region were well placed to slip across the border for that vital last half hour's boozing. And not in small numbers. The Gretna munitionettes, there in spades to save the nation during World War One, took the train to Carlisle for a drink on a Friday or Saturday night. Trouble was the train arrived five minutes before closing time. Sometimes the train drivers were bribed to leave early but the barmen of

Bousted's Bar in Carlisle knew to start pouring and lining up a thousand whiskies on the bar before all these thirsty men and women arrived.

Others were prepared to risk their lives. After the giant Solway viaduct was shut to rail traffic, a guardhouse and gates had to be constructed to stop folk running the mile and a half across the Firth to more liberal drinking hours. People dying for a drink.

Now, although the pubs are fewer, the thirst remains. Of course alcohol abuse is a terrible curse and drain on the NHS but human beings and drink are involved in a passionate and historical romance which continues to this day. Recently in Dalbeattie we were drinking our way through some of the gantry in the aptly named Cum Ye Inn and swapping some drinking anecdotes but most were either litigious or not very savoury.

My favourite story involves a visitor to Dumfries who was staying at the house of a resident and who set off on his own one October evening to explore. The next morning when he surfaced

he told a story of the pub he ended the night in. He couldn't recall the name he said but there was a horse on the sign, there was a folk band, a beautiful girl, a roaring fire and he'd won £30 worth of tokens all of which he'd spent on drink and his new friend. He couldn't wait to go back and meet her. Of course, he couldn't find it because no such pub existed. Was it drink conflating three separate pubs together? Or was it a supernatural experience? Or was he just raving drunk?

Care, mad to see a man sae happy,
E'en drown'd himsel amang the
  nappy.
As bees flee hame wi' lades o'
  treasure,
The minutes wing'd their way wi'
  pleasure:
Kings may be blest, but Tam was
  glorious,
O'er a' the ills o' life victorious!

('Tam o' Shanter', Robert Burns)

The friend and resident, from whom I gathered this tale, said the man had persisted stubbornly in this delusion, even sending in an envelope a small silver fruit machine token he'd found at the bottom of his pocket. Needless to say it didn't fit any of the fruit machines his friend could find in the town.

*See **Munitionettes, Pubs; where have they gone?***

Duke of Elsinore

> Look here, upon this picture, and
>   on this,
> The counterfeit presentment of two
>   brothers.
> See, what a grace was seated on this
>   brow;
> Hyperion's curls; the front of Jove.
>
> (*Hamlet*, Act Three Scene Four)

Beneath the staircase in Drumlanrig Castle, Hamlet and Gertrude, aka Frazer Morton and Morgan Crosbie, two 16-year-olds from Thornhill, stand using a portrait of Sir Nicholas Carew by Hans Holbein the Younger, 1532, as a mere prop. All around could be Elsinore, sumptuous wallpaper embossed in gold, portraiture worth a fortune. There's a bookcase stuffed with Sotheby's catalogues, appropriate for a man who owns 1,500 paintings and miniatures. Nearby stands the window where Da Vinci's *Madonna with the Yarnwinder*

made an undignified exit at the hands of two art thieves in 2003. They've moved the good chairs and brought in mere Chippendales for the cast to sit on.

> 'Have you eyes?
> Could you on this fair mountain
>   leave to feed,
> And batten on this moor? Ha!
>   Have you eyes?'

It's an extraordinary moment, one the students will remember. It's not everyone that gets in here to work on such a sumptuous and redolent film set, a background that stinks of real passions and history. The noise of construction outside reminds us that folk pay up to a quarter of a million pounds to get married here with the castle as a backdrop, and these young actors have got in for nothing – philanthropy and the Duke's liking for a bit of theatre triumphing in this case over hard cash.

The Queensberry Initiative is an attempt to link the Duke's estate to the young people round about, in terms of vocational training and providing one of the best outdoor classrooms in the world. Though it's not just a philanthropic thing; the estate benefits not just in terms of PR but by grooming a potential workforce. Having said that, though, the Duke was so keen to allow the kids to participate in this particular project that he involved himself in the preliminary meetings, and was even waiting for the team in the car park on their first day. They had hoped that he might play a cameo role, the ghost perhaps, on day two but he played the role too well and vanished on the days of the filming.

Only one shot remains to be filmed, and the head gardener is busy digging a grave outside. When the interior shots are over and the cast is departing, someone notices in one of the other rooms, sitting prosaically among the treasures, the board game of *Who Wants To Be A Millionaire*.

*See **Macbeth in Dumfries***

Dumfries

Dumfries, so good they named it once. Dumfries has had so many identities, so many makeovers, it seems to be a town on the run from itself, its true self only glimpsed in clues and vignettes.

When I think of Dumfries, the town of my boyhood, manhood and senility, I think of many Dumfrieses all set, to one extent or another, in my imagination. And how could they be anywhere else?

I think of my own Dumfries, Duke Swann's little cave full of comics in the High St, *Evening News* sellers like Eddie P, hot chips in Piolis after school, the closes at the end of the High Street, great for games and imagining. I think of walking my girlfriend romantically past the sewage plant to Kingholm Quay, of my mother dying in the hospital muttering quietly to her

own mother in the Highlands
dead 30 years before. This was
the Dumfries of hopes and
disappointments and death, of the
pub and the dead end, the place
to dream of getting away from,
only to find yourself back:

> When I am walking up
>   Queensberry Street in low cloud
> and tread on chips floating in an
>   oily puddle,
> I am actually on the Cierro Del Sol,
>   staring through trees
> at ponds like pearl, the roses and
>   myrtle.
>
> When I turn onto the High Street at
>   seven o'clock at night
> and neds are stoned out of their
>   brains and jeering,
> I am hearing the sound of
>   nightingales in gardens
> with the heat still singing and the
>   sun setting on fire.
>
> At midnight I am not leaving the
>   Hole in the Wa,
> fumbling my way through a huddle
>   of strange dwarves,
> but moving statuesquely through
>   the lush blooms
> of my imagination, heavy and sweet
>   as jacaranda,

> and the night will not end here, in
>   light to heavy drizzle,
> and a taxi that fines you a hundred
>   quid for being sick,
> it will not end here in damp
>   sandstone and shadows
> but surely with a last long kiss
>   below an orange moon.

('Not Actually Being in Dumfries')

I think also of the Dumfries of a
century or so ago, the town of
Barrie and Carlyle, the port busy,
the town a bustling mixture of the
squalid and the expansive, Dumfries
as a literary salon centring round
Anderson's Book shop, dances
round the bandstand, boats on
the river, the silver light playing
on trees reflected in water like
Fergusson's paintings, Dickens
about to read to a rapturous
audience in Irish Street.

I think of the medieval Dumfries,
full of folk hardened by burnings
and border wars, the Dumfries
where international treaties were
signed, Kings proclaimed, where
ancient and beautiful buildings
stood, long gone to ground, the
Chapel of St Thomas, the
Monastery of the Grey Friars, the
Crystal Chapel, the Castle of
Dumfries.

I think too of the future. Dumfries has important cultural references in Barrie and Burns, second in literary heritage only to Edinburgh you might argue, and impeccable credentials in the mad maelstrom that was Scottish medieval history and the Wars of Independence. I may have banged on about this before, but here's my vision. Let's dig up that whole block between the Friars' Vennel, Buccleuch Street and Irish Street and excavate the old Greyfriars Monastery, the place where the Scottish Wars of Independence began with Robert Bruce's murder of John Comyn. Let's turn half the site, like the Jorvik Centre, into a display of working archaeology and the other half into a lavish reconstruction, like the great hall of Stirling castle. It would become a magnet for tourists who could then go on to the Barrie and Burns stuff. I'll come and pretend to be Rab Bruce, with a dirk up my sock. Who wants to be the Red Comyn? Pow, you free?
See Barrie, JM, Burns,Robert, Chrissie Fergusson, Eddie P

Dykers

To some this is profession is a mystical calling and its practitioners are like wandering priests and poets in stone, a real throwback to our rural past. Of this type was Willie McMeekin, the dyker from New Luce, of whom much more later. For an alternative bitter perspective on the profession though, I talked to Dean Vaughan of Crocketford, the only dyker I know with a degree in Law. 'Lot of folk just being made redundant use their pay-off to get a van, next thing they're a dyker... or landscape gardener,' he adds, bitterly, as he works at that too.

Most people agree, however, that proper dykers are born, not chosen, like the one lauded by Mactaggart:

> His dykes had ne'er the sleek'd skin,
> ne'er fair without and false within...
> a rickl'd rood ne'er left his han',
> his dykes for centuries will stan'.

(Davie the Dyker: John Mactaggart)

The heart of the dyke, the bit you can't see, is the important part. When you pass a dyke whose guts have spilled, you know it hasn't been 'hearted' properly, filled with hard level stones packed tight. There's the skill, that and the coping or keystanes that lock it in place. Anyone can build a dyke that looks good, not everyone can build one that lasts. Ask Dean Vaughan.

Dykers were not always seen as reliquaries of a sacred past. In the 18th century they enclosed the land for the landowners, destroying common grazing, causing rural depopulation, and their dykes became symbols of the repression of the people. Mactaggart compared them to the walls built by the Romans to pen the people in. The Levellers, led by people like Billy Marshall, mobilised to pull them down.

Nevertheless the dykes criss-crossing Galloway, many of them hundreds of years old, are a romantic sight, and the craft nowadays is one of the few practised continuously through the generations, occasionally passed down from father to son.

The old man learned his trade the
   hard way,
I'm learning his practice in muscle
   ache.
The scholar released for the
   summer...
He built walls in bonded patterns,
simple repetitions made sense. A
   mixture
we worked well together; the wall
   grew tall.
He's on the other side now, scarcely
   visible.

('Spelling Galloway', Davie Douglas)

There still is a sense of passing something on, not necessarily from father to son, but to the landscape, a gift to time. Scott Maxwell told me he likes to do it the old way, take the dykes right down to repair them: 'Every wee bit you'd find little bits of crockery the original dykers left, or their names carved under a stone. It was like keeping history going. I always stayed up in the hills, it was cheaper than travelling back and forwards, built a lean-to against the dyke, stayed there. Puts you in touch wi nature, that, and yourself. It's what they did in the old days. I liked it, there's nothing as good.

The auld boys would hae approved.'

Another young dyker I spoke to very recently pours a tot of whisky onto the dykes he repairs as a tribute to the dykers who came before, who he's convinced are still watching him, measuring his craft, watching their measure.

*See **Levellers, Willie McMeekin***

EA Hornel

EA Hornel was a colourist and Glasgow Boy who travelled widely in Japan and elsewhere. His experimentations with bright colour and context were revolutionary for their time and very controversial. Later in life he produced more formulaic work, emphasising the beauties of rural life. He was a long time inhabitant of Kirkcudbright where he founded an extensive library on the history and literature of Dumfries and Galloway. As he got older he took a lot of photographs of small girls, and after he was dead, held a conversation with me in the Selkirk Arms.

On every panelled wall
they crouch or dance,
Hornel's little girls.
In arab dress or kimono,
in cloud or deep blossom,
their hair jet, their cheeks gloss,
their smiles frozen.
How many mothers
took them home,
scolded away their tears?
What an honour to be there
in the big house
paint piled on their faces
like ice.

('Hornel's Little Girls')

See Art, Chrissie Fergusson

Eddie P

The name of a stocky newspaper seller of the *Evening News* who worked outside Binns Department Store in Dumfries til the 1970s. Much ridiculed for his red complexion and sometimes incomprehensible delivery, 'Evnanewss', but he was a war hero of sorts. Eddie P was a sergeant in the commandos. After the allied invasion of Italy he was sent out with two men on a mission to a large house behind German lines, acting on a rumour that high ranking German officers were billeted there. In fact all they found was one very drunk German soldier and the biggest wine cellar in Southern Italy. It was six months before Eddie's platoon were rescued and he was repatriated with a chronic liver condition. The German, still drunk, was taken prisoner.

*See **Drink & Accordions***

Elephants

On my way home from Castle Douglas and sightings of ospreys and beautiful soaring red kites I am reassured that the region's natural heritage is rich. Staring at Elephant Rock earlier got me thinking of animals that are not part of our tradition, however, and how exciting it was and is to first see in the flesh creatures only glimpsed before in books. I remember the circuses that used to come to the area with awe and affection but this is not an experience to be granted weans in the future. In 2007, acting on legislation to protect animals, Dumfries and Galloway Council banned Anne, then 54 years old and the last travelling elephant in Britain, from appearing in public in the region or even getting her photograph taken. Elephants appear to me to be singular in the appearance of dignity and wisdom, and there are many references to

them in the area. 'There are as many elephants and crocodiles in Galloway as orderly persons,' wrote Claverhouse, persecutor of the Covenanters. He didn't mean it literally of course, but there are a few. Actual elephants I mean.

Apart from the Elephant Rock at Heston Island, one of the Pictish panels at Trusty's Fort near Gatehouse seems to depict part of a 'swimming elephant', the name given to a particular long trunked beast the Picts were fond of carving. Of course it can't be meant as an elephant, though the Romans did bring at least one across to Britain in the Claudian invasion.

To the Romans and Greeks the elephant was a creature of great meaning. Aristotle called it 'the beast that passeth all others in wit and mind... and by its intelligence makes as near an approach to man as matter can make to spirit.'

Elephants appear to be buried all over Dumfries and Galloway, usually as a result of having died while in travelling circuses, which were hugely popular. There's one in Stranraer, one called Rosie in Gatehouse, one called Bosco from Pindar's Travelling Circus buried in the Dock Park Dumfries, having died in 1923 'from eating poisoned grass' and another near Thornhill which died after a travelling circus from Europe was prevented from leaving the country by the outbreak of World War Two. The elephant there was buried in great secrecy to prevent the ivory being dug up by local entrepreneurs.

Emigration

As I've said before, and will doubtless say again since it is one of the motifs of this book, the major historical export from Dumfries and Galloway was its people. Arguably it still is today. Though the flow has lessened, it is still significant. How many people left from what is now Dumfries and Galloway in the 19th century? Statistics are hard to find but, for an example, out of a total of 478,224 Scots entering the United States between 1852 and 1910 some nine per cent were from the area, an astonishingly high statistic. They left from embarkation ports in Annan, Glencaple, Carsethorne, Wigtown and Stranraer carrying a steady stream of new blood to the colonies, having their own unique impact on a series of important and history changing events; the suppression of the indigenous peoples of the 'New' World, the foundation of new states like the USA, the creation of the British Empire.

I was close to being an emigrant. When I was in my final year at university my tutor in American History arranged a job for me on graduation at a local newspaper in Philadelphia. Various things happened and I didn't go in the end. I've often wondered what would have happened if I'd become transatlantic.

When there's traffic in my mind,
I end up in Philadelphia,
strolling in the Avenue of the Arts
with a well groomed girl,
or punching the air like Rocky
on the steps of the Rodin Museum
at the sight of another by line
from Scoop McMillan.
As I eat hoagies in the
unusually mild weather this Fall,
I watch leaves slowly drift to sea.
At this point I'm interrupted by a
    bum.
What is a hoagie? he asks.
And what's it like to be on the edge
of a humid subtropical zone?
He's drunk again, and on Wikipedia,
and soon he'll show me, irresistibly,
pictures of his home town.

('Hoagies')

Historically the region's children
have achieved some great things.
Unlike me, Robert, David and
William Lenox, sons of a
Kirkcudbright merchant called
James Lenox, made it to
Philadelphia. They arrived just as
the American War of Independence
was kicking off. All three brothers
served in the war, Robert and
William went to New York to join
the British cause and David stayed
in Philadelphia and was eventually
promoted to an officer in the
American Army. He later became
President of the Philadelphia
Bank. Following the war, Robert
had a career as a shipping agent,
and invested in spectacularly
successful real estate purchases
around New York City. Robert's
son James worked alongside his
father as a merchant and inherited
his father's vast fortune in 1839.
James, a bibliophile and
philanthropist, retired from work
to collect rare books. He amassed
an impressive collection which
included the first Gutenberg Bible
in the United States. The Lenox
Library was made accessible to
the public in 1870, in 1895 it was
joined with the Astor Library and
the Tilden Trust to become what
is now the New York Public
Library.

Of course you hear all about
the success stories whilst the life
stories of most of the others go
unchronicled. That's the way with
history, the famous get written
about. However we have some
evidence from others. In a
remarkable memoir Annie Jeanne
McMichael Grimes from New
Galloway wrote:

It was a chilly, foggy morning in October 1879 when the beautiful old ship, 'The Star' of the Canard Line was docked in the harbour of Liverpool, England. Among the passengers going aboard were my mother, Aunt Hetty and myself, a very small child. We had left the old farm home among the heathered hills of Scotland which had been in our family for almost a century. The name of this farm was 'Fallow Wheat', a short distance from New Galloway. My father had sailed to America a short time before to locate a home for us, and was to meet us in New York on landing.

She goes on to relate the story of her aunt and uncle Annie and James McKelvie, also from New Galloway. Annie McKelvie was on the same ship with her four young children making for Illinois where James had found a farm. In America they had six more children:

At first times were good but then things changed... Little Esther died on May 27, 1891 at the age of 2 months, 6 days. In the latter half of the 90's, Annie and some of the children took the 'consumption', and Annie died on May 27, 1897, age 47... Tuberculosis was to take its toll on the others too: Jessie, December 8, 1902, age 25; Henrietta, September 2, 1904, age 19; and Annie, May 20, 1908, age 34. Little wonder that James moved what was left of his family from Illinois.

It's this kind of thing that goes through my mind when I'm haunting the creeks and silted channels of the Solway with its rotting piers and overgrown bollards, the ghosts of ships and the legions of weans setting sail across a vast and endless sea to who knows what?

Then almost unseen
river rehearses being sea.
There are bollards sunk like teeth
in the green mudbanks
where it slips away,
where the tall ships left.
They slipped away at night
across starless horizons,
and disappeared
as even blood does, eventually.
We sigh and walk our dogs
who crap on ghosts of quayside.
What is history anyway
but a shift of tide?

('Leaving')

*See **Carsethorne, Ghost Landscape***

F

I have an influential literary anthology of the early 1970s containing the cream of Dumfries and Galloway's poetical talent: Kirkpatrick Dobie, George Macadam, Bill Shannon, Helen Woodhouse and Douglas Rome. Kirkpatrick Dobie is the best known of these but even he, by dint of choosing to live and work in Dumfries, has little reputation beyond the region in spite of being, by any sane measurement, an outstanding poet. Later in life, partly thanks to the attention of the Scottish poet Gerry Cambridge, he gained some critical attention and a major selection of his works was published by Peterloo in 1992, seven years before his death. Look at this for directness and sensitivity:

> Tall poppies grow beside the stile,
> some partly hidden by the hedge,
> and some that brush the upper rail
> are rooted at the very edge.
>
> In June of every year they come
> red-orange-tipped and irised-brown.
> They sway towards you as you pass
> and touch your hand as you step
>   down.
>
> Great gangling girls, they never
>   learn
> how much of men is purely brute,
> so every year they come again
> and some are trampled underfoot.

('Tall Poppies', Kirkpatrick Dobie)

Douglas Rome was the mad intellectual of the group. He worked as a sub-editor in the *Dumfries and Galloway Standard* until he was sacked for writing radical editorials railing against local landowners while the real editor was on holiday. With the equally insane Jim Gilpin, a Trotskyite perpetually engaged, long before it was fashionable, in writing a novel about the vampire community in Dumfries, he made up a double act well known in Dumfries in the late 60s and 70s. I blame Gilpin and Rome for the creative bat on my neck. Friends of my sister, they came to the house one night, lay in the fireplace and enthralled my mother and me with a long dialogue they made up on the spot about Stalin's purges which involved Gilpin strangling Rome with his thighs while the latter begged for his life in song. That was my creative birth. As far as I know, all the poets in the anthology, *A Fatal Tree*, are now dead, the youngest, Douglas Rome, walking into the Nith one wet Saturday afternoon just a few weeks ago. I was on a bus that was passing at the time, and wondered what all the fuss was about.

See Journalists, Makar

Feisty Women

During a village gala I overheard a conversation between two men both of whom had their backs turned to me at the time.

> Male 1: Marilyn caught up wi ye, then?
>
> Male 2: Aye, is it no obvious?
>
> (*Turns round to reveal huge black eye or keeker, with yellow and orange streaks on a black and purple background*)
>
> Male 1: She's aye been feisty.
>
> Male 2: (*Touching the affected area tentatively*) She's my dream wumman.

Although 'feisty' was used there in an undiluted and adoring fashion, it's often patronisingly applied to women with the subtext that it's a bit unnatural really for them to want to do things like explore their potential when there's embroidery or ironing still to be done. Dumfries and Galloway has had powerful women in the past who have used their wealth and position to make an impact on events in spite of expectation, like Lady Devorgilla and the heroic and indefatigable Winifred Maxwell of Terregles. Likewise in the 20th century there have been women in a variety of fields who have triumphed in areas recognised up to then as men's, for instance Dorothée Pullinger in engineering, Flora Murray in medicine, Elsie MacKie in aviation, Chrissie Fergusson in art. They've usually been a bit posh, but the history of Dumfries and Galloway is also full of stories of ordinary working class women who didn't take any crap. Women who were smugglers and levellers, for instance.

When in Ruthwell in 1777, the excise found out that a smuggler called Morrow of Hidwood had returned from the Isle of Man, they searched the man's house, finding there a lot of illicit tobacco. They were preparing to carry it away when 'a multitude of women pounced, making off with the contraband', locking the revenue man in the house. After he escaped and returned to his headquarters, he came back with ten armed men. Nevertheless, they still had to 'run the gauntlet of... a monstrous regiment... of women armed with clubs and pitchforks.'

My favourite is the tale of Maggie McConnell. In Dally Bay near Stonykirk; the Stranraer revenue officer had intercepted a large haul of cloth and brandy and, having put a band of smugglers to flight, was sitting on the beach quite pleased with himself when Maggie McConnell 'a very comely woman of about forty' wandered up, threw him onto his back, stole his pistol and, cocking it at his head, sat on his midriff pinning him to the ground and putting her apron over his head. When she took it away every piece of contraband had vanished. She then sauntered back into the undergrowth.

Often the women were smugglers' molls, so to speak, rather than smugglers themselves, but women certainly played the leading part in the food riots that took place in some Solway ports in the 18th and early 19th centuries. These centred on ships that were exporting food at times of shortage and high prices. Although men were sometimes involved on the periphery, the organisation, planning and execution of these raids, often extremely violent, were carried out exclusively by women. In 1763, seven women were charged with mobbing and destroying the rigging of a ship in Stranraer in an attack in which one crew member lost an eye and another several teeth. In 1796 Agnes Byers, Katherine Miller and Janet Nicol were charged with mobbing and trying to stop the loading of grain onto a ship in Port William. They were also accused of stoning members of the crew to the 'great effusion of their blood and the danger of their lives.' Janet Nicol ripped off one of the crew member's ears, saying later she only meant to get 'a chuggle of his hair'. In April 1801 Marie Milligan, Agnes Glover and Marion Ireland forcibly boarded a ship in Kirkcudbright laden with potatoes, taking them 'without authority' and 'distributing them at a price they deemed just'. Not content with that, they then sought out the farmer who was exporting the potatoes, dragged him to the harbour and threw him in.

See **Bodkin, Chrissie Fergusson, Dorothée Pullinger, Jailbirds, Old Aeroplanes**

Ferry Bell Tower

A small crowd, swelled by the presence of the whole of Creetown Primary School, stands in the gale and driving rain in a muddy field to hear the Ferry Bell Tower toll. It's the culmination of a year of work in the town by a collection of artists working in the community. It features a specially cast bronze bell in the style of the one which used to be in the quarry here, and a series of flags on themes special to the town. The group has done other work in the area, for instance the schoolgirl Evie Cloy was chosen as town crier and had the honour of first ringing the bell.

The piece's sculptor Will Levi Marshall, struggling to make himself heard in the wind and sleet, is at pains to remind the crowd how much Creetown has been involved in the making of this artwork. It's a theme picked up by the chairman of the Creetown Initiative in a small speech, and in a conversation I have with one of the project workers. They tell me the tower will generate a lot of interest. The tower has not been 'imposed on the landscape. The functionality of the piece, at once a flagpole, bell-tower and landmark, makes the work a really practical addition to the community it serves.'

I don't know why at gatherings like these I am reminded

churlishly of the Narodniks, a crowd of bearded and bourgeois Russian students from the city who in the 1860s travelled into the countryside to tell the peasants what to believe in. Is that too cynical? There are real artists here, after all, working with the kids and in the community, giving these weans an insight into the processes as well as the excitement of art, one they'll maybe remember and that might inspire them to be creative, too. And what's more these might be tourist attractions, if it ever stops raining. Even if it doesn't.

Nevertheless, the town is dying and this seems to me a kind of memorial. Twenty families have left in the last 18 months, since the last big employer folded. A long-term resident said, 'We used to have a police station, the doctors, the nurse, a post office, but there's nothing much now, a butcher's shop open in the mornings.' The flags designed by Lisa Gallagher, are, let's face it, funeral flags, commemorating famous things about the town that have gone into the storm and mist, like shipping, like the quarry, the Silver Band and so on.

What did John Betjeman say in *Summoned by Bells?*

> As I struggled up, I saw grey brick,
> The cemetery railings and the tomb.

> Bells take you to work and when there is no work toll the passing of hours, then the passing of life itself. So says an old poem about the ancient Kirkmaiden Bell, sunk in Luce Bay on its way to a new home, which tolls solemnly when a member of the old family of Myrton dies.

> An' certes, there are nane, I trow,
> That by Kirkmaiden bide,
> Will, when they hear the wraith-
>   bell jow,
> Gae oot at Lammastide.

> (Nathaniel McKie)

In the rain, as cars and lorries sweep by on the nearby bypass, and the flags stream in the wind, we queue up to toll the tinny Ferry Bell.

*See **Ghost Landscape**, **Villages of the Damned**, **Voice***

Festivals

I suppose the music festivals in the area are the modern equivalent of the horse or hiring fairs, when everyone lets their hair down and normal rules are suspended for the duration. Perhaps the tradition goes back even further than that to classical or pagan times. I've been reminded of bacchanalia the odd time I've been to one, or had tales recounted to me about the shenanigans that have gone on. The desire to have a good time, to be transported beyond the humdrum by music, drink or ecstasy, religious or any other type, is endemic in the human condition. So whoop whoop! The festival goer is well served in Dumfries and Galloway with the Eden Festival, Knockengorroch and the papa of them, the Wickerman, invented by Sid Ambrose and Jamie Gilroy, as a laid-back more alternative event to ones like Glastonbury, the backdrop of the 'incomparable beauty' of Galloway being a vital and unique contributory factor to the experience. As well as the big events, there are many smaller traditional music festivals, jazz festivals and even a blues festival.

Duncan, an electrician by trade, was and is, one of the area's more eccentric characters and festival goers. Once he cut two holes in the bottom of a large suitcase, a discreet eye hole in the side, dressed himself in red tights and somehow folded himself into the case. He then persuaded his friend to carry the suitcase through a festival crowd on a Saturday afternoon, when everyone was sitting with their picnics or carry outs and having a good time. Then he shot his legs through the holes and ran off through the middle of them with his friend puffing after him shouting, 'Will you stop my suitcase, it's had too much to drink.'

See Wandering Poets

Food Parcels

When I used to teach we would travel, the weans and I, down the deep dark roads of Scottish social history and they usually emerged at the end of two years with a Standard Grade Certificate and a general appreciation for the 20th century, as it was then.

'I don't know how folk lived,' I remember one girl saying during a visit to New Lanark Mills, 'I mean, how did they do their hair?'

The thing about history is that it repeats itself whether you're watching or not and the fact is that Scotland today, in terms of land ownership and wealth distribution, is pretty much the same as it was in 1750.

I'm getting a lift up the road and am squeezed in beside the main cargo in the car; food parcels bound to a town in the north of the region.

'They go as far west as Creetown,' says the driver, an ex-union official, '450 parcels a week across the region to a score of depots. What a society we live in.' The food is donated by individuals and companies. 'One of the most generous, a meat processing firm, was the only place I ever organised a strike. They must remember me.'

While we drive he tells me about his passion for Junior Football. 'The only places you can see football as a working class game for working class people. £5 entry and the clubs give subsidised travel so you can have a day out for a tenner. What a difference from paying silly money to watch millionaires.'

We lapse into silence. On the radio an utterly charming woman is telling the listening public how reasonable it is for everybody in Britain to give the Queen £52 a year, less than £1 a week each, as she's good value for money. And her only worth, according to Forbes in 2012, 44 billion quid.

*See **Duke of Elsinore, Levellers***

Foot-and-Mouth

The UK's worst outbreak was in 2001 and Dumfries and Galloway was one of the hardest hit areas. In total about 1,500 farms lost 750,000 animals, culled. Compensation for slaughtered livestock came to £171 million. However, this did not meet loss of income while farms were without stock, nor did it extend to farms which were not culled, but where farming was disrupted by movement restrictions. Those additional losses were estimated at around £60 million. The culls were not restricted to commercial animals. On the 4 May 2001 vets began slaughtering five pet sheep which had been kept in their owner's house for five days. Carolyn Hoffe of Glasserton had barricaded herself and her five Dutch Zwartbles sheep in her home. On the 15 May Juanita Wilson of Mossburn Animal Sanctuary won a reprieve for her 14 goats and three sheep. Looking back on those days, she said, 'It was a most appalling situation to find yourself in in Britain, you just didn't expect it – the Army breaking peoples' doors down to slaughter their stock, those of us who went through it probably have never fully recovered emotionally. I personally cry far easier than I used to do, it did leave huge emotional scars on us.'

Liz Niven's poetry from the time captures some of the trauma:

A farmer at Ae still
goes out on his quad bike
with his sheep dogs
every day, same time,
though the fields are empty
of beasts.

The farmer at Auchleand
feeds his beasts though
he knows fine they'll be killed
in the morning
'You wouldn't leave them starving
even though,' he tells you.

A farmhouse window is coated
with grease, fat from the burning
animals.

('Merrick Tae Criffel', Liz Niven)

Of course Dumfries and Galloway has always been a frontier, a land within lands, staring out to Ireland, England, Scotland and Man. The kingdom of heaven too, some savants said, and claimed you could see five kingdoms from the Mull of Galloway. And within the place are borders too: the Deil's Dyke, and many other earthworks, like the demilitarised zone on either side of the forts of the River Urr; archaeology that has yet to be completely figured out. The region still feels like a frontier sometimes, especially if you're standing on a wind-lashed shore at Garlieston and the sleet is driving horizontally at your knee caps and every person seems to have been swept from the landscape as if by a plague.

Red-kneed, red-necked? Today I read, the day after the Euro Elections 2014, that Dumfries and Galloway has the greatest support for right-wing parties of any other area in Scotland. 'In a place where depopulation is a tourist attraction it's inevitable that it should be filled with white settlers or hippies,'

someone said to me. The frontier that saw 500 years of invasion, destruction and famine in the wars against England now appears committed, apparently, more than any other, to the union and conservative values. Or maybe they're just bucking the trend, being pig-headed. There has always been a rough and ready libertarian streak in the area, back to the times when there were few laws to enforce from any government.

Scott Walker was telling me recently about another lawless frontier, St Kilda, where he was stationed in the radar base:

> I was there at the same time as Willie Wright, from Dumfries, who was the National Trust Warden. There were many times the seas were so bad we couldn't land supplies and had to have them flown in. They dropped them in army kitbags. Once the mailbag went over the cliffs and Willie abseiled down to get it from the rocks. He came back up, sorted them out and threw all the bills back over the cliff into the sea.

Another time a bag was dropped and it split open, all these prawns spilled out. The officer said pick them up, because they were for the officers' mess, and we did. You can imagine picking up prawns off the ground for that bastard on an island full of big seabirds! Later, though, there was a bit of rough justice. We were standing in a line

and a bag of frozen chickens came down, shattered the officer's shoulder, as well as the Land Rover windscreen. He had to be lifted off by helicopter.

See Bank Managers, SR Crockett and the British Union of Fascist Lifeguards

Funerals

I've attended a lot of funerals in the last two years, which I suppose is a result of getting older, as well as making friends in too many pubs, which are still the places in this area where different generations can meet and mingle. The funerals are all sad affairs, no matter the style, the content or place, for how could they be anything else? It's the ceremony that counts, the sense of some kind of decent end.

In spite of living next door to undertakers, in separate locations, for nearly all of my adult life, I've never felt the urge to go for a pint and have a chat about what they do. However, death is everybody's business and always has been. Dumfries and Galloway is littered

with the evidence of people coming to terms with each other's death since 3000BC and before. Cairn Holy is the most spectacular example but the landscape is littered with cysts, barrows and chambered cairns. Evidence of the Ritual Landscape is everywhere. Later Christian burials incorporated behaviour and traditions imported direct from the pagan past. In 1911, Maxwell Wood in his book *Witchcraft and Superstitious Record in the South-Western District of Scotland* tells us that in the 18th century:

The nearest relative bent down to the dying face to receive the last breath. The door was kept ajar, although not too wide, that the spirit might be untrammelled in its flight. The spirit fled, the poor dead eyes were closed, also by the nearest relative, and generally kept so by means of copper coins placed upon them. The looking-glass in the death-chamber was covered with a white cloth. The clock was stopped, or at least the striking-weight removed. The daily routine of work was discontinued, such days of enforced idleness being known as the 'dead days'. On the farm, for example, no matter the season, the appropriate labour of ploughing, seed sowing, or even harvest, at once ceased. The household companions of dog and cat were rigidly excluded from the stricken house; indeed, it was not uncommon for the cat to be imprisoned beneath an inverted tub, for it was believed that if either of these animals should jump or cross over the dead body, the welfare of the spirit of the deceased would certainly be affected. The body was then washed, and dressed in its last garments, the hands of females being crossed over the breast, those of the other sex being extended by the sides. Last of all a plate of salt was placed upon the breast, either from the higher idea of future life being signified by the salt, which is the emblem of perpetuity, or from a more practical notion, however unlikely, that by this means the body would be prevented from swelling.

To the relief of cats everywhere, such customs are gone. One tradition remains, and that is the wake, or watch, that began as relatives keeping vigil with the corpse until burial. This wake was once a solely Catholic tradition but was adopted by all in the form of a remembrance of the deceased that sometimes involved strong drink taken. Two hundred years ago a drunk funeral procession wound its way for miles through deep snow on Eskdale Moor to arrive in Moffat without the corpse which had fallen off the end of the wagon en route. An account from a Wigtownshire farmer's book of expenses in 1794 showed that though the coffin was the singularly most expensive item, the different drink taken, including a gallon of brandy and a gallon of rum, added to three times as much. This tradition continues now and then. A local storyteller and musician remembers that during the wake that followed the folk singer

Lionel McLellan's funeral in Moffat, 'the whole town ran out of lager'. Lionel's funeral in 2012 was also unusual in that it involved a four letter word – a quote of course – from the pulpit and a 30 piece New Orleans jazz band escorting the coffin from the church to the graveyard.

Funeral customs have changed in a radical way since the 1960s, when it was more common to see a funeral in a house rather than in a church, and where the local joiner would be the undertaker, a practice common still in some rural places. John Wilson from Whithorn in a recent interview said:

> If we had a funeral, say, at the Top of the Town where the streets narrow, the funerals were always well attended... and what would happen at the Top o the Town, they would stand around the door-way and the Minister, we would get the Minister to stand at the door-way so the people, the relatives could hear but also the people outside could hear what was being said.

A service was held in the house for the women folk and then the minister would give the service out in the street to the men before the body was put in a hearse.

Funeral processions are serious matters of course, but on one notorious occasion in Dalbeattie in the 1970s, according to long-term SNP activist Ian Rodgers, a malfunctioning loudspeaker van canvassing for the election got lodged behind one, with the music stuck at maximum volume on 'Will Ye No Come Back Again?'

*See **Ritual Roads, Stanes***

G

Garlieston in Darkness and Light

With the demise of local shipping, railways, milling and agriculture as major employers, there are few jobs in the locality. Young people have to leave the village to find work, and the remaining population becomes increasingly elderly, augmented by retired people from throughout the United Kingdom, coming to enjoy the tranquil village life; and of course, despite the deterioration of some of the scenic parts of the area this 18th century Georgian village still displays traditional pleasantries absent in urban areas.

(*Garlieston*, David Kirkwood)

Traditional pleasantries may have been lacking in the hearts of some in Garlieston a few years ago in an episode which provides a dark example of life imitating art, imitating life. The writer Des Dillon who lives in the town wrote a play entitled *Village of the Damned* in which Robert Thompson, one of the killers of the child James Bulger, is relocated and subsequently exposed in a coastal village in south west Scotland. Fear and suspicion among some in the village led in real life to a campaign of harassment against a man from Bolton, 36-year-old Scott Bradley, recently an incomer into the town, who was alleged by some to be the killer and a paedophile. Bradley killed himself, according to his mother and a diary he had left in his room, as a result of these accusations. His mother was at pains to say that while she directly blamed some in the community for what happened to her son, others had given her great comfort after his death.

Geniuses

Genius springs from the hills and farms of Galloway said Mactaggart. Though he had a wide definition of genius, as a statement I think is true. My own little class in school contained many clever folk at least two of whom I would consider geniuses. Mild mannered Peter Ellis became a scientist and part of the team that invented

Viagra, the drug of choice for lovelorn pensioners, and the other genius would be Professor Christine Bold whose studies of cowboy novels have led to many authoritative books and exalted academic posts. I am not jealous of Peter because I have never understood science, and to me the switching on of a light bulb seems an act akin to shamanism. I am highly jealous of Professor Bold, though, because I have always aspired to the life of academe; perhaps a little plant-lined office in Seville or Philadelphia. I remember the day in 1974 when she became a genius and our routes parted forever, when she refused to come to the pub and said instead she was going to the University Library, a place I had, in spite of being a student there for two years, never visited.

We all had very good schooling, however, and mostly supportive parents to help us on our way. The greatest geniuses are those who seem touched at an early age by some inexplicable source of power and light. One of Galloway's was James Clerk Maxwell, the brilliant mathematician and physicist, voted in the Millennium Poll by the world's hundred most prominent scientists as one of the three greatest of all time. Much of his work was carried out near Kirkcudbright. When he was 14 he published a paper on ovals which improved on the work previously done by the great philosopher and mathematician Rene Descartes. When he was two years old he was described as doing:

> great work with doors, locks, keys etc., and 'Show me how it doos' is never out of his mouth. He also investigates the hidden course of streams and bell-wires, the way the water gets from the pond through the wall and a pend or small bridge and down a drain.

Another prodigy was Alexander Murray, son of a shepherd in Minigaff. His 70-year-old father taught him the alphabet using a wool card and a charred heather stem for a pen. He taught himself languages from a book which had the Lord's Prayer printed in all the tongues of the world, and by the age of 13 he could read Greek, Latin, Hebrew, French and

German. By 16 Abyssinian, Welsh and Anglo Saxon. Through the help of an itinerant second-hand book peddler and part time smuggler named McHarg, he was introduced to Edinburgh and given a bursary to study at the university. He added Icelandic, Sanskrit, Persian and Chinese to the languages he knew, eventually becoming Professor of Oriental Languages at Edinburgh University. He specialised in the dialects of Abyssinia. In fact when George III received a letter from the Governor of Trgri in Abyssinia, the shepherd's boy from Minigaff was the only person in Britain who could read it.

Inventors are another ilk. Their talent involves having an idea and having the determination to pursue it. I suppose Kirkpatrick Macmillan would come into this category. A blacksmith from Keir, he is generally credited with inventing the first mechanically driven two-wheeled bicycle, though some mean-spirited folk dispute this. There's no disputing, however, that he is the first person to have committed a road traffic offence with a bicycle. In 1842 a Glasgow newspaper reported an accident in which an anonymous 'gentleman from Dumfries-shire… bestride a velocipede… of ingenious design' knocked over a little girl in Glasgow and was fined five shillings.

I know for a fact that the spirit of genius and invention is alive and well in the countryside of Dumfries and Galloway today. Only last week in Port William, in the Monreith Arms, a man took the time to explain to us his invention of the fashion shoe with a retractable high heel so that, 'Lassies can get back fae the pub steaming wi out brakking their heids, ken?' He later added that 'Ah hivnae made a prototype yet, it's at the dreamin stage.'

That's what it's about as well, though. Dreaming.

> What makes the difference
> is letting go:
> whether peddling or dreaming,
> letting go of the ground.
> I wonder what's in this landscape
> that turns whiskered sons of the soil
> or manse into dreamers?
> Not far from here are cottages,
> yards apart, that in the space of
> 50 years

turned out an Oxford Don
and an Admiral of the Turkish Navy,
not posh boys,
village boys from a village school.
I suppose it's imagination that makes
ordinary things into marvels,
a Dandy Horse into a bicycle,
a road from Carronbridge to
    Holywood
the runway to infinity.   ('Both Feet Off the Ground')

Geofantasapsychiatry

The longer I have been a writer, the more I realise that I don't have to go to Dumfries and Galloway but that Dumfries and Galloway comes to me, in all shapes and forms, in day to day reality and dreams. You can't function anywhere without some kind of interaction with people and place, and where that happens it's sometimes a cause to write. However the process goes beyond that to a kind of magic, or at the very least a succession of leading coincidences. Or has this obsession and sleep deprivation finally taken its toll?

Recently I got a parcel of William McIlvanney novels I hadn't read. As I set out yesterday I absent-mindedly stuffed one in my bag. I had planned to have a wee search for Dirk Hatteraick's cave, on the coast just past Auchenlarie. No car, but juggling with buses, a finely honed art form of which I think I am, by now, one of the world's finest exponents. I had a wee lunch in Gatehouse, then caught the bus. It was a nice day on the coast, if a little overcast, and when I got off I wandered about on the shore. The road was invisible from there, and there was only silence and the Solway glittering and clouds running wool white overhead. After a while I sat down and for the sheer hell of it gave a loud howl, frightening the family I hadn't spotted who were walking along the shingle kicking a ball for their dog.

Out of embarrassment I took out the novel, *A Gift from Nessus*, opened it randomly and began to pretend to read. I saw the word 'Dumfries', skipped a few pages, followed the main character, whom I later discovered to be a window salesman from Glasgow, on the road south. A few pages later he was in a hotel, The Angel, in the middle of Gatehouse. Then, on the foreshore before Creetown 'looking through a rock cleft that was open to a bay, where the wind was farming empty acres of dun sky.' Of course, at the end of the chapter, he was disturbed by a family 'throwing a ball that was being tirelessly retrieved by a dog'.

Even if I hadn't just been sold a new set of windows, I would have found this a bit odd. I think I'll invent a new term for all this. Geofantasapsychiatry. There I've done it.

and in his brain, –
Which is as dry as the remainder
    biscuit
After a voyage, he hath strange
    places crammed
With observation, the which he
    vents
In mangled forms.

(*As You Like It*, Act 2 Scene 7)

Ghost Landscape

There are many landscapes folded together in Dumfries and Galloway. There's a working landscape, drastically changed through the years. There's the mythic landscape of fairies, druids and heather ale. There's the historic landscape of cup and ring and carved stone and ruined castles. Then there's the ghost landscape:

When the eye is robbed
of its vista of distant hills,
when the foot stops and the ear
listens into the stillness.

The mind to be held firm
against encroaching images,
of those old ghosts that move upon
    the moor
defying a pragmatic nothingness

('Greyness', William Neill)

Part of the attraction of Dumfries and Galloway is its desolation. All the brochures tell you that. 'Lonely', 'undiscovered', 'vast tracts of emptiness'. The ghost landscape is one we're all supposed to enjoy. But it wasn't always as ghostly: the layering of place names of Dumfries and Galloway tell not just of waves of settlers but also deep penetration and habitation, lasting from antique times. The area, we can guess, had a shifting but large population based mainly on farming and hunting.

I spoke to someone involved in a community archaeological project which last year examined the geophysics of the 'lost' town of Innermessan near Stranraer, a town thought to be *Rerigonium*, the seat of the Novantæ tribe mentioned by Ptolemy in the 2nd century AD and described by Symson in 1684 as 'the most considerable place in the Rhinns of Galloway, and the greatest town thereabout, til Stranraer was built'.

'There's nothing there,' he told me, 'a few farm buildings, but this was a Royal Burgh, the history's all there, underfoot, the houses and roads, all of it. Hard to imagine how it could disappear.'

I recommend travelling to Laggangairn, a moor five miles north of New Luce, if you're looking for ghosts. There are two ancient stones there, probably part of a bigger stone circle which has disappeared. Two Christian crosses are carved on the stones, dating from the 8th century. This was a stopping-off point they say, a village on a pilgrim route from the north to Whithorn. Dotted in the hills round about are the ruins of later cottages, moss-covered stone. Sara Maitland, an author who lives nearby, wrote:

> This beautiful wild silence exists under the shadow of the people silenced in order to create it. The silence of oppression... exists inextricably entangled with the jouissance, the bliss of solitude.

(A Book of Silence)

Everyone's heard the story of the Highland Clearances. Ironically much of the symbolism of Scottish nationality, tartan, bagpipes and so on, comes from a culture that was annihilated, mostly by lowland Scots, after Scotland ceased to exist. Scottish cultural identity is focused to an exaggerated extent on the Highlands. In comparison, the south of Scotland is often seen as an area of marginal importance. However the trauma of economic change was as bad here as in the Highlands, if not worse:

> The key to understanding Scottish modern history is to grasp the sheer, force, violence and immensity of social change in the two centuries after 1760. No country in Europe underwent a social and physical mutation so fast and so complete. Tidal waves of transformation swept over the country, Lowland and Highland, drowning the way of life of hundreds of thousands of families and obliterating not only traditional societies but the very appearance of the landscape itself.

(*Stone Voices*, Neal Ascherson)

In the 18th century, after the Treaty of Union between Scotland and England, landowners adopted the improvements they'd seen in England and enclosed the land. As farmland became more profitable, rents increased and many tenants couldn't afford them. Cottars and cottagers were replaced by smaller numbers of full-time farm labourers who lived in farms or in new planned towns like Thornhill or Castle Douglas. These planned towns were market towns, providing goods for local use, but soon with improved communications it became cheaper to import goods and so a further decline of the region's population began. With industrialisation some towns in the region grew in size but have shrunk in the last fifty years as traditional industry has died. In 2010 a study by the New Economics Foundation (NEF) named Dumfries a 'ghost town'.

The population of Dumfries and Galloway reached a peak of 158,890 in 1851. This was 5.5 per cent of the total Scottish population of 2,888,742. The most recent figures for Dumfries and Galloway give the region a population of 148,060, which is 2.8 per cent of the total Scottish population of 5,295,000.

The emphasis on wilderness and eco-tourism, dark skies tourism, wilderness art and so on relies on a perpetuation of the ghost landscape. The furore over wind farms is interesting in this context. The new government legislation that a wind turbine can be no closer than 2.5 kilometres from a home makes Dumfries and Galloway potentially the most attractive place in Scotland to build wind farms because of its lack of population. Another irony – groups protesting that wind farms, built because there is no population, might damage the number of tourists attracted to the place because of its lack of population. Of course there are valid aesthetic reasons to object to wind turbines but there are also vested interests committed to keeping the ghost landscape alive, if you'll excuse the pun.

See **Emigration, Levellers**

Ground Control to Major Gong

'Samye Ling is an oasis of calm,' says Jill Dobbie. 'In a frantic world you can get space and time, if you need it.' Set near Eskdalemuir, Samye Ling was the first Buddhist monastery built in the west and has been operational, if that's the word, since 1967. There are peacocks and bright prayer flags and a community of about 60.

It was founded by two monks. One, Trungpa Rinpoche, left in 1970 amidst scandals involving heavy drinking and sex with underage girls. The other, Choje Akong Rinpoche, was the spiritual head until he was stabbed to death in 2013 in the Chinese city of Chengdu in a dispute over money. Odd events to surround major religious figures, but Buddhism has always seemed to me to be a code for real people, flawed ones, too. It seems to recognise people are imperfect but can still achieve a kind of spirituality or peace divorced from dogma, unlike Catholicism and Presbyterianism.

Both Leonard Cohen and David Bowie stayed here in 1969, Bowie almost becoming a monk. Bowie said:

> I had stayed in their monastery and was going through all their exams, and yet I had this feeling that it

wasn't right for me. I suddenly realised how close it all was: another month and my head would have been shaved.

He should have gone for it, with the example in his mind of the legendary Buddhist teacher Ji Gong. This 12th century monk rolled about the hillside with monkeys, sang songs in the wine shops and dressed as a beggar, always waving a fan and slugging from a gourd holding wine.

Hurrah, Move over John Calvin. Ground Control to Major Gong.

H

Haaf Netting

Haaf net fishing was brought here by the Vikings and was once carried out all along the Solway, but is now restricted to the Nith and the Annan. The word 'haaf' is the Norse word for channel. Haaf netters stand in the river making a human barrier to catch salmon in a net that was once framed by wood but now is usually of aluminium. Haaf netters were also sometimes 'shaulers', who used 'leisters' or harpoons to spear the fish. It was such a man that Allan Cunningham described in his spooky tale of 'The Haunted Ships':

> As we looked, we saw an old man emerging from a path that winded to the shore through a grove of doddered hazel; he carried a halve-net on his back, while behind him came a girl, bearing a small harpoon with which the fishers are remarkably dexterous in striking their prey. The senior seated himself on a large grey stone, which overlooked the bay, laid aside his bonnet, and submitted his bosom and neck to the refreshing sea-breeze; and taking his harpoon from his attendant, sat with the gravity and composure of a spirit of the flood, with his ministering nymph behind him. We pushed our shallop to the shore, and soon stood at their side.

In the autumn of 2013, I went to Annan to meet with an artist, fisherman and teacher I've known for years. He was in reflective mood and told me he wanted to take some time off to do a series of paintings on haaf netting, maybe get an exhibition together. 'Time I did some real work,' he said with a smile.

He told me that haaf netting was a dying art on both sides of the Solway. 'Once there were 34 nets on the Solway near Annan, but now there are only four. Most haaf net licenses aren't taken up. It's too much like hard work for some folk. Nobody does it for a living, it's more of a hobby. And it's a convivial sport, you get to chat. An the salmon are mostly safe. Bloke I knew got six fish from 14 tides last year an he's good at it.'

Since I knew him to be a man of strongly expressed opinions on art and every other topic I brought up, for a laugh, the piece of public art in Annan depicting the sport, a statue commissioned by Tesco entitled the *Haaf Netter* which has created, it would be fair to say, a great deal of controversy in the town. 'Dinnae talk to me about that,' he spluttered. 'Somebody I knew got his Manitou out and some chains and tried to pull it down. It's a laughing stock. There's a fish stuck on his groin. What did the bloke say in the paper? "The fish had to be welded on somewhere!"' He guffawed and ordered up a few more pints.

Haunted

Empty and resonant, as in 'it's empta noo, haunted only speerits'.

Near New Galloway I am chatting to an elderly lady as she surveys the compact rose-red building that had been her school. It's now a holiday home with a very pretty garden, clematis gleaming in the afternoon sun. It doesn't look spooky to me, but to her, of course, it will be forever haunted by her young self and the children she knew and played with, long dead or scattered. 'I wakked three miles to get tae yon cross country, hail rain or snaw. If the snaw was too deep we'd a come in a wagon pulled by the tractor. The maister would put a fire on an we'd stand roon til we warmed up. "When your brains are defrosted boys an girls," he'd say, "we'll start work." We'd aye pretend to be numb a bit langer.'

A sad sight are closed schools, some demolished most converted to houses or other uses. When I was at university I used to get the bus to Edinburgh up the Dalveen Pass, the old walking, riding route, north to south west and vice versa, and the driver would carry the milk crate and take it out in the morning to where two weans were waiting to cart it in. He didn't like it; 'fucking pony express,' he used to say to the passengers, but he had always some sweet to give to the children. If you watched, he'd smuggle it to them. A wee kindness, a wee secret, a wee history, unrecorded.

The school's a house now, a lot of money spent on it. A lovely garden. Another layer of reality gone to memory and myth.

*See **Ghost Landscape, Levellers, Teachers***

Hollows Tower

Hollows Tower at Canonbie is a keep or Peel Tower that dates from the 15th century, and gives a great sense of where these scallies the reivers lived. Well actually for scallies, substitute thieves and psychopaths, because the reivers were no joke as neighbours. They were like the *Cosa Nostra*, driven by a peculiar sense of justice and honour which saw them have more in common with their English counterparts across the border than with any government. Violent times, but haven't they always been? Whenever I visit a site with these glossy weatherproofed boards that instruct you how to think about things, I recall the great Willie Neill's words:

> Eyes looked at me through time
>   from Lancet windows;
> across long centuries their harness
>   jingled.

I walked away from grey
   imaginings
till safely out of bowshot, hearing
   the sentry's voice:
'What better now, in your own
   squalid day?'

('Peel Tower', William Neill)

These were stateless lands, though, debatable lands, no-man's land. The shifting territories brought about by raid or feud was a late medieval mirror image of what ancient Galloway must have been like, where borders ebbed and flowed like the tide. Hollows Tower is close to the site of Gilnockie Castle and both are associated with a Godfather of the Reivers, Johnny Armstrong. When James v became king of Scotland, he brought an army of 12,000 men to Teviotdale and Annandale and offered safe conduct to Johnnie Armstrong for a meeting. It was a trick of course. Johnny held sway through the area and was a patriotic Scot in his way; unlike many of his compatriots he confined most of his dodgy activities to England. Violating a safe conduct, to the reivers, was about as bad as it got. 'I have asked grace at a graceless face,' he is said to have shouted at the treacherous king when he realised the game was up. Johnnie and his men were hung in the trees of Carlanrig churchyard. There is a legend that the trees on which they were hung withered and that the same has happened to any trees planted since. This is apocryphal, a bit like no birds singing at the site of Auschwitz, as there seemed to be lots of healthy trees when I visited. Pacification is seldom meant ironically, but the reivers are remembered fondly on the whole, and the Stewarts less so and the spirit of the reivers lives on where the fudges and deceits of the Stewarts remain only in textbook form. At Annan Rugby Club I talked to someone who was reminiscing about his playing days. He recalls as a boy going to play an English boarding school in Cumbria. He said:

> Where we changed, next door was all these neat piles o clothes, blazers at their pegs, and a these pairs o wellington boots, lined up ready to wear. Well they murdered us, but we pished in their boots.

*See **Frontiers***

Insane

My father was badly affected by his experience of the war. I am reminded of this by a message sent today by Neil MacDonald, a boyhood friend who lived next door to me in Queen St, Dumfries. He was asking me to look over a eulogy he had written for his father Ross, another RAF veteran of World War Two, who had died aged 93 after spending most of his adult life in the Crichton Royal Hospital. One of the sentences struck me forcefully: 'Both my sister and I have houses full of his works of art.' Such was my experience too, and I wondered at the coincidences – madness, painting and the Crichton. I suppose it may have had something to do with the great William AF Browne, who died in Dumfries in 1885.

When Elizabeth Crichton's plans to build a university in Dumfries were stymied by the existing Scottish universities, she founded in 1838 the Crichton Royal Hospital for the Insane and had the insight to staff it with some brilliant doctors and administrators. William AF Browne was one of these. Browne believed in occupational and art therapy and his time as Supervisor in the Crichton saw innovations massively ahead of their time. He actively collected the art work of patients, ensuring it was exhibited and published. He wrote insightfully not just about how art could be used as a therapeutic aid but also how madness affected the life and work of existing artists. As such he prefigured much of the current work on 'outsider art'.

As a boy I had seldom clapped eyes on Neil's father and when he was talked about, my mother used to do a strange Hebridean face which simultaneously suggested that it was an awful shame but that the matter shouldn't be pursued. After all, we had our own maniac upstairs. 'Where there is art there is no madness,' said Michael Foucault, an assertion quoted by Dr Maureen Park, in 2010, in a book about Browne called *Art in Madness: Dr WAF Browne's Collection of Patient Art at*

Crichton Royal Institution, Dumfries.

My father did some very strange and violent things but I always thought that one of the greatest outlets for his turmoil was a huge picture of a tree which he painted and which resided for most of my life in the attic of our house. It was mad, all right, crusted in oil paint, vivid and harsh and beautiful. My father painted birds faultlessly but they always looked as if they had been stuffed and stuck on the branch. There was no energy. The tree, however, boiled perpetually in the attic:

> That painting he left in the attic, a tree
> dissected against a nightmare's sky,
> with a thumbprint sunk in oils like a calderon,
> the centre of a brief but violent storm
>
> ('My Father from Extant Sources')

See Midnight in Stavanger, War

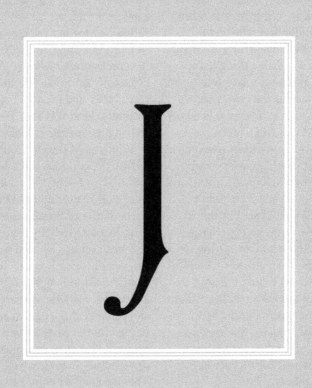

Jailbirds

The brother of a friend of mine was a plumber who once worked in Germany. While he was there, staying in Bochum, he met a stunning looking girl at a nightclub. They hit it off, one thing led to another and after a few weeks she moved into his flat. He couldn't believe his luck. They seemed very much in love, and were inseparable apart from weekends when she would go away without saying where. He understood, and when one Monday she didn't return, he was upset but put it eventually down to experience, happy to have shared his life for a while with such a funny, beautiful and vivacious woman. About a year later as he was taking a flight back to Scotland he saw her again. On a poster. She was a member of the Baader-Meinhof Gang, wanted for murder and armed robbery.

Avril lives on the Colvend coast. She too fell in love in Germany, and lived there for ten years. When her boyfriend tragically fell off a balcony, the police accused her of pushing him and charged her with murder. After eight months in custody a specialist legal firm took on her case and raised bail for her release. She fled to Dumfries and Galloway and the case against her was eventually dropped. She doesn't seem bitter and is chuckling as she recounts the story. They're still chasing me for the bill, she says.

Winifred Maxwell, Countess of Nithsdale, conducted the best jailbreak in history. Her husband, Lord Nithsdale, had been captured at the Battle of Preston during the First Jacobite Rebellion in 1715 had been sentenced, and was awaiting his death in the Tower of London. On the night before his execution, his wife appeared and she persuaded the guards to let her see him in private for a last farewell. She then smuggled him out dressed in women's clothing. They escaped to France to join the Jacobites there and the court of the exiled James. The Nithsdale Cloak used in the escape is still held by the family.

See Feisty

Bill Herbert, former writer-in-residence for Dumfries and Galloway, once wrote the following on the subject of Burns and women:

His gender views were something brassy
his suppers toast the female chassis
thi semm wad turn ma wife's fiss glassy
gin et reached her lug –
Eh'll hae tae raise ma gless tae Lassie
that filmic dug.

('Epistle to Twa Editors', Bill Herbert)

Interesting he should mention Collie dugs because according to some, Burns' first meeting with Jean Armour featured one of them, as well as giving as an insight into what Burns looked for in a woman.

It happened at a dance in Mauchline during April 1784, where he was supposedly, and unbelievably, acting like a bit of a gooseberry. His Collie arrived and as he sent the dog home he was heard to remark that he wished he could find a girl who would love him as faithfully as his dog did. A few days later he was approached by Jean who had overheard him, asking if he had found one yet.

The words dug and mug differ only by a single syllable and in this politically correct age, in any age for that matter, Burns' treatment of women is pretty terrible. In the four years that elapsed after meeting Jean he had made her pregnant, been called before the Kirk Session, been summonsed by her father, made Highland Mary pregnant, thought about running off to Jamaica, seen Mary die possibly in childbirth, heard Jean had been delivered of twins, published the Kilmarnock edition, and made Jean pregnant again. Whilst flirting furiously with Clarinda in Edinburgh he heard that Jean had been thrown out by her father. On 3 March 1788 he writes to his mate Ainslie:

Jean I found banished like a martyr — forlorn, destitute and friendless; all for the good old cause: I have reconciled her to her fate: I have reconciled her to her mother: I have taken her a room: I have taken her to my arms: I have given her a mahogany bed: I have given her a guinea; and I have fucked her til she rejoiced with joy unspeakable and full of glory. But — as I always am on every occasion — I have been prudent and cautious to an astounding degree; I swore her, privately and solemnly, never to attempt any claim on me as a husband.

At this point someone usually comes in and says, 'she was a big hearted woman, that'. History does record her manners and gentility but not her mental strength. One of her few quotes was 'Our Robbie should have had twa wives.'

I'm a poet and I'm all for people believing that we Parnassians should not be judged by mere mortal standards but he was pushing it a bit, wasn't he?

Jane Brown, President of the World Burns Federation, tells me it is all about passion, his priapic activities round women, Jean's love for him, his love for poetry. Jane Brown is a powerful modern woman and passionate too on the subject of Burns. She is the landlady of Burns' favourite pub, the Globe Inn in Dumfries. When I spoke to her, at the start of February, she had done 19 Burns Suppers and had eight still to go. She had travelled all over the world, doing immortal memories, toasts and other speeches. More and more women were involved in Burns groups and societies. 'It's about time too,' she said, 'getting away from chauvinism. Love of Burns and what he believed in shouldn't be a gender issue. It's all about the poems.'

Burns wrote more than a dozen poems and songs about Jean. The best known is 'Of a' the Airts the Wind can Blaw'.

I see her in the dewy flowers,
I see her sweet and fair:
I hear her in the tunefu' birds,
I hear her charm the air:
There's not a bonie flower that
    springs,
By fountain, shaw, or green;
There's not a bonie bird that sings,
But minds me o' my Jean.

('Of a' the Airts the Wind can Blaw', Robert Burns)

Jane says, 'I'm not an academic Burnsian, but I'm passionate, that's what they're getting this year.' She pauses to answer the phone, it's another engagement. 'Of course I would have given him a harder time,' she says. She moves off to talk to another group of visitors and before I go I overhear her saying, 'I usually pause half way through my job title. I say I'm President of the World...'

See Burns, Plagues

Jarama

There's a Valley in Spain called
   Jarama,
It's a place that we all know so
   well,
It's there that we gave up our
   manhood,
And so many of our brave
   comrades fell.

We're proud of the British Battalion
And the fight for Madrid that they
   made,
Where they fought like true sons of
   the soil.
As part of the Fifteenth Brigade.

('Jarama Valley', Alec McDaid)

When I was a young leftie, it was a badge of courage to be able to sing all the verses of that song, along with *Viva La Quinta Brigada*. Of course all we were doing was skulking about the Nith thinking what it would have been like to have been in the Spanish Civil War, then going for a pint quite pleased we had missed it all. Being a member of the Workers Revolutionary Party or the International Socialists in the countryside was a way of rebelling against what we saw as the tyranny of smug small-town conservatism while never having to do anything very onerous to aid the class struggle.

It seems as difficult as ever now to make sense of the politics of Dumfries and Galloway, that ever changing frontier always on the cusp, or in the middle of invasions and wars and now, perversely, or maybe because of that, one of the most politically conservative areas in the entire country. I like war memorials, and find them very moving, but in Whithorn I found one which packed an extra punch. I've always known of the Scottish contribution to the International Brigade which fought in Spain and hadn't realised there was a small contingent from Galloway. I'm a pacifist – I think my last fight was in Primary Two about a stolen gym shoe – but it seems to me particularly brave and honourable to go to a war you don't have to, to support people you've never seen, purely out of principle and a spirit of fraternity.

George Dickie was born in 1912 and grew up in Whithorn where he left school at 13 and joined a local butcher's. He enlisted in the Cameron Highlanders but then deserted and drifted to London, soon becoming involved in the Socialist movement. In 1936 he volunteered, under the name of Jack Brent, for the International Brigade and fought against Franco, being shot in the spine during the Battle of Jarama in 1937. His injuries gave him terrible pain and he walked with sticks for the rest of his short life, eventually dying in 1951, aged only 39, as a direct result of his

wounds. Despite the pain he became national secretary of the International Brigade Association helping Brigaders still in prison or suffering after the war. He was a prominent member of the Communist Party in London, and was involved in the campaign to give Londoners access to the Underground during the Blitz. He returned to his home town after the war. A memorial was unveiled to him there in 2006.

This being Dumfries and Galloway though, there were plenty of people around who thought that raising a monument to a communist and a deserter was a disgrace. Echoing some of the issues of the Spanish Civil War itself, some thought it was sacrilege to celebrate a communist and atheist so close to the Whithorn Priory, one of the historic centres of Scottish Catholicism and Christianity. Several people resigned from the Community Council over the issue. One opponent said:

> If it was a question of somebody of worth and if he had been a hero, fair enough, but he did nothing for Whithorn and nothing for Great

Britain. He went away to fight for the communists in Spain. He's hardly a role model. Whithorn's most famous literary son, Alasdair Reid disagrees. 'Boy, this is Whithorn's most distinguished son', he is quoted as saying, 'He went further than anybody in Whithorn ever dreamed of going.'

George Dickie didn't hack it as a
    butcher,
swapped the blood and offal
for a uniform, and when its shade
    didn't suit him,
vanished in London among the
    dispossessed;
the distaste back home was
    palpable,

Then George Dickie became Jack
    Brent,
and took a bullet in the spine
for the poor at Jarama
limped back, battling still for the
    flag
red as carnations,
as the blood of Spain.
On the sodden streets of Whithorn
    now,
there's a splash of colour and a
    communist star:
'Un heroe de la guerra civil de
    espanola'.
How disgusting some said,
so close to a shrine of Christ
who gave his life and was reborn to
    save us all.

('Reborn')

Jerry Rawlings

Dalbeattie, 1967. A youthful and handsome African dressed in an air force uniform visits a house in Dalbeattie to enquire after a chemist called James John. He and his girlfriend are directed to a pharmacists in Dumfries. They board a bus, get off at the Whitesands and walk up Buccleuch Street. Someone shouts 'nigger' from the other side of the street. It's a moment the man will remember and recall with bitterness years after. They arrive at the pharmacy, where they are told by an elderly man behind the counter they have just missed Mr John.

That young man was Jerry Rawlings who would go on to stage a military coup in Ghana, murder hundreds of his opponents and serve two terms as president of the country. He remains to this day one of the most influential men in Africa.

The chemist, James John, was his father and the man who spoke to him in the shop was also his father who had gone to The Gold Coast in 1935 with his wife Mary to work for the United Africa Company. Six years after he arrived he started a relationship with Victoria Agbotui, a caterer at the State House. This relationship lasted six years and ended in 1947, the year Rawlings was born. He was baptised with his father's name, Jerry Rawlings John, which later, when he was training with the RAF as a pilot, became inverted to Jerry John Rawlings.

I heard this tale walking in Castle Douglas with James John's nephew, Tony Barbour. He told me Rawlings may have met his father once, when he was a child, but that John had, for the sake of his marriage, never admitted paternity. After John's death, there had been contact between Rawlings and the family through an intermediate, the poet and playwright Maude Sulter, who lived near Castle Douglas herself and wrote a play based on Rawling's life, *Service to Empire*. Tony himself travelled with his family to Ghana and met Rawlings and his mother, whom he described as an 'extremely dignified 90-year-old'.

I've just finished an essay by Alexander Grant which includes a section on the great bastards of Scotland. It's a scholarly work, of course, not some kind of defamatory list. Needless to say a good proportion of the Great Bastards are from Dumfries and Galloway, men like Sir Archibald Douglas, Archibald the Grim, son of the Black Douglas, who began the construction of the great fortress at Threave. Such was the wealth of his properties that Grant says 'Archibald third earl of Douglas may have been fourteenth-century Europe's most successful bastard'. The illegitimate sons of nobles had it lucky, however. Though they were usually deprived of succession to any throne, they did have title and were customarily honoured and acknowledged by their fathers. The sons of chemists were not necessarily so lucky.

You hear a lot about Dumfries and Galloway being the birth place of great leaders and kings through history. In the modern age we have a more complex legacy, as seen in the controversial figure of Rawlings. He purged the judiciary and the military and at least 300 people were summarily shot. It's too simplistic, surely, to imagine that two incidents in a single day in Dumfries in 1967 could have led to the formation of an African dictator, isn't it?

See **Barbados House,**

Journalists

Up to about 20 years ago, the region's two major towns, Dumfries and Stranraer, had staffers, full time reporters for the national newspapers. There was a friendly rivalry among them but they cooperated too. In Dumfries the *Record* and *Express* reporters Frank Ryan and John Ennis couldn't stand sitting at rain-swept Palmerston Park every second Saturday, so got the freelance reporter Bert Houston to go. In return they fed him some tit-bits to flog to the *Scotsman* or *Herald*. They used to do 'an awful lot of hanging about in pubs,' one of their friends told me. 'In these days the papers would report divorces, so they were always on the lookout for tasty gossip. As well as having a good wee drink.'

A photographer who was attached to the *Daily Record*, Jack Johnstone, once showed me to the Record office, in Great King St in Dumfries, up a very narrow staircase. 'Many a reporter ended face down at the bottom of these,' he told me. Jack also told me a story of the news room in the *Daily Mail*, just after the Dalai Lama had been ejected from Tibet by the Chinese and reporters were desperate to get hold of him. Jack recalled entering the newsroom just as an Australian reporter had reached the great man. 'Hellaw,' he was bellowing, 'Is that the Dalai Lama? This is the Dalai Mail!'

The region was home to many ace reporters, including Jack Johnstone's son, also called Jack, who went on to produce the television news programme *Border News and Lookaround*. Last time we met, we talked about probably the most talented of them all, Philip Mulvey, an award-winning young journalist whose sensitive and insightful writing on the Lockerbie disaster won him many friends and admirers. He died tragically young in an accident while working in Vietnam. He had attended St Joseph's College from the age of 12 and in the words of his obituary in the *Herald*, thought of Dumfries as his 'spiritual home'. Philip was a raconteur of international class and radiated wit and bonhomie. He could create a party just by sitting beside you. He had a mischievous streak too and loved pricking bombast and small town hypocrisy. In his early days he had the job of editing a hugely respectful obituary of a local bigwig, notorious in the town for his drunkenness. Of course the paper was only meant to reflect the respectable side of his life but at the end instead of 'sadly missed' Philip substituted 'sadly pissed', claiming it to be an unfortunate typing error.

*See **Disasters***

K

Killantrigan Lighthouse Keeper, 1913

I once wanted to be a lighthouse keeper. It seemed a very romantic pursuit, plenty of time to write poems while you polished the lanterns and walked down the track to meet the daughter of the local innkeeper bringing you pasties and a flask of beer. My friend Colin Bryson actually did work for Northern Lighthouses however and his story of being forced by his co-workers in his first week to climb the outside of a lantern room to sit on top of a lighthouse, the ventilator at the very tip of the tower between his thighs, and let go, disabused me of this notion.

The lighthouses of Dumfries and Galloway look romantic, especially the ones in the far west, the Mull of Galloway, Corsewell and Killantringan, perched on rocks and lashed by the Irish Sea, but it's easy to imagine the harshness of the life led by the men who manned them, as well as what problems the job caused, including chronic boredom verging on borderline insanity. The keeper of the Killantringan

Lighthouse, one DA Mowat, spent long nights counting moths and entering the results in his official Log Book, as per the evening of 19th September when he scrupulously counted 293 moths near his lamp.

> I imagine sailors
> watching the lamp's eye,
> envious as they creep
> along the breast of the sea
>
> like shadows.
> From this high place
> they are a plank's width
> from death,
>
> all questions
> drowned on their lips.
> I know:
> I've seen it.
>
> I am beyond marrying,
> watch moths instead of time,
> beating on the glass. At night
> I sit in the watchroom,
>
> throw my beam of light
> like a rope
> across the back of the ocean,
> and catch hope after hope after
> hope.

('Catcher')

In Kirkcudbright, in horizontal sleet. The fleet's in and fuelling up for the Isle of Man tomorrow, scalloping. They work a stretch from the Shetlands to the Bay of Biscay and being here, watching the boats, and hearing the throb of engines and smelling the stench of the fish, as well as eavesdropping on the banter in the Steam Packet Inn, it's obvious that this is a proper working port with a proper history and hopefully a proper future. Fourteen trawlers operate from here, mostly steel-built beam trawlers, and three smaller lobster boats. Normally the catch is turned over to local shops and manufacturers.

Historically, Kirkcudbright was one of the most important ports in Scotland. Its burgh charter, granted in 1455, gave it the right to international trade. It traded wool and wine with Ireland, France and Spain. The Armada planned to put in here to spark a Catholic rebellion. The region's best known sailor and part-time American, John Paul Jones, landed here in an abortive

seaborne commando raid to capture the Earl of Selkirk.

When the railways came, and Glasgow and Liverpool became the predominant ports in the west of Britain, the port of Kirkcudbright nearly silted up and died like so many others on the Solway. But it was saved by the imagination of John King who, in the '50s and '60s, trawled for sole and skate for eight months of the year and dredged for scallops in the other four, expanding into fishing scallops full time, bringing others from Kirkcudbright and Annan to explore that market, with all the huge beneficial expansion of ancillary trades like fish packing and processing which that fuelled. There are pleasure boats here, too, but they tie up at a floating pontoon downstream. They know their place.

There's a wooden memorial on the shore showing a woman and child staring out to sea, a poignant reminder of the cost of this trade. The sea has taken many of the Solway's sons and daughters. Some refuse to be taken, mind you. Just before Christmas 2013, late on a Monday night, 30-year-old Andrew Smith fell off the Kirkcudbright trawler the *Aztec*, 16 miles south east of Douglas, Isle of Man, and was in the water for hours. 'I crossed my legs and floated on my back,' he said, 'I knew they would come back for me.' They did, and Andrew was winched off the *Aztec* and taken to hospital in the Isle of Man. He signed himself out after ten hours and is now back at his trade, and to hear him speak you would think it had all been nothing. 'I've worked on boats for ten year,' he said, 'In far worse weather. It was just one of those things and it won't put me off.'

In 1995 an Annan fisherman, Tom Willacy, showed the same sangfroid when, shrimping alone near his home town, he got caught in a winch cable which severed his right leg below the knee. He cut his clothes away, freed himself, and phoned his wife on his mobile. A spokesman for Liverpool Coastguard who coordinated his rescue said:

We were chatting with Mr Willacy throughout. It was amazing how he kept calm. He was fully aware of everything and directed us to himself. He told us he had lost part of his leg. I don't know how he kept going.

The sinking of the *Solway Harvester* shows us the ultimate price the sea can demand. Another Kirkcudbright scalloper, it sank off Ramsay, Isle of Man in a force nine gale on the 11 January 2000 with the loss of all hands. All were from the Isle of Whithorn.

It is the saddest thing
gin loved yins dinna come hame,
whither sea, or soil, or sky
has taen them.

This time it's the sea's turn.
The Solway is the harvester,
haulin in a fine catch o
seeven young men fae sooth west
   villages;
brothers, cousins, husbands, sons.

Fae boyhood days they kent the
   sea,
fir leisure or labour,
fae skytin stanes abuin it
tae skippering ships across it.

In Machars hames an kirks,
faimilies an freens haud hans,
fin words tae mend crackt hairts
dark as the deepest ocean.

Bit nane will dae sae weel as
time and tears,
wavin in wi the Spring tides
ower Ninian's land.

These mists o watter,
are mair nor jist a haar
comin in fae the wild sea,
as Gallowa folk greet thegither
fir thir deid sons.

May licht brak,
in days tae come,
as the year grows.

Fir it is the saddest thing
gin loved yins dinna come hame,
whither sea, or soil, or sky,
has taen them.

('In Memoriam Solway Harvester',
Liz Niven)

Cockling can be equally dangerous.
They were telling me in the Steam
Packet Inn that many local men
were involved in cockling and in
the north of England: It's big
business and there was money to be
made. People operated on both
sides of the law, and as well as the
legit ones there were plenty of
dodgy people involved. Morecambe
Bay changed that a bit but to be
honest, there's still plenty illegal
stuff going on, even locally.

In 2004, 21 Chinese cocklers
were drowned when they were cut
off by the tide.

See Disasters, Pistapolis

L

Lachy Jackson's Bet

On hearing that the brother of the proprietor of the Swan Inn in Stranraer was going on a round-the-world tour, Lachlan MacPhail Jackson, a retired slaughterman and regular there, slapped 20 pounds on the bar and said to the adventures, 'I'll bet you that amount again that you'll meet someone I know in each continent.' Suspecting that the world was a bigger place than Lachlan was thinking, they readily agreed. The proprietor, Nick, takes up the story:

> Their first port of call was Perth, Australia. Before they even got out of the airport, in the airport bar, they met the man who had taught Lachy to be a butcher in Aberdeen. From Australia they went to South America and in a bar in Buenos Aries met a whole load of rig workers one of whom was an ex-slaughterman from Aberdeen who, having heard they were from Stranraer, immediately asked if they knew a man called Lachy. Chastened, they went north and in Bourbon St in New Orleans met another Scotsman. Reluctant to ask anything that might reveal a connection with Lachy they nevertheless eventually let slip where they came from. Of course the man's next question was about Lachy... and so it went on. On their return they handed the money over to Lachy, who took it without a word.

Lauren in Snaw and Flud

A failure in communications leads to another extended stay in Newton Stewart. The bus to Dumfries sneaked off from Stance Two while I was standing in Stance One, my eyes fixed on a strange tableau unfolding outside the Star Inn, which is too exotic in nature to write here. I am not unduly bothered because Newton Stewart is a good town with many McMillan connections, though the McMillan Inn which I used to pretend to own has closed. Newton Stewart seems to be hanging on in there, and hanging onto some of its young, in spite of the conversation I had with a young man here on an earlier visit.

In the Crown Hotel in Newton Stewart I get to talking to Lauren, a friendly and vivacious young woman who clearly loves her life and loves living here, and who, for my benefit, is running through her highlights of the last year, 'those I cin remember'. Some of these seem to centre on extreme weather events, such as last March when unexpected blizzards shut the roads and the Crown became an emergency centre for travellers stuck in the vicinity. 'They were sleeping everywhere.'

Electricity was cut off for a week in the Machars and there was panic buying of gas camper stoves. 'They were getting a' angry but ye canna expect the shoap to hae a hunnert camping stoves, just in case o snaw! They ate us oot of everything, we had tae bring stuff frae home.'

Lauren lives near the Cree and was flooded in November, or at least the flats below her were and she had to be rescued. 'It was a big boat, I was that embarrassed. I had to be brought out wi ma two dugs an everyone was lined up on the road watching, takin pictures an putting them on Facebook. Ah just kept ma heid doon, feeding ma dugs biscuits frae ma pocket in case they jumped overboard because the firemen said they could na go after them if they did cos of the undercurrents. When I saw these folk watching I thocht I'd end up on Facebook, I tried no to look an said to my dugs "just keep your heids down girls."'

Maybe it's the result of not working so much with young folk, but I can't describe how great it was to talk to Lauren for a short while and be bathed in sheer, youthful joie de vivre, all delivered in the most lovely Galloway-Irish-Scots. I don't want to get carried away, but after days stalking ghosts it was almost like touching Galloway's soul.

See Stagecoach – not the Company, the Means of Transport

Not for the first time I overhear the words, 'the land was here long before the Duke'. It's in relation to the loss of an old tar curling rink called the Common Ground in upper Nithsdale. There's a longstanding resentment among some over the privileges of the landowners in the region, strange since so many of the indigenous folk who are left work for them, strange also because the region can hardly be termed as it once was 'insouciant, endemically out of the control of any government'.

I'm taken back to the words of the inspirational savant and Dyker Willie McMeekin, 'the land is ours'. Much of what was deemed 'common land' has disappeared, a process begun under the old enclosures initiated by landowners who sought to maximise profits at the expense of the folk who lived and worked there. The Levellers, a group who tried to overturn enclosures and destroy the dykes that parcelled out the new boundaries, led by semi-mythological figures like the gypsy anarchist horse trader Billy Marshall, weren't just trying to turn back the clock but hold onto a sacred communality of purpose and land which still finds an echo in the sentiments I've just heard in this pub.

One of the things my mother taught me, to my initial terrible embarrassment as she burst through the rhododendrons onto posh peoples' lawns with her leaking Wolsey, was that as she said, 'the land belongs not to a few but the folk who were born on it, who bleed on it'. Dumfries and Galloway is not alone in having a tiny number of folk who own most of the property and land, but it seems to me to be the area most in danger of becoming extinct because of it. By that I mean through depopulation, by an economic process that is leading to the aggrandisement of existing land ownership and the colonisation of what remains by wealthier people from outside.

The European Common Agricultural Policy was meant to preserve small farms and a rural way of life but in Dumfries and

Galloway where, since the 18th century, larger and larger farms have been the norm. It's not had that effect. Short-term land management, designed to provide shooting estates, and investment forestry and windfarms, further promotes the place as a ghost landscape. The future direction of tourism either in history, books, art or the environment seems currently to be predicated on perpetuating and maintaining the ghost landscape as a theme park.

...Look now,
the gardens gone to stumps, crab
  grass grows lush.
Only the peat smoke, a tweak at
  absence, lingers; tripping
some tongue-tip memory, tactile,
  succulent and stirring.

('The Cottage Garden,
Clatteringshaws', Davie Douglas)

Where are today's *Levellers*?

See **Curling, Dykers, Ghost
Landscape**

Love and Death

Somewhere in the rain last Saturday rushing for a bus to Gatehouse I saw the parade for the festival the Big Burns Supper making its way through Dumfries, giant puppets and all. It was a good event, held in the calm between storms. Among the children were some dressed as poppies, a bit bravely given the season. I read later that one of the themes of the carnival was love letters written by an unknown British soldier from the trenches. The mix of poppies, weans, soldiers and love is a dangerous

one. I've always thought that the hijacking of the powerful symbol of the poppy by the Earl Haig Fund was an atrocity, as was the association with the Field Marshal's name itself; a bit like having a Jack the Ripper Fund for murder victims.

Poppies whose roots are in men's
  veins
drop, and are ever dropping

Isaac Rosenberg said, and does anything have to be added? I never wear a poppy, though of course I put money in the cans in pubs. I'll run a mile from the sight of some child in uniform selling poppies: the First World War was a celebration of child murder.

Love and death are powerful themes, interlinked. 'The sweetest honey is loathsome in its own deliciousness. And in the taste destroys the appetite. Therefore, love moderately,' Friar Lawrence advises in *Romeo and Juliet*. Some hope.

Poor Helen of Kirkconnel was destroyed by the all-consuming passion of Robert Bell, a posh bloke whom her family favoured to marry her. She, however, had fallen in love with another man, Adam Fleming, whom she used to meet at twilight in the old churchyard, the twin symbolism of which, though a gift to poets, obviously escaped them.

Robert Bell used to sneak about and watch them, and tormented beyond endurance by the sight of their canoodling, produced some kind of musket, took aim and fired. Helen threw herself in front of her lover and was killed instantly. In the 25 minutes or so it took Robert Bell to reload his arquebus – this was

the late 16th century remember – Fleming had plenty of time to kill the murderer. Some sources say he then fled, turning up much later to die of a broken heart on her tombstone. Kirkconnel's not in the upper Nith Valley, by the way, but old Kirkconnel near Eaglesfield.

I wish I were where Helen lies!
Night and day on me she cries;
O that I were where Helen lies,
On fair Kirconnell Lee!
Curst be the heart, that thought the
    thought,
And curst the hand, that fired the
    shot,
When in my arms burd Helen
    dropt,
And died to succour me!

('Fair Helen of Kirkconnell' Walter Scott)

I suppose Dumfries and Galloway's greatest love story is meant to transcend death.

Lady Devorgilla's love for her departed husband, John Balliol, was so great she had his heart excised from his body so she could carry it around in a silver and ivory box. After her death in 1290 she was buried in the sanctuary of the abbey church she had founded – Dulce Cor, or Sweetheart Abbey – and on her instructions the casket containing her husband's heart was buried beside her. A hugely powerful and wealthy woman in her own respect, descended from the Princes of Galloway as well as the royal line of Scotland, the mother of King John Balliol, an educated woman speaking four languages and the biggest landowner in Europe, yet she spent much of her life mourning lost love. A bit of a waste, suggests Liz Niven:

> Here she comes now,
> wading through the Nith,
> his heart in her hand.
>
> It's a long time since she held
> her own heart in her mouth.
> He'd been away so often.
>
> Her waiting, watching, weeping,
> never brought him back.
> He came when he wanted,
> As they all do.
>
> ('Devorgilla's Legacy')

As powerful as love and death is love and loss. Two of Scotland's greatest love songs were collected, re-composed and put to music in Nithsdale by Robert Burns, 'My Love is Like a Red Red Rose' in 1794 and 'Ae Fond Kiss' in 1791. Agnes Maclehose, an unhappily married woman of 29, was involved in a passionate but unconsummated love affair with the poet. She outlived him by 45 years but, like Devorgilla, never forgot. On their last meeting she wrote: This day I can never forget. Parted with Burns, in the year 1791, never more to meet in this world. Oh, may we meet in Heaven! Burns wrote and sent to her the poem *Ae Fond Kiss* before she sailed for Jamaica: it's a poem about emigration, in a way.

Some years ago I unwrapped a fragile letter brought to me by a school pupil in Annan, which had been in her family's possession for some time, an heirloom. It was from New England in 1842, a letter written by a man to his wife. It was most delicate but I was able to photocopy it and am looking at it now. It reads:

> I cannot wait for you all to join me here in the sun, it is all my heart's desire. The land is good and rich, and all I have need for now is you and your kindness.

The pupil couldn't add anything beyond the fact that the reunion had never happened, the man had died. I wrote a poem about it.

Here is a letter
come across the membrane of ocean
over the back of a world
curved like a whale.
I unwrap it, like tissue,
and sentences spill out,
as though the seal on a jar has
    broken,
coils of cornflower blue
on paper thin as shell.

I saw a sailor's valentine once
in a museum in Nantucket Sound,
a mosaic of broken scallop
glued in a compass rose.
'Writ from the heart' it said.
Words come best like that:
in ink or blood,
when the source is from a major
    vein.

I read, and understand this much:
if ink sees off time and miles, then
    so must love.

('Letter')

Let us not part this chapter with a snivel, however, and the steady pulse of our people haemorrhaging west and south. Let us not be cynical. Let us leave with a modern love story, an American girl from Los Angeles who dreamed of love and bookshops and Scotland and who flew across the sea on the cyberwaves of Google, then in person.

Jessica Fox now lives in a bookshop in Wigtown, where, according to an interview with *The Guardian* newspaper, 'she doesn't feel the cold anymore, just a warm sense of accomplishment'. With no connection at all to Scotland, or any experience of it, she dreamed an existence for herself there, then made it happen, contacting the first bookshop she came across in a list on her computer screen, then visiting during the Book Festival, then falling slowly in love with the owner, then coming finally to stay in the dream landscape of Galloway.

*See **Emigration, War***

M

Macbeth in Dumfries and Alexander Montgomerie

Whaur's your Willie Shakespeare noo?

This question, shouted from the crowd during the first performance of John Home's *Douglas* in Edinburgh in 1756 reminds me of a conversation I once had with a man who claimed William Shakespeare had visited Dumfries, causing the street which contains Scotland's oldest theatre, *The Theatre Royal*, to be named Shakespeare Street. I always dismissed this man's theories about anything, not least because he lived in a cave for a while outside New Abbey. Even though his mother used to bring him breakfast, I felt this behaviour did not qualify him to be respected in his literary views.

An article by Richard Whalen published in the *Oxfordian* in 2003, however, puts forward the very same theory. He and the authors he cites claim that the intimate knowledge of Scottish weather conditions, geography and history shown in the play *Macbeth* must have meant its author was familiar with Scotland to the extent he'd actually travelled there. Some of the evidence is a little tendential. The line 'So fair and foul a day I have not seen', he says, displays an awareness of the subtleties of Scottish atmospheric conditions that could only be gained through personal experience. He then goes on to quote sources that suggest Shakespeare could have travelled to Scotland in the years 1601–2 when he disappeared from England and might have toured, even premiered *Macbeth* in Edinburgh. None of this proves that Shakespeare was anywhere in Dumfries and Galloway of course, even if this early appearance at the Edinburgh Fringe is true. Whalen himself, however, favours the theory that *Macbeth* was written by Richard de Vere, 17th Earl of Oxford, who definitely was campaigning in the Scottish Borders as a soldier and would have known details of contemporary events in Scotland such as the death of Mary Queen of Scots' consort Darnley, evidence of which Whalen finds in some of the plot features of Macbeth.

Oxford participated in two invasions of Scotland in 1570. Was the author of *Macbeth* therefore really in Dumfries and Galloway?

All very vague and difficult to prove you might say. One thing is for sure and that is that Chrys Salt, from Gatehouse of Fleet, today brings Shakespeare, in the form of the famous Globe Theatre Touring, Company to Dumfries in the grounds of the Crichton campus, providing as she says, 'a world class theatrical experience' to the region. 'It's such a thrill to see famous actors bringing the plays alive,' Kasia Ritchie, a school student, told me after last year's performance of King Lear, 'sheer class.'

So who needs Shakespeare in person and, in the spirit of the anonymous heckler, who cares? We have our own poet of the time of Shakespeare, Captain Alexander Montgomerie, and he was a lot more exciting. His home is said to have been Compston Castle near Kirkcudbright. He was a soldier during the minority of Mary Queen of Scots and was named by James VI as his 'maister poete', a

kind of Laureate, the most skilled of the court circle of poets that included the monarch himself. Unlike Shakespeare, Montgomerie, typical of Scottish poets perhaps, couldn't keep his mouth shut and had a relatively short and stormy life in which he fought with other poets, served as a soldier in the Netherlands, was robbed of his pension, took part in a Catholic rising to seize Ailsa Craig, was outlawed and then denied burial on holy ground. Refreshingly, many of his poems and sonnets were aimed at the chiselling lawyers and judges he thought had robbed him in his life or at poets he thought inferior to him. His poem 'The Cherry and the Slaye', a very long debate about whether he should eat a cherry from up the hill, or a sloe that didn't involve such a long walk, was very popular at the time but his shorter lyrics are best in my opinion. He had a 'fluent and radiant talent for love poetry' according to the *Encyclopaedia Britannica*.

Na thing thair is in hir at all
That is not supernaturall,
Maist proper and perfyte;

So fresche, so fragrant, and so fair,
As dees and Dame Bewtie's air,
An dochter o delight;
With qualeteis and forme Devine
Be nature so decoird,
As goddes of all feminine,
Of men to be adoird:
Sa blissed that wissed

Scho is in all men's thocht,
As rarest and fairest
That eur nature wrocht.

('Ye Bankis of Helicon', Alexander Montgomerie)

*See **Makar***

Machars

A strip of coastline on the Solway simultaneously bleak but haunted. Even leaving aside the history and the folk tales, there's something about the Machars, even in a force 12 gale, even if you've been dropped off by a bus in a village where the pub's not open for another five hours, and there's no sign of life beyond two men trying to cut up a giant turnip with an axe.

The silt and water shine,
and in this type of weather
look more like steel than silver.
Venture out and the wind goes
through you like death,
leaves you breathless.
In every wet corner of this shore
they are clinging on.
The holiday homes are
sealed for better times,
but here and there,
flowers in the window,
checked curtains,
a porcelain horse,
and in the slick street
an old man with a stick,
and by grass lit for a moment
like emerald,
a boy and girl holding hands.
Life brings love and longing,
along with all the rest,
in the Machars, or carried about
prosaically, on a stagecoach bus,
in the heart.

('Life and Longing in the Machars')

Magic and Michael Scott, Superhero

Many folk have tried to emulate the great magician Michael Scott and it has proved beyond them.

Michael had the benefit of supernatural powers, but modern magicians, less well endowed, have had to scratch for a living at children's parties and magic shows. The strain of trying to produce magic experiences for children who daily, in film or television, and nowadays online, get extraordinary and wonderful imagery, has proved destructive to many of them. Many years ago one magician in particular, now sadly dead, covered parties, festivals and galas all over the region specialising in rabbit tricks and balloon twisting until the strain got too much for him and he suffered a mental breakdown during a children's show. One of the organisers said, 'it was a terrible embarrassment. One minute he was fine, the next he was swearing like a trooper, saying the most terrible things, like a blue comedian. And I won't tell you what he was doing with the balloons. We had to storm the stage. Three days later I heard he was in an institution'.

Magic seemed so much easier in the old days, when it was just the Deil you had to face, as with Michael Scotus, Michael The Scot.

Going to sleep at night is much easier in Dumfries and Galloway knowing that Michael Scott, mathematician, renaissance scholar and wizard is looking after us. The Cornish have got their King Arthur – well actually Galloway has got him too – but we also have Michael Scott, sleeping still beneath the hills ready to come out and amaze us if we need him. What's King Arthur, anyway, but brawn and a pretty face? Michael had the lot; brains, wit, skill, magic and impeccable supernatural connections. A respected scholar and mathematician by day, he would transform by means of some medieval telephone box at night and emerge ready to do battle with the forces of darkness.

Fluent in Latin, Greek, Hebrew and Arabic, Michael was a star in the intellectual crucible that was the court of the Emperor Frederick II in Sicily, supervising new translations of Aristotle and giving a hand to Fibonacci when he was having difficulties with his famous sequence. Offered the Archbishopric of Canterbury, Scott preferred to hang about in the south of Scotland building a library, and confounding Satan by a series of clever tricks. Scott acted as the devil's social worker, keeping him busy doing useful if endless tasks like knotting sand in Luce Bay rather than corrupting people's souls. Scott was everyone's favourite superhero. His namesake, Walter, commented in the 19th century that 'Every great project in Scotland is said to be the work of William Wallace, the Devil or Michael Scott.'

Scott's reputation as a wizard was probably caused by his interest in astrology, a pursuit which brought criticism from some quarters including that killjoy Dante. In *The Inferno* he is to be found in the Circle of Hell reserved for shysters and con men.

Michael Scott said:

> Every astrologer is worthy of praise and honour, since by such a doctrine as astrology he probably knows many secrets of God, and things which few know.

What did Scott do? What did he not do?

> After his death the legend grew.
> When the light was jagged on the hills,

a contrast of sun and black shadows,
and heaven seemed poised skewered
on the razor tips of mountains,
his horse, scattering bairns and silencing the bells,
was said to clatter down the road to Hell.
In his grave in seven silver books
were the secrets of light and alchemy
gathered from a journey round the world
on the back of a kelpie.

The truth is scarcely less fantastic.
He wandered from Oxford to Palermo,
translated Aristotle, argued the toss
with the cream of Arab scholars,
found time in Toledo to discover
the secret of 'aqua ardens',
(whisky to you and me) then came back,
bringing the Renaissance to the borders,
200 years before the rest of Europe.
No wonder among the dubs and moss
and wet sheep, they thought he was magic.

('Michael Scott')

Michael Scott moved easily through that grey area between science and magic, logic and superstition. It was his milieu. His quick wittedness set him apart from other wizards. Easily tricking the devil, he did the same to the Pope, riding a fairy steed from Scotland to Rome to find out the date of Shrove-tide, a secret which for some reason the Pope was hiding from us. In an unusual exchange, Scott notices the Pope is wearing a woman's shoe rather than his own. In embarrassed confusion the Pope then reveals the date of Shrove-tide.

Unfortunately Scott died just before he could have done service during the Wars of Independence, turning the English into boulders or something even more imaginative, though some say he is sleeping still beneath the hills until his country calls. In which, case where was he when that charlatan Uri Geller used telepathic powers to shift the ball just as Gary McAllister was about to equalise from the penalty spot against England in the 1996 European Championship? Probably he was reading.

See Books: Existing, Lost, Made up, Vanished, Made of Wood, Plagues, Stanes

Magna Carta

There is much in the news about the anniversary of the Magna Carta which, as radio commentators are fond of saying, forms the basis for British democracy, but which in fact was just a charter for rich folk which all sides renounced within five minutes of signing it. It does remind me of Galloway also, however, as all things do, because Alan Lord of Galloway, John Balliol's granddad, was instrumental in helping prop up King John of England in his wars in England and Wales, sending, in the days when Galloway was a Princedom operating its own eccentric foreign policy, a huge fleet into the Irish Sea and unleashing his renowned and feared Gallowglasses on the King's enemies. These Gallowglasses, from *gallóglaigh*, 'foreign warriors', were ruthless mercenaries of mixed Norse and Gaelic stock, the people who gave Galloway its name. The men of Galloway, operating for profit in Ireland or at home under their princes, had a military reputation second to none. Alan of Galloway was very close to King John, a trusted confidant, and helped advise him how much wriggle room he had in the immediate aftermath of the over-hyped Magna Carta. Not that the Galloway princes would ever have subscribed to such a lily-livered document, in 1215 or any date.

Makar

A poet, who weaves in words an artefact. Makars are more than writers, but craftsmen and craftswomen. From its origins in the Scottish Renaissance, a makar was taken to be a poet skilled in form, like Henrysson or Dunbar. Usage nowadays implies any poet either writing in Scots or a language in Scotland, for the term is exclusively Scottish. Recently there has been a National Makar of Scotland, first Edwin Morgan and now Liz Lochead. Over the last ten years or so a Makar has been appointed in certain Scottish cities such as Glasgow, Edinburgh and Dundee. After a Highlands and Islands Makar has been appointed, someone will eventually decide that that forgotten corner of literary excellence, the bottom left hand bit of Scotland, should get one too. I think there has been some premature jostling for this non-existent role already but surely the odds-on favourite must be Peter Angelini whose poem about Peter Pan so marvellously complemented the unveiling of a chain saw sculpture of the eponymous hero outside Gardenwise in Dumfries in 2011.

What can we say though, but that the region which saw Burns and James Hogg, Mactaggart's favourite Allan Cunningham, SR Crockett, and so on has continued to breed or pay host to poets of great talent.

Hugh MacDiarmid was the giant of Scottish literature in the 20th century, re-establishing the writing of Scots as a form and scribbling feisty political verse which did not necessarily always go down well in his hometown of Langholm. In his various works he makes reference to his hometown, however:

> I had the fortune to live as a boy
> In a world a' columbe and colour-
>   de-roy
> As gin I'd had Mars for the land o'
>   my birth
> Instead o' the earth.
> Nae maitter hoo faur I've travelled
>   sinsyne
> The cast o' Dumfriesshire's aye in
>   me like wine;
> And my songs are gleids o' the
>   candent spirit
> Its sons inherit.

(Dedicatory Verses to the book *Stony Limits*, Hugh MacDiarmid)

In one of my favourite MacDiarmid poems, *Crowdieknowe*, he's referring, according to another Galloway scholar and poet John Manson, to his ancestors' graveyard at Waterbeck. He visualises the hard men of his youth giving God a hard time at the Last Trump, glowering at him – 'an aa his gang o angels i the lift, thae trashy bleezin French-like folk wha gar'd them shift.'

Three makars vie in the last 40 years, Alasdair Reid from Whithorn, a poet of international class, Kirkpatrick Dobie in Dumfries, seeking the universal in the parochial, and the Stewartry's Willie Neill, an extraordinary talent, craggy, feisty like the landscape, a poet who spun gold in all three languages of Scotland. If I was handing posthumous makar-ships out I would give Dumfries and Galloway's to Willie Neill.

> I remember the black chains that
>   hung
> on the swee above the fire, and I
>   remember
> the men who sat in the farm
>   kitchen;
> they wore stout boots, and their
>   hands were no less rough.
> They could not read, or would not
>   read
> except what they read in the sky, on
>   the moor and the hills
> and the noise of ploughshares
>   ripping the winter turf
> was a kind of music to them.

('The Ayrshire Farmer', William Neill)

In the last 20 years there has been an explosion of writing in the region, three separate anthologies from the area have been published and there is a regular literary magazine called *Southlight*. The Crichton Campus in Dumfries plays host to two writing groups and there are others throughout the region. In Dumfries, Hugh Bryden began the prizewinning Roncadora Press, publishing artists' books and poetry collections. Both the Bakehouse at Gatehouse and the Wigtown Book Festival have hosted many events encouraging local writers and writing, and posts have been created to develop literature networks throughout the region.

The current father of Dumfries and Galloway poetry must be Tom Pow. I know this because every time I meet him he strokes my arm in a warm and paternal manner. He is a beautifully lyrical writer whom I have quoted in this volume and who has written much about the landscape of Dumfries and Galloway and the internal landscape too. Scots language poets of excellence are Liz Niven from Castle Douglas, John Burns from Dumfries and Rab Wilson, ex-holder of the Robert Burns and James Hogg Fellowships. They have recently been joined by Stuart Paterson who now lives in Sandyhills, adding his muscular vibrant Scots to the mix. Writing in English are Donald Adamson and Chrys Salt in Gatehouse, Douglas Lipton in Moffat, and there are many others, too, some of them graduates of Tom's creative writing class at the Crichton Campus, or members of two long standing writers groups in Dumfries. Alasdair Reid, James McGonagle and Alison Fell are poets from the region who have moved on. I'm not sure the number of poets there are per square foot in the region but it is strangely ironic that while the region has become depopulated of people with real jobs, the number of poets has seemed to multiply. This cannot be a coincidence. I moved to the small village of Penpont in order to be the only poet, the Makar of Penpont so to speak, only to find that there were two poets already living there, a few doors down. It was a bitter disappointment.

Of course, if Mactaggart is

anything to go by, there were as many poets kicking about 200 years ago and they were probably just as competitive. Certainly the *Encyclopaedia* is packed with verse, more so than this volume here. In fact with so many poets about now, I often like to imagine that I lived 200 years ago and am striding through the moors in my trews, carrying a parcel of bannocks or square sausage to meet the Makar Tom Pow in the learig or some other pub, like James Hogg meeting Sir Walter Scott. What did Wordsworth say of Hogg after the great man had died?

> The mighty Minstrel breathes no
> longer,
> 'Mid mouldering ruins low he lies;
> And death upon the braes of
> Yarrow,
> Has closed the Shepherd-poet's
> eyes.

('On the Death of James Hogg', William Wordsworth)

Being a typical poet he couldn't resist sticking the boot in as well though, adding that Hogg had 'coarse manners and low and offensive opinions'. Ouch.

Reminds me, for some reason, of Rab Wilson's poem, 'Tom Pow on a Bike'.

> Tam Pow on a bike, Tam Pow on a
> bike,
> Puffin an pantin, just what is he
> like?
>
> Tam Pow on a bike, pop eyed an
> pechin,
> Cam via Annan? Or Ecclefechan?
>
> Tam Pow on a bike, a mid-life
> Adonis,
> How lucky we are, to hae Tam
> among us,
>
> Tam Pow on a bike, bypasses
> Penpont
> In case Shug Drumsleet, might caa
> him a 'clown'
> Tam Pow on a bike, his neb red as
> a rose,
> Nae bursaries gaun the day I
> suppose?

('Tom Pow on a Bike', Rab Wilson)

And the moral? To be a makar, amongst makars requires fortitude.

I confirm this again on a grand tour of Wigtownshire to inform an eager public about the Mactaggart project. It gets off to an inauspicious start in Wigtown Library where the staff are shocked to see me. There is no audience, and I retire into the local collection to research furiously to overcome my humiliation. I look in a mirror and am shocked to see myself, to tell you the truth it's been a long bus journey without a toilet stop and a large man bound for the Stranraer boat spent the whole journey telling me how desperate he was to get out of Scotland because it's destroying his liver.

This is not the first time this has happened to me. I was once invited to a reading in Wick when only the janitor came, and, unlike these discreetly embarrassed librarians, he insisted on making things worse by telling me Edwin Morgan had been there the fortnight before and they had been 'queued round the block'. Worse I suppose, is a story that Tom Pow once told me about a reading in The Edinburgh Festival at the Art College, entitled *Bards o Gallowa* featuring himself and the great Willie Neill. In spite of extensive publicity no one turned up at all and the poets were about to leave quietly and in a dignified way, when the organiser said 'wait a minute' and, pointing to the door of the bar from where extravagant noise and laughter issued, said, 'I'll see if anyone wants to come for free'. After what seemed an eternity he emerged furiously shaking his head, muttering 'no, no one'.

So you see, there is little shame in having no audience at all for a reading on such a pleasant sunlit afternoon when there are no alternative attractions. Not even in a Book Town full of book shops and book lovers. Not even feet from the office of the Wigtown Book Festival, who commissioned the book I was planning to read from.

I am disappointed most for my companion John Mactaggart's sake, but like him I do not have 'a hinging lugg' about it. As he said, 'The kicks and thousand rebuffs of this world, thank God, I can take with pleasure, and give none.' This phrase comes from the way dogs, and some other brutes, have, of letting their ears or lugs droop when on the eve of battle.

See **Big Shuggie MacDiarmid, Book Town**

Mermaids

I like Allan Cunningham's poem, 'The Mermaid of Galloway'.

> There's a maid has sat o' the green
>   merse side
> Thae ten lang years and mair;
> An' every first night o' the new
>   moon
> She kames her yellow hair.
>
> An' ay while she sheds the yellow
>   burning gowd,
> Fu' sweet she sings an' hie,
> Till the fairest bird that wooes the
>   green wood,
> Is charm'd wi' her melodie.
>
> But wha e'er listens to that sweet
>   sang,
> Or gangs the fair dame te;
> Ne'er hears the sang o' the lark
>   again,
> Nor waukens an earthlie ee.

('The Mermaid of Galloway', Allan Cunningham)

I suppose the nearest I've come to witnessing this kind of thing is when a beautiful girl once attempted to drown a friend of mine in the stream that runs through Kirkgunzeon. The circumstances were very different, mind you, and it is highly unlikely she was a mermaid, or if she was, she must have been the type that wades ashore for a few pints in the Anvil Inn before going about her murderous business. Besides, he was asking for it.

But I wonder why there are so many mermaid stories in Dumfries and Galloway? It's even more unusual because most of the mermaids are inland, in rivers and streams, rather than hanging about the extensive coastline where they could really do some damage to local shipping. But that's confusing a mermaid with a siren, and there are no siren stories, though I know a good one about a foghorn. Sirens are always bad, mermaids, like fairies, are a mixed bag. In 'The Mermaid of Galloway', recently recorded in an excellent version by the Nithsdale folk singer Emily Smith, the Laird of Cowhill, about to be wed, is seduced by a bad, bad mermaid, trapped by her golden hair and dies.

The Mermaid of Barnhourie was a proper ocean-going mermaid, perhaps because she came from an Irish family that lived in the middle of the Solway. She fell in love with a young married sailor who used to ply the trade routes between Whitehaven and Kippford. He fell in love with her, too, after she rescued him from a shipwreck, and spent the night cosily with her in the kelp, but was forced by economic circumstances to go to America. The mermaid, who by this time had borne a son by the sailor, waited patiently, but on his return his lugger was driven onto the sandbanks at Barnhourie and broken up in the storms. She searched for him in the wreckage and found him drowned. Using herbs and flowers and seaweed she brought him back to life, and he turned into a merman as a result, the family living happily ever after in the Solway, spending their days alerting other ships to the dangers of the sandbanks. And the sailor's wife married a prosperous a sea captain so that was alright too.

Old tales. Scan as you might now the smirr on the Galloway coast you'll not see a flash of long red hair or a beautiful girl combing her hair on a rock and staring out to sea. Or will you? The Mermaids from Whithorn are sisters trying to make it in a tough industry but getting there on the basis of raw talent. They write and sing their own music, have played at the Celtic Connections festival, and have just issued their first EP. While acknowledging some of the difficulties in terms of travel and so on that living in the Machars causes, they see the landscape as integral to their art. 'It's the peace and the countryside here that lets us write'. And the name? 'It all started in the summer of 2012, we were thinking of entering a battle of the bands type competition, messing about with what names we'd give ourselves... we found ourselves entering Wigtown's Got Talent in October 2012, our first ever public performance together! After our performance we were given this lovely feedback by one of the judges. "They look like mermaids and sing like angels,"' and *The Mermaids* were born.

The Mermaids look the part, and sound the part, and there's no doubt which side of the mermaid divide they're on. 'In our view we are going to spend our lives doing something that will not only make us happy but others happy as well, so what's better than that?' What indeed?

See Away with the Fairies

Midnight in Stavanger and Eric Booth Moodiecliffe

A legendary painting, with its exact duplicate *Midnight in Lerwick*, one of a pair made during the Galloway artist Eric Booth Moodiecliffe's purple and blue period, during the late 1980s, a time when he only had purple and blue paint. At one time there was a coterie of artists working out of the Tam o' Shanter in Dumfries. Prominent among these were Ronnie Fisher, a fisherman and painter transplanted from Newcastle, Frank Murphy, a retired art teacher who did painfully intricate miniatures, Hugh MacIntyre, a proper professional painter widely acknowledged in this country and internationally, and Eric Booth Moodiecliffe, an ex-mental nurse who had spent many years in Charters Towers in Australia and liked to paint historic landmarks. Ronnie and Eric were really only in it for beer and baccy money.

Ronnie was a proficient wildlife painter, who did a lot of stags and geese. Eric, I think it's fair to say, was a prolific but very bad painter. Opinions differed as to why this was, from the fact he was rushing it or was too skint or mean to use a lot of paint, to the more widely held theory that he just had no talent for it whatsoever. Eric was so world weary and likeable that he did shift some paintings, and whenever he sold one he would think he was onto a good thing and paint many other versions on the same theme. Therefore the selling of *Cairnholy June 86* was followed by *Cairnholy 2* all the way up to *Cairnholy 9*, all similar but, as the series progressed, rendered in less and less paint. There was a kind of ghostly and otherworldly aspect to these later paintings. I spoke to someone who owned *Caerlaverock 8* who said there was now nothing at all on the canvas, and I often think of this as the zenith of Eric's artistic career, kind of like Salvador Dali selling pictures with only a signature on them, but one step better.

Ronnie used to take the micky out of Eric's paintings, affectionately, because the two were good friends. Once, when a celebrity story was all over the newspapers concerning a drowning in a private swimming pool, Eric wondered aloud why the celebrity had a swimming pool since it was common knowledge he couldn't swim. 'Well,' replied Ronnie in his thick Geordie accent, 'you've got paints!'

Eric was a rotten driver, too. We once went on a tour of the Machars in the course of which he nearly ploughed into a milk tanker. After we'd swerved into a lay-by he leaned across to me. 'Thank God I woke up in time', he whispered.

Eric was a beautiful poet, however, and could recite long screeds of his own work all from memory. As far as I know, none of this was written down and all has been lost, though he did go through a wee period of painting poems onto little canvases. Presumably they have all disappeared too. The only snatch that remains I wrote down, to try and capture in a poem the amazing story Eric once told me of nursing the American poet Robert Lowell after he had been committed to a mental institution in London.

Greenways, St John's Wood, 1970.
When Eric Booth Moodiecliffe enters,
Lowell is standing naked on the bed.
Moodiecliffe picks up the paper

discarded in panic by another nurse,
and begins to read.
After a minute, Lowell shouts
'Don't you know me?

I'm Robert Lowell, I'm famous!'
Folding the paper neatly on his lap
Moodiecliffe quietly says
'So? I'm better than you are.'

'Prove it' Lowell replies,
his face wax, wet with sweat.
Moodiecliffe then recites from memory
part of his epic poem set,

'Time is a Thief'.
'Time steals', he begins, 'that which
    anyone
would hold most dear..'
Soon, Lowell is shouting

'Moodiecliffe, you are one of the
    four
greatest poets since Shakespeare!'
By part six, however,
'as we must follow the wake of his
    insidious spoor',

Lowell is half dressed and
Moodiecliffe no better than Empson.
and as the clock strikes ten,
'borne along to that unknown

shore where night and darkness seal
    the door',
Lowell, clean shaven,
his hair combed and suitcase on the
    floor,

is asking, 'you finished with the
    paper?'

('The Healing Power of Poetry')

When Eric was drinking he'd
mutter 'how would ye be?' in his
quiet hybrid Australian accent.
This would progress to 'who
would you be?' then inevitably to
'why would you be?'
    His was a rumpled and
ultimately tragic life, looking back
on it, but who am I to judge what
counts as success?
    Folk still talk about him, and I
for my part am still searching for
that still elusive masterpiece
Midnight in Stavanger.

Minerva, Dumfries Academy and JM Barrie

In the middle of Dumfries a
splendid antique goddess points
her torch to the heavens and
clutches at her side a book
containing the wisdom of the
ages. It is an inspiring sight for
anyone trudging the rain-swept
streets of Dumfries to watch the
sun shine on her slender golden
body. She is of course the goddess
of wisdom and she presides over
that splendid palace of the pagan
spirit, Dumfries Academy, the
region's oldest school, with roots
that stretch back to the 14th
century when John of Greyfriars
was appointed headmaster. The
school has been on its current site
since 1804, was a boarding
school, and operated essentially as

a grammar school until 1983, taking the most gifted pupils from the surrounding area. The Minerva Building was built in 1897 over the foundations of the older school which faced out towards what is now Irving Street. If you penetrate into the cellars of the newer building you can actually see the cobbled road which used to lead into the old school, the same road that was captured on the only photograph of that school, wending its way between some young boatered chaps who appear to be playing cricket on the lawn.

This is the very road along which the 14-year-old Jim Barrie walked into school from his house in Victoria Avenue, or left to go to his mate Stuart Gordon's house, Moat Brae, next door to the school. Moat Brae, on the point of demolition, has been rescued by a hugely successful campaign and, as I type, the idea is to re-open it as a centre for children's literature. A fantastic idea since, on Barrie's own admission, the gardens of Moat Brae, sloping down to the Nith, were the inspiration for that strange and morbid work, *Peter Pan*, which continues to frighten children to this day:

> When the shades of night began to fall, certain young mathematicians shed their triangles, crept up walls and down trees, and became pirates in a sort of odyssey that long afterwards was to become the play *Peter Pan*. For our escapades in a certain Dumfries Garden, which is an enchanted land to me, were certainly the genesis of that nefarious work.

Barrie in fact wrote his first work while at school, a 100,000 word novel called *A Child of Nature*, which he later ripped up. He drew inspiration from the local bookshop where he read Fennimore Cooper, RM Ballantyne, as well as 'penny dreadfuls', lurid tales of adventure like *Spring Heeled Jack*. He also got involved in the theatre, attending the local Theatre Royal, and founding a drama club in the school. I think one of the things about Dumfries then was that it was an exciting literary environment. It wasn't just the Burns legacy; Barrie used to pass

Thomas Carlyle, then acclaimed as one of the best literary talents in the world, as the latter visited his sister in Hill House opposite Barrie's home. And the uncle of one of Barrie's best friends, James Anderson, captain of the *SS Great Eastern*, the largest ship afloat, had just been the subject of a bestselling story by Ballantyne.

Jim was a bit weird, mind you, even in terms of his own day. The Barrie legacy at the Academy amounted to some photographs and documents and, as I've mentioned previously, a priceless work of vandalism, his name carved onto a piece of desk, which was carefully preserved over the years. When we were establishing an archive room in the school, a group of 6th year girls volunteered to paint the walls, which they did very enthusiastically, using the precious Barrie memento as a door jam and completely ruining it.

In the very first year of the campaign to save Moat Brae, pupils and a few teachers from the Academy published a booklet of poems, *On the Grass Cloud* to fundraise. It sold out two print

runs and showed the depth of talent that still exists under Minerva's sandals.

> Recently we've been captured
> held hostage by snow
> away from biros and dull
> monotony
> dressed up as work.
>
> In leggings shirts and scarves
> we shirk in Neverland,
> white as a flickering screen
> a blank page that cries adventure
>
> then reality calls a mutiny
> the snow melts,
> we're chased back to life
> where we're all lost children
>
> terrorised by the ticking crocodile.

('Snowed In', Charlotte Singleton)

Although the pupils no longer have access to the cupola of Minerva, and don't dress her in ladies' underwear as they used to, they remain a gifted and vibrant lot, giving the centre of Dumfries a much needed sense of vitality and life, even though the locals don't often appreciate it much. Jim Barrie might be hard to beat but people of quality have always come out of the gates here. A wee committee formed by senior pupils were recently given the task of finding distinguished former pupils to add to the roll of honour outside the gates, which includes names such as John Laurie the actor, and Jane Haining a heroic teacher from Dunscore who, refusing to abandon her pupils in Budapest during World War Two, died in Auschwitz. They came up with quite a few but as yet the head teacher has not consented to add the name of Peter Ellis, the co-inventor of Viagra.

*See **Barrie, J.M., Geniuses, Teachers***

Mining

Rab Wilson, a poet from Ayrshire, but Dumfries' Robert Burns Fellow for several years, has written eloquently and elegiacally about the mining industry in south west Scotland. His film *Mining the Seam* has been critically acclaimed, though I warn you against googling this title because it is a euphemism for an another activity altogether, one which cannot have been on Rab's mind when he wrote so movingly about the decline of one of Nithsdale's most historic traditional industries and the human cost of this.

The Romans probably started mining up in the Leadhills, first lead, then gold. The communities mining there through the 18th century were among the most impoverished and unhealthy in the country. As Alasdair Livingstone writes in *Green Galloway*:

> The inhabitants of the lead villages purchased five times as many antiscorbutic preparations per head to ward off scurvy as the other customers of the Sanquhar chemist's shop in 1742–3, and the risks of lead poisoning also led them to take twice as many purgatives as the general community.

The Duke of Buccleuch, whose land they mined, took about a sixth of the lead and made a sizeable fortune during the wars of the 19th and early 20th centuries when bullets were in great demand. The end of the First World War saw the closure of the mines though some workers managed to be absorbed into the booming coal mining industry based round Kirkconnel, on land also leased by the Duke, in pits at Gateside and Fauldhead. Mining was hugely hazardous. Sarah Butt from Kirkconnel wrote:

My Grandad James Crawford worked at the Fauldhead pit, but sadly died before I was born... myocarditis, nephritis, bronchitis and uritis listed on his death certificate... all of them related to working down the pit, but no compensation then.

In Kirkconnel there is a memorial to 79 miners killed in the area between 1872 and 1969 mostly in the Fauldhead pit. Inscribed on it are the words:

They served their day unseen unsung
In caverns of the deep
Till early laid the mools among
They through the ages sleep.

One example of a miner laid in the 'mools' was Thomas Bennie, killed while trying to rescue a workmate and awarded the Edward Medal. Bennie and his injured comrades had to be carried to the surface from a mile and a half underground.

The Queen has been pleased to award the Edward Medal to the late Thomas Dalziel Bennie in recognition of his gallantry in the following circumstances:

As the result of a fall of roof in Fauldhead Colliery, Dumfriesshire, on 22 May 1953, a miner was trapped by a large stone, but the dirt in the sides of the road prevented the full weight of the stone bearing on him. The fall displaced timber supports and left the roof in a dangerous condition, with every indication of further collapse. Despite the risk, Bennie, who had been working with the trapped miner, remained in order to try to release him, but a further fall occurred and Bennie was fatally injured. His disregard of personal risk in his attempts to rescue the trapped miner was in the highest tradition of the mining industry.

(*The London Gazette*)

Gateside Pit closed in 1964, Fauldhead in 1968. The human cost of mining was huge, but the social cost of its collapse equally devastating.

In Gateside the village primary

school closed and the few remaining pupils transferred to the school in the adjacent housing development of Kelloholm. When Fauldhead Colliery closed, many families moved to other coal fields in Nottingham, Lothian or South Yorkshire. As the school roll plummeted, Kirkconnel Junior Secondary was shut in 1971 and the pupils transferred to Sanquhar Academy. Now the only miners work in an open cast mine in Kirkconnel or cross the border to others in Ayrshire. The death of the coal mining industries in the north of the region brought another wave of depopulation. In Wanlockhead, there's a black plaque on the old library wall dedicated to the vastly underrated poet Robert Reid, born Wanlockhead in 1850, died in Montreal in 1922, who left for the same reasons folk continue to.

the weary and wae...
fain to be laid, limb-free,
In a dreamless dwawm to be airtit
　away
To the shores o' the crystal sea;
Far frae the toil, and the moil, and
　the murk.

('Kirkbride', Robert Reid)

See **Emigration, Ghost Landscape**

Miracles

The supernatural is never far away in Galloway and it's late at night, and we're talking, as you do, of miraculous happenings. The man I am speaking to is telling me a tale of his younger days when, smitten by a young woman, and a bit drunk after a ceilidh, he called upon her in a lonely country location on a hopeless errand of love and, having been gently rejected, found himself alone near Kirkbean, far from home after the last bus had gone, 'nothing in my pockets but an empty tobacco tin'. He had wandered into a graveyard and slept on a stone, '1697, it said, I remember it well, though I couldn't take you back to where I was. It was a warm evening and I put my jacket under me, and decided to just go to sleep and dream of her all night. I was heartbroken.'

He woke to birdsong: And the strangest thing was there was my jacket was still where I put it but in the pockets was my tobacco tin, stuffed with baccy and in the other pocket a half bottle of whisky. I mean I can't call it a miracle because surely miracles don't help you smoke and drink? But I have absolutely no explanation. None at all. There was no shop nearby. I can't explain it. Not then, not now. It was sent to help me in my time of need!

No Christian miracle would have worked out like this. Not far from where this happened, St Ninian, according to Rievaux's 'Life' caused a field of leeks to appear because his monks had no vegetables for their evening meal:

And in the yard soon had sene
caile and leikis afire and greene,
an al that of had neid,
then cummyne of new sadine seide.
The monk that saw this ferly
was then in extasy.

('Life', Rievaux)

Aye, all very good, let's leave them to that ecstasy. The first miracle was clearly the work of the fairies, still alive and kicking when they're needed apparently, rewarding the lovelorn, the damaged and the weak, taking the complete pish out of the cocksure, the privileged and the conceited.

See Away with the Fairies

Money: Lost, Made, Burned

It's Thursday, one of the weans is having a sleepover for her mates, the other's going camping. A range of opportunities and activities you would think designed to encourage them as healthy and sociable young members of the community. Yet as I ransack the lining of my coats and search for that fiver

I know I hid somewhere I am reminded that what underpins all our aspirations for ourselves and our children is the need for base coinage, and how if we hide our money we should at the least be able to recover it. I always find this hard to explain to the kids and it's not getting any easier.

I wonder who hid the 300 medieval coins found just before last Christmas in a rain-lashed field near Twynholm by two treasure hunters? They date from the two Scottish Wars of Independence, from the reigns of the Scottish King Alexander III to the English King Edward III, and I assume they were hidden during the fighting, never to be reclaimed. It's a haunting feeling, especially now when I'm looking under the floorboards, to think of all the gold and silver probably still out there, just a metal detector away. Or a pair of dowsing twigs. I'm utterly convinced by dowsing twigs since the day we used them to trace perfectly the path of a buried defensive wall round a spur of land near Crocketford. It was a day that turned up currency of a sort, and I don't mean for the following poem I then wrote:

> It sits near a brochure for gites,
> an angry percolator
> and a child in the corner
> with a cube of light,
> beeping.

I found it this morning,
prised it from the kiss of clay,
saw the thick grooves for fingers,
felt the balance, perfect in my palm.
Was this the bark-splitter,
the stone-breaker?

At last
in this passing wizardry,
silence,
strength,
power.

('Hand Axe')

I suppose one way of trying to make sure you've got enough cash is to make your own, like Thomas Watling, art teacher and forger of Dumfries. Sentenced to transportation to Australia in 1792 for forging banknotes, he had many adventures en route, ending up in New South Wales as one of Australia's earliest wildlife archivists and artists. When freed in 1796 he returned to Dumfries and was rearrested for forgery. In spite of some half-finished bank notes being found in his bedroom, he was mysteriously acquitted. The other great Galloway banknote story is Bill Drummond's. Bill Drummond is the coolest person ever to have come out of Dumfries and Galloway. In fact, according to Select Magazine, he was the coolest person ever to have come out of anywhere, anytime, by 1993:

> Like the Monolith in 2001: A Space Odyssey, Drummond has always been a step ahead of human evolution, guiding us on. Manager of TheTeardrop Explodes, co-inventor of ambient and trance house, number one pop star, situationist pagan, folk troubadour, pan-dimensional zenarchist gentleman of leisure... and then, ladies and gentlemen, he THROWS IT ALL AWAY, machine-guns the audience and dumps a dead sheep on the doorstep of the Brit Awards and vanishes to build dry-stone walls. His new band The K Foundation make records but say they won't release them at all until world peace is established. Deranged, inspired, intensely cool.
>
> (*Bill Drummond, Number One in the 100 Coolest People in Pop, Select Magazine 1993*)

Bill Drummond was the son of a Church of Scotland minister and spent most of the first 11 years of his life in Newton Stewart. In the late 1980s he co-founded the avant-garde pop group KLF and its successor the KLF Foundation. In 1994 in Jura, Drummond burned the profits of KLF, a million pounds, and filmed it as a piece of performance art. Drummond renounced pop music to concentrate on his art and has been involved ever since in hugely inspirational, or deranged, depending on your point of view, projects. These projects are often symbolic, transient and only recorded by Drummond and the people who happen, often by accident, to become involved with his art. *The Soup Line* involved Drummond coming to anyone's house sited on a line drawn arbitrarily across Britain to make them and their family and friends soup. Drummond also drew *Cake Circles* on maps. Cakes were then baked and delivered to people who lived inside the circle with the words 'I have baked you a cake, here it is'. Each spring Drummond travels to a number of different cities to distribute to complete strangers 40 bunches of daffodils. His latest project is a tour, beginning in Birmingham in

March 2014 and ending at the same place in April 2025. He will travel to 12 cities in 12 different countries, each bit of the tour lasting three months. By the end of the tour he plans to have produced 25 paintings.

Drummond's art activities are perpetrated under the name the Penkiln Burn, which is the burn at Cumloden, near Newton Stewart where he used to play as a boy.

Speaking to the BBC in 2004 about burning the million quid he said, 'It's a hard one to explain to your kids and it doesn't get any easier.'

See Art

Mons Meg, Munitions and CND

I once wrote a poem about Devorgilla's Bridge in Dumfries, a romantic and historical construction and a unique piece of technology of its time, the 13th Century, and in the course of this I was idly wondering who had crossed it over the years. I suppose the answer was everybody. Or at least everybody who wanted to cross the Nith and move west to Galloway or Ireland between the years 1280 and 1793, a period which saw invasions, pilgrimages, all the shenanigans of 500 years of history. One of the things that stirred the imagination most is the idea of the huge cannon Mons Meg drawn by 20 oxen with its retinue of hundreds being dragged across the bridge by James II's royal army to reduce the treacherous Douglases of Threave in 1455. Mons Meg was a huge state of the art cannon, I suppose the modern equivalent of this would be carting a cruise missile or nuclear bomb into the Stewartry. It stirs the imagination, this scene, but could it have happened given the narrowness of the bridge? Historians doubt it but they're a dour lot.

When I was a boy, and looking at Mons Meg where it used to stand in Edinburgh Castle, hanging off the battlements and pointing in a vaguely threatening anti-capitalist manner at Jenners in Princess Street, somebody pointed at one of the giant stone cannonballs at its foot and said 'good Galloway granite' and went on to say that the weapon had been built at Carlingwark near Castle Douglas by a large family of blacksmiths called McKim who were anxious to rid themselves of the tyrant Douglas family, and built the cannon from scratch after a brief examination of a smaller model. This story is quoted by Alan Temperley. Apparently it needed only two shots to bring about Threave's surrender, the second of which burst through the walls and removed the hand of Margaret the Fair Maid of Galloway, Douglas' wife, just as she was about to drink a rather cheeky glass of chablis. Just joking, of course, Mons Meg being made, as the name suggests, in Mons in Belgium, engineers of the Low Countries being supposed experts in building this type of stuff. I suppose the Fair Maid had her revenge when James II was eventually blown up by another dodgy cannon nicknamed the Lion as he was trying to bombard the English in Roxburgh.

Unpredictable ordinance takes me in two directions. While it's easy to imagine that sweaty cannon train inching across Devorgilla Bridge in the summer of 1455, it's harder to imagine a small group of CND activists in 1985, huddled round a cruise missile launcher in Castle Douglas car park in the early hours of a cold November morning. However it happened, because I was there. After the deployment of cruise missiles from 1983 at bases like Greenham Common, the peace movement had mobilised and had mounted a series of highly public and effective protests. One strategy had been to build a dummy cruise missile launcher and tour it around, showing the public what it would be like to have this lethal piece of ordinance doing what it was designed to do during wartime, lurking about country lanes pretending to be a refuse truck or whatever. This expensive and very effective piece of propaganda was in high demand and Dumfries and Galloway CND were delighted to have booked it for a short time, as the centrepiece of a local protest. Due to an administrative error, however, this was between five and six o clock in the morning in cold and rainy November. The only member of the public was, I recall, a passing drunk, who shouted 'what are you freaks daeing?'

Equally dodgy but far more dangerous are the munitions that have been supposedly decommissioned but are still around to haunt us. An unsavoury and highly dangerous legacy of military activity has been the dumping of chemical weapons off the Galloway coast. Europe's biggest underwater dump for surplus ammunition lies a mere six miles offshore. The munitions dump in the Beaufort's Dyke trench, off Stranraer, holds more than one million tons of bombs, rockets and shells, including 14,000 tons of rockets with phosgene poison gas warheads. These don't stay put. Davie Proudfoot tells of dredging up phosphorous shells in a scalloper and them 'combusting on deck when they came into contact with oxygen'.

The artist Hugh MacIntyre told me he had a class from Gretna Primary School at the estuary of the Sark a few years ago sketching the coastline when two of the boys came running up carrying a rocket. 'It was about three feet long,' he said, 'with a warhead about eight inches in diameter. I said put it down boys, very gently, and step away.' They called the bomb disposal unit at Powfoot which came up with a series of boxes 'like a russian doll' into which they gingerly placed the missile. A man from Colvend also told me recently that as a boy he had filled his beach hut with octagonal shaped rods he'd found washed up on the shore and used to play with. On a visit to Aberdeen he'd been horrified to see a poster of one of these things with the lurid caption

IF YOU SEE ONE OF THESE ON THE BEACH DO NOT APPROACH.

THEY ARE EXTREMELY DANGEROUS AND LIFE THREATENING.

Even if it didn't have the glamour of being the most southerly part of Scotland, the Mull of Galloway is an exotic, otherworldly place. Earthworks across the neck show it was an ancient defensive site and there's a sense of the last ditch about it. There's nowhere to run to here, just cliffs and needle-sharp rocks and the sea. Here's where the last Picts supposedly committed suicide rather than give the thirsty Romans or the thirsty Scots the secret of heather ale.

Just along the coast is where the last fairies abandoned Scotland to the farmers and the fishermen and later the holidaymakers. It's an eerie place, I think:

> Here, in this fastness,
> light and oceans blaze,
> tides collide,
> heathers swell like the sea,
> and there are sounds
> on the edge of hearing;
> gulls like old regrets,
> soft wash of water
> like a mother's breath.

('Fastness')

Dean Vaughan, one time warden at the tiny nature reserve here, is more prosaic about it:

> I was here before they built the big cafe and car park when it was even more isolated but I never felt any sense of weirdness, but then I'm not a poet. My job was to maintain a tiny visitors' centre and count the seabirds, with a hand-held clicker. 'Razorbills, guillemots, kittiwakes, fulmars, shags and oh yes, four puffins.
>
> It did get a bit lonely here during the foot-and-mouth. The farmer put boulders across the track. Every time I wanted to drive into Drummore to go for a pint or the shop I had to phone him and he'd come with his tractor and move the boulders. I used to visit the pub quite a lot so I think he got a bit sick of me! There were no visitors on the Mull so I used to walk about stark naked. I used to wave to the lobster fishermen not realising I hadn't put my clothes on that day.'

*See **Drink & Accordions, Festivals***

Munitionettes

Some 25 years ago Annan Academy History Department, under the inspired leadership of Ian Gilmour OBE, a man whose single piece of professional advice – 'always drink the red at staff functions you'll get more that way' – has stood me in good stead through the years, decided to do some research on the Munitionettes of Gretna and Eastriggs. These government-constructed 'new towns' were designed to house and entertain the many thousands of female workers who flocked to the area during World War One to supply the British army with shells.

At its height there were 20,000 workers there in a complex nine miles long and two miles wide. Designed to answer serious shortages of cordite and acetone which were stymying the British war effort, the factory was a dangerous place to work but also saw a glorious collision of newly partly or fully emancipated women from every background and geographical area. The resulting apocalypse was a sociologists' dream, whether charting the number of drunken women staggering about Carlisle after shutting time, the illegitimate births, the literature spawned there, the women's football teams, the workers' love of cinema and so on. Though the shutting of the factories led in some practical ways to a return to the pre-war social and economic norms, some things had changed for good. Gretna and Eastriggs had brought new freedoms and a new confidence. Though there was much worry at the time about the immorality and 'weak character' of some of the girls, here was an environment where women could go to the cinema, pub or ice cream parlour with other girls or even by themselves, and mingle freely in many environments with people of their own age and their own or the other sex.

In an article written by 'A Lady Worker' which appeared in *Blackwoods Magazine* in 1916, the author writes:

> Answering the strident challenges of the town they live in, they go to

rinks and cinemas, they read and chatter, they kiss and quarrel and follow new fashions and new ideas... as far as the cinema and halfpenny press can make them so, they are up to date: in that measure of life afforded to them they are alive.

We recorded an interview with Mrs Graves, from Annan, in the early 1980s. She'd been 20 in 1917, and looked back on that time with great fondness. She thought the 'daftest girls' were from Ireland and Glasgow, 'the further from home they were, the wilder.' She dismissed the dangers. Looking back it was 'a great exciting time with money in the pocket and fun to be had.' She was local, 'a home-loving girl,' she said, not given to much in the way of wildness 'but it was creating history you could tell... the women were creating it.'

See *Alcohol, Dorothée Pullinger, Feisty, Munitions*

Myrton, Magic and Monreith Bay

Myrton is another word for magic, or should be. Look at it on the map. The White Loch of Myrton is moody and tree-lined water flanked by hills and the greatest concentration of pre-Christian antiquities in the region, maybe anywhere in the country, outside Kilmartin in Argyllshire. To the north and west are Torhouskie and Drumtroddan standing stones, to the south west, the Wren's Egg at Blairbuie and a bit further on, overlooking the steel grey sea is Barsalloch, an iron age fort perched on a cliff where people have lived for 6,000 years. On the White Loch itself is a crannog, a man-made defensive island a mere 3,000 years old. In the summer of 2013, work on the Black Loch of Myrton, the White Loch's older brother, drained to peat and woodland, has revealed groups of buildings, a completely unique find, a loch village, like Glastonbury's. All round Myrton in the rocks and glens are groupings of enigmatic cup and rings markings, astral sculptures or whatever the current interpretation is.

When Christianity came, the new god appeared as usual in old guises, and in old places. On Monreith Bay is the remains of Kirkmaiden church, one of the oldest in Scotland, named after St Medana, who has a sacred well on the beach. Story goes she was an Irish princess who was fabulously beautiful, her eyes especially radiant and magical, and who was pursued by some alpha prince all over Ireland til she escaped to Galloway. He was persistent though and after some strange shenanigans, including her floating away on a rock over Luce Bay, he tracked her down to Monreith where, to get away from him she chose, rather disappointingly given her previous exploits, to climb a tree. 'Why do you give me such grief?' she cried. 'Your eyes compel me,' he replied. I take this rather lyrical response to suggest that she was actually being chased not by a prince but by a poet, an altogether different though equally persistent creature. Her heart was not softened and, having become a religious maniac over the last few months, she tore out her eyes and threw them at him.

Apparently he then gave up, which actually suggests he wasn't a poet, because a poet would not only have been relishing jotting down all this great material for a slim new volume on the theme of his handicapped girlfriend, he'd also be bound to think he stood an even better chance with a blind girl.

From Dowies, the tower house to the east of the loch that overlooks Monreith Bay, one of its Maxwell owners repeated the boast of being able to see five kingdoms, Scotland, Ireland, Man, England and Heaven. The old castle close to the loch, the Castle of Myrton, romantically overgrown, was where Sir Godfrey McCulloch once received the tetchy deputation of fairies I have described earlier in this book. The McCullochs also hosted James IV on his pilgrimages to Whithorn. I wonder whether he was fun to have in the house? The Stewarts as a family would have been taken into care by the Social Work Department if they'd lived nowadays: James was scarred with guilt by the death of his father, in whose murder he was deeply implicated.

Gavin Maxwell of Elrig's father was killed by a German shell in Belgium just after he was born in 1914 and Maxwell was a tortured personality too. I suppose you can argue they make the best writers. Possibly bipolar and certainly, for many years, a repressed homosexual, Maxwell poured his energy into dangerous driving and hopeless schemes – a shark processing plant, a Sicilian baronetcy – and produced a series of best sellers inspired by them, the greatest of which was *Ring of Bright Water*, a book which revolutionised people's attitudes to wild nature. On a visit to the Marsh Arabs in Iraq he was given the gift of an otter which he brought back to Britain and used to walk on a lead in places as various as Monrieth beach and King's Road in Chelsea, moving it eventually to the Highlands. A bronze otter, a tribute to Maxwell, now stares over the Solway from Monreith, a commemoration of the countryside which had inspired him as man and boy. The title of *Ring of Bright Water* came from the brilliant and beautiful poet

Kathleen Raine who was passionately in love with Maxwell:

> He has married me with a ring, a ring of bright water, whose ripples travel from the heart of the sea ...

(*The Marriage of Psyche*)

Raine, who had a Scottish mother, adored Maxwell from first sight:

> another had crossed the magic threshold; had, it seemed, been there from the beginning. I had met by miracle another person who came from my first world; and because he came from the places where Eden had been, it was as if he came from Eden itself.

(*On An Ancient Isle, Kathleen Raine*)

For Eden, read Scotland, Elrig, Myrton. The relationship was a disaster. Medana's in reverse. It even involved a tree. Shut out of his house during a wild night in Sandaig, Raine cursed Maxwell on a rowan tree, 'Let Gavin suffer in this place, as I am suffering now,' she said. His life after that was a collapse to disaster, the destruction of his home, the death of his pet otter, his death by cancer. Raine was forever guilty that she had caused it all.

This is a deeply resonant location, one of the many places in Galloway where myth meets mystery meets history meets coincidence and together it produces shivers down the spine, especially when you're walking on a grey day and the water's like a mirror of the bending branches and sky and there's not another soul in sight, just soundless echoes.

…You share
instead something of the deep unruffled
stillness of the water, the bluish haze
of bulrushes, the load line between the trees

and their reflections. Hold to that lightness
and see how easy it is to love at the White
Loch of Myrton, where you have no history

but this moment…

('Pilgrim', Tom Pow)

*See **Away with the Fairies, Badges, Stanes***

N

Dumfries and Galloway is a revolving door, people leave, people come, but the demographics have shifted nowadays in favour of people who come here to holiday and retire, not to fight for a fierce living on the barren soil or on the sea. It's a reason why so many of the small towns and villages are in discreet decay. People do still come here to work though. I've spoken to two in the last week.

First there is Erin of the Seals who works at the Corsewall Lighthouse Hotel, a converted Stevenson Lighthouse not far from Portpatrick, jutting into the Irish Sea. From there you can see Ireland and the Mull of Kintrye and that ridiculous half-eaten cupcake that is Ailsa Craig. Erin has come into the region from Glasgow, though she has relatives in the area already, round Leswalt. 'The thing I like aboot here, apart frae the folk I work wi, they're a like a family really, is the beasts. It's amazin. I'll be driving tae ma work and there'll be broon seals just lying aboot like big dugs in the sun, and these huge birds wi the crooked wings, what are they called? Skuas. It's a here, wildness, but I'm telt it's hard in the winter... I'll soon fin out, but I'm loving it.'

Then there's Hania's parents. Hania is my youngest daughter's best friend and the first person she ever invited to a sleepover. As such she is honoured, and therefore honourable. Hania is 'Half Scot but whole Pole' she told me. Her parents came here from Eastern Poland to work on the land near Gairlieston. Their English was and is limited, but their smiles broad. They like it here because of the 'kindness, not weather', as her mother told me. I hope they get kindness because they deserve it. There are large numbers of Poles in the region and their reception, judging from what I've heard on my travels, is mixed. Hania arrived at the school speaking no English or Scots and now after a mere two years has both in abundance, and a lovely gravelly Scots accent. When Hania was taken away after the sleepover her mother left gifts, beautiful home-baked cakes and sweets. Hania gruffly said thanks, and declined to shake hands. Half Scot now, right enough.

See Love, and Death

Nicknames

I think nicknames, so prevalent in Dumfries and Galloway, are an old throwback to Celtic times when everyone was called the same names and were distinguished by their occupation or by their unfortunate disfigurement. Even the pubs have nicknames. In the Back Bar I am sitting with Bob the Water, Rooster, Hazy and Furry. Nunk and Chuff have just gone out. Bob the Water, a professorial type, is holding forth.

'It is manifestly a product of your employment,' says Bob the Water. 'For instance I was always regaled as Bob the Water when I worked for the Water Board but now I am content to be called Bob the Bun, as I work for the bakers. I am fairly confident that this epithet will stick because of its alliterative nature.'

Bob the Water returns thoughtfully to his bottle of Peroni, before continuing.

'Of course it's not always to do with that. Sometimes it's a play upon your given name. For instance Furry here is called Furry because her name is Jennifer and she has long hair. And Hazy here is thus acclaimed because she is called Hazel and has a well-earned reputation as a party animal.'

Bob takes a long and thoughtful sook of his bottle. 'Often it's a habit, too. For instance Cheesy was called that because he was in love with cheese sandwiches, and Rooster here...'

'It's cos my hair stands on end,' interjects Rooster quickly, and an awkward silence falls.

Nith Cross

I'm standing in a muddy field one late afternoon. I've been diverted from my walk along the main road from Penpont to Thornhill by a monument that no one seems to care about but is really quite remarkable. I'm nearly always diverted by it, trying to catch it when the sun is sliding across it for good photos or to make out the carvings of the amazing zoomorphic shapes of winged beasts. It's remarkable for a lot of reasons including the fact that nobody seems to care about it. No protective glass panels for it like the Kirkmadrine stones, or interpretation boards to tell us what we're looking at or what we should be thinking. The locals tend to think it's a monument to people who lost their lives in an accident here, on the ferry that used to run before the Nith Bridge was built.

The truth is just as remarkable, because it dates from the 10th century and is the Ruthwell Cross's poor neglected scabby cousin, a Northumbrian cross shaft, with its bestiary of carved symbols and bible stories being slowly eroded by wind and rain, its warm stone turning smooth as a plum.

What it's doing here I don't know, but this appears to be its natural location. Its neglect is a crime against history, but I also can't help thinking how romantic and lonely and enigmatic it is standing here with its necklace of rusty fence, and a backdrop of fields and gentle slopes and torn pink and grey sky furling round the dark fortress of Tynron Doon. It seems a suitable sentinel for that strange quasi island between the Nith and the Scaur that I call home.

Leave the world between bridges:
the narrow one across the Nith
with its sentry box and the old
crossing at Scaur squatting on its
    Roman haunch.
There's a shaded cup of fields
    between the bridges,
moss and trees darkened on every
    side by hills.
The royal holm is here where Bruce
    camped on his way
to heaven via Whithorn, and
    Penpont, still scratched

on maps after seven hundred years.
  Penpont,
an island, and The Nith Stone,
  totem of this pagan space.
Rain has swept the dogma from its
  sides
and smooth as a grape it stares
  from a bright clasp
of weeds, sizing up visitors and
  their burdens,
daring them to stay for a night here
in the blaze between the bridges,
below our thin, bright slice of moon.

('Nith Stone')

It's also a kind of totem pole for
the forgotten landscape. 'Children,
let us do a creative writing
workshop standing here, ankle
deep in glaur. Place your hands
upon this cold stone and trace the
carvings. Take your earphones
out, Daytona, there is a place for
Pixie Lott but this is not it. Take a
deep breath, extend your arms
against this chill January sky,
imagine, imagine, imagine…'

See Pubs, Where Have They Gone?

No Deid Yet: Two Galloway Memorials

The traditional response of a local
'auld heid' to the salutary greeting
'How are ye?' is 'No deid yet.'
This sums up in just three words
the indefatigability of the human
spirit while simultaneously giving
a glimpse of the depths of terrible
suffering experienced by them in
the course of their long existence.

No deid yet could be also said
to provide the inspiration for two
interesting memorials in Galloway.
Memorials are usually about dead
people but some unusually buck
this trend, commemorating some
other thing, in these cases luck,
and frugality.

Near Port o Warren is a
memorial to Captain Samuel
Wilson. It reads:

> *The Schooner Elbe* Captain Samuel
> Wilson of Palnackie after
> providentially landing her crew
> here backed off the rocks and sank
> off Rascarrel 6 December 1866

You might read that as meaning
the captain saved his crew before
sacrificing himself as the ship
went down, therefore being well
worthy of a nice granite stone,
but in actual fact he survived
along with the crew and as a
consequence there's a kind of

implicit ruefulness about this memorial. 'Providential', it says and seems to be adding, 'how lucky were you lot to be no deid yet?' Captain Wilson lived to the age of 94, by the way, and even then only died as a result of an accident in which he cut off his hand.

The other memorial is not far away, near Colvend School, a bench commemorating a couple called Sarah and Willie Robertson. I'd always thought I'd like a seat overlooking the sea as a memorial to me and I mentioned this to my companion while we were passing this place and he muttered, 'Aye, except he's no deid yet. When his wife passed away, he just got his name put on it too to save time.' Apparently Willie is still walking about, no deid yet, and so the bench is also a memorial to that great Scottish virtue, thrift.

From my vantage ground I could scan the whole moor right away to the railway line and to the south of it where green fields took the place of heather. I have eyes like a hawk, but I could see nothing moving in the whole countryside. Then I looked east beyond the ridge and saw a new kind of landscape – shallow green valleys with plentiful fir plantations and the faint lines of dust which spoke of highroads. Last of all I looked into the blue May sky, and there I saw that which set my pulse racing.

(*The Thirty Nine Steps: John Buchan*)

I am making a brief journey off road somewhere near the old Loch Skerrow Halt between Water of Fleet and New Galloway and can imagine Richard Hannay's fear when he saw that aeroplane circling, searching for him. When I read that passage I always visualise the scene from *North by North West* when Cary Grant's character Thornbill, there but for a consonant a good Dumfries and Galloway name, was chased by a crop-dusting biplane, but the comparison is spurious. The German plane merely scares Richard Hannay half to death, doesn't shoot at him, and besides it's a monoplane, a most exotic bird for 1914.

Suspension of belief is an important thing in fiction, but when I read *The Thirty Nine Steps* as a boy even I thought, what would a German aeroplane be doing in Galloway anyway? I was young at the time and was visualising it as a warplane, covered in the black iron crosses of the Fliegertruppe. Bizarrely though, while I was sifting through various esoteric works trying to work out where exactly on the old Paddy Line Hannay was describing so I could re-enact the whole thing for a laugh, I came across an article in the Dumfries and Galloway Standard from the 18 November 1914, only three months after the outbreak of war, which actually mentioned the possibility of German air bases in the Galloway Hills:

Last night about half past seven o clock persons resident along the road between Dumfries and New Abbey observed singular moving lights, associated it was suggested with an airship that seemed to be manoeuvring over Criffel.

There seems to have been a frenzy of aeroplane scares in the early part of the war. As Charles Hill Dick says in the great *Highways and Byways in Galloway and Carrick*, published in 1916:

> There were strong suspicions, amounting almost to imperturbable conviction, that the enemy had a base in the Minigaff hills. Over-strained eyes saw hostile aeroplanes over Glentrool, and there were even rumours of hydroplanes disporting themselves on our lochs.

Wildernesses have always been a great source of mystery and rumour, whether it be monsters, Nazis or UFOs, but old fashioned aeroplanes have been here in strength. Here, I want to include Elsie Mackay. Even though she's strictly speaking an Ayrshire girl, she often used Dumfries and Galloway airspace so she qualifies as a part-time resident even if it was a thousand feet up. She was a dashing girl, daughter of the Chairman of P&O and she lived in a castle, but she was a serious flier. She was one of the first women to be granted a pilot's license and as a consequence was made an advisor to the British Empire Air League. She often did aerobatics over Wigtownshire. Jayne Baldwin of Kirkcowan, who wrote a monograph on Elsie, describes an incident in which she looped the loop, her safety strap broke, and she cut her hands to the bone hanging on to the aircraft's bracing wires. Elsie's favourite plane was another monoplane, a Stinson Detroiter, which she shipped over from the USA. It was black with gold tipped wings and she named it *Endeavour*. She'd hooked up with a one-eyed war hero called Captain Hinchliffe and sneaked back from a family holiday in Egypt to make an attempt to be the first woman to fly across the Atlantic, east to west, far more dangerous than in the other direction because of the headwinds. The whole thing was meant to be a secret but she was such a glamorous and newsworthy figure that the press tracked her down. On 26 March 1928 *Time Magazine* said:

> Elsie Mackay, madcap daughter of James Lyle Mackay, Viscount Inchcape of Strathnaver, muffled herself almost beyond recognition and stealthily departed with one-eyed Capt Walter GR Hinchliffe on the treacherous flight across the Atlantic, Westward.

Unfortunately they never made it, a piece of wreckage washed up in Ireland eight months later being the only evidence of the aircraft ever seen again.

Old intrepid Galloway fliers are still with us. Only a few months ago one of them was out flying over the Atlantic in an antique plane 22 years younger than he was. Tom Lackey, a 93 year old former builder flew from Castle Kennedy to Ireland strapped to the upper wing of a 1943 Boeing Stearman biplane, the oldest wing-walker in history. The flight took an hour and all he said at the end of it was 'noisy but refreshing'. History remains silent on the question of toilet-facilities and related matters eg the development of massive bladders.

See Feisty, Things that Go Blink in the Night

Old Tongue

Mactaggart laced his original Encyclopaedia with old Scots words and native usages. In fact it was largely written in Scots and, apart from the toffs, the Galloway that he inhabited was Scots speaking. A hundred years after his book was published, the language had become marginalised, undermined in the education system – by the 1940s, the Scottish Education Department's language policy was that Scots had no value '… it is not the language of "educated" people anywhere, and could not be described as a suitable medium of education or culture' – and by the growing popularity of English, or American films and music.

Nowadays a minority of people in Scotland consider Scots even a language. Attempts to reverse the process have begun and though there is no education through the medium of Scots, it is at least more accepted in schools that speaking Scots, even writing it in exams, is a perfectly valid thing to do.

In my travels through the region it was clear that Scots still trips off some young tongues in the rural north east and west. And of course, old tongues in the pubs. As an homage to the original Encyclopedia, and in the fervent hope that these gems of language hang on, I have gathered together some of what I've heard in everyday conversation, stray words, sayings and idioms:

As likely as a Bookie on a Bike – something too ridiculous to be true; **Bouroch** – from the Gaelic, a right mess; **Broth** – a filling vegetable and meat soup; **Coup** – to fall over or spill; **Crabbit** – angry or habitually bad tempered, applied to either sex; **Cuddie** – a horse; **Dwam** – state of mild confusion or uncertainty; **Face for frichtin the French/ rats; A face like a welders'** bench; A face like a well skelpt airse'; A heid like a guiser's neep; A face that would soor milk; A tongue that could clip cloots; A neck like a fairmer's bull; Hands like a guddled troot; Hair like a bothy cat; A **flea heugh** is a fly hook, '**Duin up like a flea heugh**' is to be dressed gaudily or showily; **Footer or Plooter** – to potter about at something, not really caring if it is achieved or not; **Gantin for It** – desperate need; **Hingin Ee** – unspoken desire; **King or Queen of Clatteringshaws/ The Laird of Cockinch** – Generic terms for a hopelessly deluded person, mad but occasionally entertaining, who has lost his or her reason; **Leerie** – licentious behaviour; **Ludgin Hoose Cat** – a creature of an extremely lazy and languorous nature, like a **Storehoose dug**; **Mawkit** – an ugly or disagreeable looking person whom you suspect has poor sanitary arrangements likewise **howlin, loupin or mingin**, all giving rise to sayings like 'so ugly they had to feed him wi a catapult', or 'we had tae hing pork chops roond his neck to get the dug to lick him'; **Pauchle or Pockle** – to unfairly gain an advantage by underhand methods eg 'England pauchled the 1966 Football World Cup'; **Poacher's Pooch** – an expansive undercover area of a coat which might accommodate a large fish. Also applied to people who have eaten and drunk too often and too well, as in 'ye've got a gut like a poacher's pooch'; **Scunnert wi, or of** – feeling of being fed up with some activity you have been unsuccessfully engaged in for a long time; **Shilpit** – thin and cowed, like a dog that has been badly fed and treated; **Skelf** – a splinter of wood; **Snell** – very cold or biting weather; **Trachled or Trauchled** – beset by tiredness or pressure, exasperated; **Wabbit** – excessively tired, physically and or mentally such as after listening for three hours to the Laird o Cockinch or the King of Clatteringshaws on a bus journey.

I'm wandering through Palnackie with Stuart Paterson. It's a grey day with a hint of mist, but the views are still good. Down the hill the river bank and green folds of land slashed with water stretch gently to the horizon. It is very quiet. The pub is shut. Unfortunately it looks like the perfect place for a retired major from Andover to come and live with the online *Daily Telegraph*.

There are a dozen wee silted inlet-ports off the Solway like it, though this is still a working harbour the sign says, and there are two boats, though they're only laid up for repairs and the surface of the dock makes it useless for landing fish. As we walk there are few signs of life but we hear furious hammerings from a very old building, the oldest building in Palnackie it transpires, the boat shed. The source of the noise turns out to be a strange man of indeterminate age, a little tuft of a beard (like a faun, he is at pains to say), and a boundless and unfathomable energy. This is Tim Dennis,

round-the-world traveller (his Toyota truck with its anti-rhinoceros bars or whatever they are, is out the front, guarded by his stuffy and long suffering looking Jack Russell) and, perhaps, saviour of Palnackie.

Tim wants to rebuild the harbour, turning part of it into a commercial facility for fishing boats and part of it into a heritage area with smuggling museum, 19th century buildings and so on, recapturing the feel of the place at its busiest, when ships from all over the world came to load granite and fertiliser from Dalbeattie. There's a case to be made for smuggling heritage: Robert in the Anchor Inn at Kippford told me that after the recent flood damage in the pub he was considering, during his renovations, 'discovering' the skeleton of a pirate with a doubloon in his fist. 'I'll glass it over,' he said, 'so people can look at it during their bar meals.'

The most unusual part of Tim's scheme is to make Palnackie one of the hubs of Fairtransport, a

Norwegian-based organisation which uses a sailing ship to transport fair-trade goods between Europe and South America and back again. He wants to see ships under wind power plying the Solway again after an absence of a century or so, under the flag of his own Quetzal Shipping, and he thinks this will prompt tourism and local industry and stimulate creativity. He wants his boat shed to be a performance space and hostel for artists, poets and musicians, as well as a... boat shed. He also doesn't have any money, grants or bursaries or whatever, he owns up to not being very good at that sort of thing. He hopes that his sheer enthusiasm and hard work will bring it all about, or create the conditions where it will spontaneously happen.

You can dismiss him as a hippy dreamer and weirdo, as I suspect some in the village already have, ticking as he does every alternative box you can think of, but there were two things that made me think that this was a person of substance. One was his passion. When he described his idea, you could practically see on that deserted street the pubs, the blacksmiths, the chandlers, and behind you, the big horses pulling the boats along the river bridle path. It was what he was seeing, you could tell, and that degree of vision is almost infectious, you can catch it. The second thing is that, completely voluntarily, some men in the village had already contracted the disease and were helping him build. One, an ex-sailor himself, a ships engineer turned local businessman, was hard bitten, someone you could tell didn't suffer fools gladly and he was wading in. That tells you something about the power of vision, unsupported even as it might be by money, common sense or whatever. I left with the impression that schemes like Tim's, and others in the region, are intent less on commemorating communities, but empowering them. This wasn't part of the ghost landscape. He wanted tourists but he also wanted a working village with its pride intact, united again with the sea. Good for him. Long live the Quetzal Shipping Line.

See Ghost Landscape

Pies

Pies are a great and traditional Scottish dish involving baking a variety of ingredients in pastry and they come in many shapes and sizes and types: Haggis, chicken, venison or game pies, for instance, many of which are gastronomic delights. The Scottish classic is, however, the individual steak or mince pie. In Thornhill the family butchers firm of Renicks won The World Scotch Pie Championships in 2012, but the quality of the pies out there range from this blue riband variety to the horribly vitrified things you see in some pubs that have been there since the previous Christmas. Robert Burns, contrary to what many butchers imply, was not a fan of the pie, which he saw as an effete English invention. To Burns, in fact, pies were a class issue. Allan Cunningham, in his introduction to *Tae a Haggis* in the *Collected Works*, says:

> The haggis of the north is the mince pie of the south; both are characteristic of the people; the ingredients which compose the former are all of Scottish growth... the ingredients of the latter are gathered chiefly from the four corners of the globe; the haggis is the triumph of poverty, the minced pie the triumph of wealth.

I was once horribly poisoned by a mince pie I purchased one windswept evening in the caravan park at Auchenlarie so I am on Burns' side here. Poets are generally fond of pies, however. A photograph was taken once in Wigtown of the poets published by the highly successful and award winning Roncadora Press, based in Dumfries, and every poet in it, including myself, was so fat that the firm's nickname became Roncadora Pies. The poet Andrew Forster, a talented Roncadora writer, is the only writer in my recollection, perhaps in history, to have cancelled a poetry reading after burning his mouth on a pie.

Stop the presses: Kerr Littles of Dumfries win 2014 World Scotch Pie Championship... the pie successes just keep coming.

Pine Martens

I'm speaking to a very jolly and enthusiastic representative of the Vincent Wildlife Trust, an organisation specialising in the conservation of our rarer mammals; otters, dormice, voles and best of all the pine marten. A cuter and cheekier looking fellow than the pine marten is hard to imagine and I've always seen their sad disappearance from the region as a parallel development to the disappearance of our own people and it's happened for similar reasons, clearance of land for sporting estates and so on. As our native languages declined, as the emigration ships left, so did the pine martens.

So it's encouraging that, extinct in Galloway for the last 200 years, the species is making a comeback. One group in Galloway was deliberately reintroduced in the 1980s but the reason the chap from the VWT is drinking pear cider is because a new colony has appeared in the east of the region, in Annandale and Eskdale, a consequence of 'natural spread'. The martens are on the move. I see this as an astute political move by the pine marten, and I hope people recognise it for the important augury it is. People of Dumfries and Galloway, pine martens are moving among you as we speak, spreading optimism about the future! The VWT and Scottish Natural Heritage have even produced a pamphlet for those lucky folk who have a pine marten in the attic. It's called *Living with Pine Martens.*

I reproduce here one of the strangest passages from recent Dumfries and Galloway literature which is nevertheless apposite. It's an excerpt from a sword and sorcery novel for kids, written and sold to raise money for the Mossburn Animal Rescue Centre. I think it embodies some important conservation issues as well as emphasising the fact that the pine marten represents part of our cultural history. In this passage, the hero, Oliver, a rabbit, encounters a pine marten, Rab, employed by Dumfries and Galloway Council:

'Hello,' said the voice in a friendly manner, 'did ye ken that when there's nae clood cover ye can spy fae here mair than ten thousand stars skinklin in the sky here?'

Oliver blinked. 'What?' he said.

'Wid ye nae be better byling a pot fir that? Looks gey sair on the teeth.' The creature looked round. 'Damp wee hoose ye hae.' He extended a paw. 'I'm Rab. Pleased tae mak yir acquaintance, Maistir Mowpie, though' he indicated Oliver's sword with a slight inclination of his head, 'yir awfie weel tooled up fir a common or gairden mowpie.'

'What are you?' stuttered Oliver.

'Am a pine marten. Ye no seen yin afore? There are yin or twa o us aroont these pairts.' He grinned widely. Oliver looked at the very sharp teeth of the animal. He was like a weasel but bigger, with a bushier tail.

'Bein a student o animal behaviour I ken yer wunnerin whether am gang tae try and eat ye.'

Oliver nodded slowly, keeping an eye on the hilt of the sword. The pine marten shook his head. 'Dinnae fret. Yer no ma type. It is time fur tea, tho. Cmon tae ma hoose. Ma wife'a a wunner in the kitchen.'

Half an hour later Oliver was cosy and warm in front of a blazing fire in the pine marten's well appointed house deep in the forest. They were seated round a rough wooden table and were finishing off a bowl of excellent vegetable broth. At their feet several kits were playing, and their father would give them a playful kick on the rear now and then.

'That was brilliant,' said Oliver. 'Thanks very much indeed.'

'Nae bother,' said Rab. 'Squirrel?' He pushed a bowl of roast meat towards the rabbit.

'No thanks,' said Oliver.

'Tryin tae gie them up eh?' laughed Rab. 'Must be a bind bein a veggie.'

Oliver shrugged.
'Wouldnae dae to be a veggie in these pairts,' said Rab's wife. 'He's aye bringin back squirrel. Tests ma skills tae the max: Squirrel fricassee, squirrel pie, baked roasted boiled squirrel, squirrel Cantonese style, ye name it ah make it.'

'Aye,' agreed Rab, 'Jean's a wonder wi the squirrels.'

'I must ask,' said Oliver, who had to ask, 'why squirrel?'

'Rab wirks fur the council,' said Jean proudly, pouring him and Oliver a frothing beaker of beer. 'He's yin o they bounty hunters.'

'Aye.' Rab inclined his head modestly and showed Oliver a badge pinned to his chest.

'001 Dumfries an Galloway Regional Cooncil.' He took a draught of his drink. 'Dumfries an Galloway: The Natural Place tae terminate grey squirrels.' Both he and Jean laughed.

'Ah,' said Oliver. 'I see.'

'Yon big saucy American gowks chasin oor wee plucky gingers intae oblivion a ouer Scotland. This is the final frontier.'

'They aye like grubbin aboot fur food on the forest flair though, that's their mistake,' said Jean. She made a cutting motion at her throat.

'A in a guid day's work,' said Rab. 'Hae a drink ma freen.'

Pistapolis

Having once been chased along the Whitesands in Dumfries by a baying mob I know exactly how the Reverend Thomas Blacklock felt about Kirkcudbright back in 1765. My offence was, having written a paean of praise to the region which was published as a book called *Dumfries, a History and Celebration*, jointly authored with Pete Fortune. I was stupid enough to write an additional chapter satirising the town. Needless to say this was meant for private circulation and not for a full page spread in the *Daily Mail, Daily Record, The Dumfries and Galloway Standard* and sundry other publications I was too embarrassed to open. I have tried to erase all memory of the infamous 'Chapter Six', from my mind but retain some of the fan mail I received during this tempestuous period, one line of which reads:

Please republish so that it can be enjoyed by those who long to see the term knock-kneed hoor brought back into common usage.

Strangely enough I do believe this episode helped forge civic pride in Dumfries at a very difficult time for the town. Complete strangers would find common cause to hurl abuse at me and croon to each other about things that enriched their lives like The Stane Man and Burns Mausoleum.

Thomas Blacklock's *Pistapolis: A Hyperpindaric Ode with Notes by Scriblerus Redivivus* was a much better effort all round, swingeingly slagging off Kirkcudbright:

Pistapolis, mother of Patriots and Sages,
The glory of Nature and wonder of ages,
With all its high worthies, a numberless throng,
At once shall inspire and ennoble this song.

But if in thy view thy procession should pass,
Though their tongues were of iron and their lungs were of brass,
To praise them like thy subject refin'd,
Were to piss in the ocean, or fart at the wind
He then went on to pick off its inhabitants one by one.

Miss B........ of veracity ever sincere,
Whose words reach the heart ere they pass through the ear,
For what tongue can be feeble, what heart can design,
Whose language and feelings are prompted by wine?

But Balbus, ye muses, remains yet unsung,
of pregnant invention and voluble tongue;
whose skull tho' retentive, why should he complain
since bodies opaque still preserve what they gain?

(*Pistapolis*, Thomas Blacklock)

He added footnotes just in case you weren't sure who he was talking about. Balbus for instance is 'a tobacconist in Pisatapolis whose hesitation of speech is remarkable, and seems to be caused by the barrenness of his understanding'.

Thomas Blacklock was a scholar, a Minister of the Church and a poet. He was observed by Samuel Johnson during his tour of Scotland, who recorded the moment by noting in his diary:

I saw at breakfast Dr Blacklock, the blind poet, who does not remember to have seen light and who is read to by a poor scholar in Latin, Greek and French. He was originally a poor scholar himself. I looked on him with reverence.

Blacklock's crime in Kirkcudbright, for which he exacted such telling literary revenge, was to have been ordained minister while simultaneously being blind. The good citizens of the town felt their spiritual needs could not be met by the visually handicapped scholar who was: unfit by reason of his stone-blindness of discharging his duty as a minister of Jesus Christ in any parish at all, and more so in a Royal Burrow.

As the appointment was made by the Crown, the town council couldn't overcome it but generally made Blacklock's life so uncomfortable that he abandoned the parishioners to their 'burrow' and retired to Edinburgh to nurse his wrath, there, by the way, making the acquaintance of Robert Burns and possibly saving the poet's life. He wrote the letter that persuaded Burns not to sail to Jamaica on a ship that sank on the way. Arguably therefore the mean-spirited burgesses of Kirkcudbright were responsible for saving Scotland's greatest poet. Maybe that's pushing it a bit. What's clear though is the message to small towns everywhere: Beware of Poets. *Dinna meddle wi us.*

See **Burns, Dumfries**

Plagues and Radiation

In the 14th century the wizard Michael Scott is said to have attempted to rid Dundrennan Abbey of the plague by imprisoning it in a dungeon and leaving it to starve to death. Since a third to half of the population of Europe died in the Great Plague of 1348–9, and its repeat visits in the 15th century, it was fair enough maybe to take drastic measures. The poet and chronicler Fordun, watching with grim satisfaction as bubonic plague ravaged England, thought it was God's revenge on them for 50 years of carnage wrought on Scotland. It crept over the border, though, and was devastating here too, despite desperate attempts to stop it. The Packman's Grave, a mound in Kirkwaugh, Wigtownshire, is supposed to mark the spot where a merchant, bringing cloth inland from a plague ship, was ambushed by locals and buried alive with his goods to prevent the disease from spreading.

My sister reminded me recently of the time we looked out of our house in Dumfries and saw men with full chemical warfare suits taking geiger counter readings in Queen St. This must have been 1986 after Chernobyl. The pattern of fallout from the Chernobyl nuclear disaster followed the patterns of the Scottish weather. The greatest concentrations were in the west, particularly on high ground where the poor, peaty soils of upland areas meant that radioactive caesium-137 in the fallout cloud was taken up by plants rather than being locked safely away in the soil itself. Caesium-137 can easily enter the

food chain and be taken up by the body. Sheep grazing in the badly affected areas on upland grass, especially in the summer months, were likely to build up levels of caesium-137 that exceeded the limit of 1,000 becquerels per kilogram of sheep meat set by the European Commission in 1986.

The government gave a warning that people should not drink rainwater, and after surveys showed that sheep had absorbed so much radiation that they were unfit for human consumption, the sale of sheep was banned across the whole of Dumfries and Galloway. Ten years later radiation was still a problem. In June 1995 Parliament was told that there was still a ban on sheep sales because of radiation on 41 holdings (farms) across Scotland, covering an area of 43,000 hectares. Monitoring restrictions weren't lifted until June 2010. Farmers were compensated for each sheep tested but the amount paid did not increase as time went on. Money was important but major fears of cancer clusters persist today, as in the Dundrennan area over the use of depleted uranium shells on the Ministry of Defence testing ground there. Officially Chernobyl was only responsible for 56 deaths worldwide, but the actual figure probably reaches into hundreds of thousands.

When the disaster occurred I remember talking to Pete Fortune, a gifted and award winning short story writer and fellow member of Dumfries and Galloway Campaign for Nuclear Disarmament. In these dark days in the mid '80s, with the effects of Chernobyl and the constant threat of war breaking out in the Middle East, Pete and I used to meet in the Waverley Hotel in Dumfries, drink frantically, and compare what we'd bought that day for our fall-out shelters – torches, wind up radios, tins of beans, that kind of thing. One day he announced 'This has turned me into a poet.' He published a terrible piece of doggerel called *Chernobyl Mutton*, then stopped writing completely and remains silent to this day. I am put in mind

of that story by an excellent piece of research written by Kevin Williamson about the events of the summer of 1783, when the Icelandic volcano erupted, sending 120 million tonnes of sulphur dioxide to mix with water in the atmosphere and form a sulphuric acid cloud which at one point covered a quarter of the surface of the earth. This coincided with Robert Burns' failure as a farmer, and the onset of his pulmonary problems. In fact two of his younger brothers died in the years following the eruption. It also coincided with his birth as a poet. The several years after 1784 saw him writing in a fever of creativity, producing his best work, and embracing the poetic life. How strange that environmental catastrophe could produce the creative death of one and the birth of another. I have to say that through all these trials, I continued to write steadily, the same sort of drivel as ever.

See Burns, Munitions

Thomas Carlyle once told Queen Victoria that the most inspirational road in Scotland was the road from Carsluith to Creetown. This is not true. For inspiration and exotic insights into life, that road, lovely though it is when the tide's in and the sun is shining silver on the waters of the Solway and on the battlements of romantic ruined castles, pales into insignificance when compared to the A76 trunk road from Holywood to Kirkconnel.

The A76 actually has a historical poet at each end of it. It passes Ellisland where Burns lived for a while and produced a massive number of songs and poems, and Friars Carse where his poem 'The Whistle' recalls a gigantic drinking competition:

> Six bottles a-piece had well wore
>   out the night,
> When gallant Sir Robert, to finish
>   the fight,
> Turn'd o'er in one bumper a bottle
>   of red,
> And swore 'twas the way that their
>   ancestor did.

('The White Whistle', Robert Burns)

At the other terminus we have the railwayman poet Alexander Anderson, born in Kirkconnel in 1845.

> Langsyne, when life was bonnie,
> An' a' the warld was fair,
> The leaves were green wi' simmer,
> For autumn wasna there.
> But listen hoo they rustle,
> Wi' an eerie, weary soun',
> For noo, alas, 'tis winter
> That gangs a twalmonth roun'.

('Langsyne When Life was Bonnie', Alexander Anderson)

Anderson was a surfaceman who later became chief librarian at Edinburgh University. His poems, in Scots and English, are often gently sad reflections on the passage of time, on the dampening of the fire.

> Love, turn thy gentle feet away,
> How can I be thy lover?
> A low wind grieves among the
>   leaves,
> And the time of the rose is over.

('The Time of the Rose is Over', Alexander Anderson)

Drink, weather and the death of love, all on the A76.

It is the blend of the beautiful and the inevitable detritus of living that makes the upper Nith valley so appealing. It's a lived-in landscape and that's where poetry is best born. The Nith is beautiful, but didn't Burns write about a dead horse floating down it?

> But now she's floating down the
> Nith,
> For Solway fish a feast

('Willie Nicol's Mare', Robert Burns)

Upper Nithsdale's finest living poet, Rab Wilson wrote on much the same theme, a discarded shopping trolley:

> Nae shoogly wheels
> wi a mind o thair ain,

brocht you here.
Aiblins some joke
bi Setterday nicht boys,
oan a tear frae Dumfries,
drucken stag-nicht oan-gauns,
they'll mind langsyne
at some Silver Waddin...

Why cam ye here,
tae this idyllic spot?
This place o mallards,
buzzards, an oystercatchers,
craws an wrens,
an mythical kingfishers;
if nae tae drag ma thochts
tae that
frae whit
ah fain wid
win awa frae

('Shopping Trolley in River Nith, Mennock', Rab Wilson)

Pubs, Where Have They Gone?

I'm walking with my friend Jennifer over Dunreggan Brae towards Moniaive, the mist over Tynron Doon behind us, and in front the village set at the junction of the three glens like a stone in a clasp. It's twenty to noon and a familiar fear has seized me, that of reaching my destination and finding the pub shut. I should

have learned by now that gone are the days of warm hostelries open at all hours for the footsore rambler or hopeless alkie. In the event, we force the cleaner to open the Craigdarroch Hotel and have some lager. Closed pubs are the curse of Dumfries and Galloway. How would HV Morton, the Rev Dick or even

John Mactaggart have managed with the shutters closed and little leafs of paper in the window saying open at six, or Friday or on Bank Holidays only? I have wandered for months along the Solway Coast and the pubs have too often set their faces against me. An ex-manager for one of the brewers who distribute in the region told me, 'so many of the pubs have shut… Sorbie, Kirkinner, Dalry, Carsphairn, the beating heart of all these communities gone, for good.'

My own little pub in Penpont, the Volunteer Arms, has been shut these last three years. It's an historic coaching inn, frequented by Burns and the scene of the meeting of the 'three kings', George v, Edward vii, and George the vi, who had a few pints there after a shooting party on the Drumlanrig Estate in the mid 1930s. The last people who bought the Volunteer Arms fell out with the locals, banned the football team, the darts team, shut on weekend afternoons, closed it temporarily, then permanently, are are now living in it. All proper and legal of course. There's no law or moral obligation to stay open just because you own an historical and cultural asset and the community depends on you. I just say, sell it and pass the asset on.

Moniaive does have pubs. The town/village is a quirky, arty place, known for its folk festival, but I remember it best for the second hand clothes shop that used to be here, called Second Hand Swank. When someone stole the letter S, the owner didn't replace it, convinced that the shops unique name would bring greater custom. She was a great character with a vibrant sense of humour. A friend of mine was at a party there once and admired the huge spread of food laid out. 'Help yourself', she was told, 'what a week we've had with the dysentery, though'.

*See **Things that go Blink in the Night***

Q

> The Queen of the South will rise at the judgement with the men of this generation.

So says the Book of Revelations, and Queens remain the only football team mentioned in any of the great religious works, though someone once tried to tell me that Alloa Athletic appears in the Buddhist Diamond Sutra. I remember the team best from the '70s, when they had players like Peter Dickson, Alan Ball and Ian McChesney. Queen of the South is a proper football team which inspires the kind of love and devotion that makes football less a hobby and more part of the cultural framework. I stopped going to Palmerston for a while, when I was in Edinburgh for years, but more recently, like everyone else, I found myself carried away with the tide of enthusiasm, skill, grit and determination that took Queens to the Scottish cup final in 2008. I was at Palmerston to see Queens' quarter final over Dundee, including the most amazing goal I've ever witnessed, a shot by Ryan McCann from nearly 80 metres out, one of the longest distance shots ever recorded. Then I was at the semi-final against Aberdeen at Hampden. Queens took the lead four times, Aberdeen equalised thrice. At the end my lasting impression, apart from dizziness, was the generosity of the Dons fans who cheered the Queens players at the end. Queens took more than 15,000 fans to the final which was almost a repeat of the excitement, Queens fighting back from 2–0 down to 2–2 before going down 3–2. It seemed the wrong end to the story, somehow, but it was a carnival for the Queens supporters and gave them not just memories, but another convivial outing in the Europa League, in Denmark, the following season.

As with all wee teams the minutiae is fascinating, like the players on the way up or the way down, who have graced Palmerston Park Players such as Andy Goram, the Scottish international goalie and Marvin Andrews, capped more than a hundred times for Trinidad and Tobago. The classiest player I ever saw at Palmerston was Pat McCluskey who served out his career at Queens in the mid '80s. He was so fat he could hardly move but he had such classy feet he would spray passes around from a standing or crouching position, always slightly (and poignantly I felt) to the left of midfield.

R

Ritual Roads

I am reading the excellent report authored by Catriona McMillan on the pilgrimage routes to Whithorn ('The Whithorn Pilgrimage: A Report'), specifically her belief that 'pilgrimage still holds significance in our evolving culture', and I am suddenly reminded of the broad smiling face of Andy Paterson. He was a history teacher, socialist and hippy turned Church of Scotland minister from Annan, and a man who used to excite my interest for having a three-legged dog and a motorbike that ran on cow-pats. Andy was responsible for a lost treasure in Dumfries and Galloway literature, *A Planet Through a Field of Stars*, which details his pilgrimage on the eccentric motorbike from Galloway to Santiago De Compostela in Spain. It's a great read, full of Andy's exasperated insights into history, politics and religion. Here he is in Crosshaven in Ireland:

> That night I saw a stranger sitting in the shadows, and weariness left me silent. I read a newspaper article which exposed the scandal of a Saudi businessman who had invested £1,000,000 in a dog food firm owned by the Taoiseach in an attempt to purchase Irish citizenship... my shoulders slumped and I was tired, tired of Irish contradictions as much as fatigued by wind, weather, and the long miles since Larne.

Andy's a typical example of the modern pilgrim for whom the spiritual quest may only be one part of a restless examination of the cultural and historical landscape they are born into. His journey to the great shrines of Spain is a disappointment:

> On the lonely Galician beach I had listened to a cuckoo mock my visit to Compostela, and in the great Cathedral of Spain the ecclesiastical accretions of the centuries had left me unmoved.

Instead he finds inspiration in the alternative technology centre in Machynlleth in Wales, a place he identifies as a modern example of the Celtic Christian tradition of 'self sufficiency, frugality and co-operation', a template for a potentially new prosperous and spiritual Scotland. Not every pilgrimage has a set purpose. Who can pass by a path that leads through the trees? What hidden stream or bridge or well or tumulus lies down there, just out of reach? We are always exploring, even when walking where we have always walked before.

*See **Badges***

S

Land use in Dumfries has changed over the centuries and this has had a big effect on social structures. Sometimes if you're eavesdropping at a festival, or at a convention of didgeridoo makers, people will talk of that time in history when the Celts lived in yurts and were at peace with nature and owned land communally and practised crystal therapy and made artefacts out of copper and ceramics, some of which they sold at open mike sessions in the local clarsach player's house. This is pie in the sky, of course, but it is true that title deeds arrived with the Norman landowners, and both the Norman landowners and title deeds are still with us. How many people who ruled us in the 14th century still own the land, sometimes the brick and mortar, we live in? Surprisingly many. I thought I'd paid for my house but it turns out the Duke of Buccleuch has just lent it to me for 990 years.

As the Normans busied themselves taking other people's land and building centres of power they made sure to provide themselves with enough space for their leisure activities, in particular hunting. Royal forests or estates were created, and closed to ordinary people who would face dire punishments if caught poaching. These Norman families weren't the first people to hunt but they were the first people to need hundreds of thousands of acres of private land to do it in. Their hunts were a complex reflection of their status and beliefs, and the hunt was often a symbolic chase as well as an actual one. In the story of Helen of Livingstone, set near Loch Ken, the hunt brings the handsome young nobleman Edward Glendinning a stag, a bride and his death in quick succession, in the fulfilment of a witch's prophecy:

> The slime of the Dee for his bridal couch,
> For his pillow a cold, cold stone;
> And heirless remains the wide domain,
> Who would wed the maid of Livingstone.

('Helen of Livingstone', Scottish Ballad)

When the nobility realised they no longer needed foot soldiers or so many hands to keep the mills and harvests going, they enclosed the land and embraced technology in order to make serious money for themselves no matter the human cost. They were loathe to give the hunting up though, and soon realised that it was a marketable asset. Huge tracts of land across the region today are used for stalking and shooting. The land is advertised in one brochure I read recently as a 'blank page for adventure'. You don't have to be a communist to think depopulation for profit and fantasy tourism is a bit dodgy, but it does employ a fair number of people and has been an intrinsic way of life for a long time in rural communities.

There are stories of course, as there are in any playground. I was speaking in the Stewartry to someone employed by a northern European millionaire, who is on permanent standby so that, given a few hours' notice, he can staff and resource a giant hunting lodge in the centre of the region for the arrival at any time night or day of a private-plane load of Scandinavians.

I was speaking to another man, further west, whose house was at the edge of a shooting estate much used by foreign visitors. 'It was aright,' he said, 'a wheen noisy at times but when the Italians cam there was aye a stream o casualties tae the back door. Yince they shot a beater, three dugs an one o their ain men.'

In amongst all the carnage though are always the local auld heids. I was in the Cross Keys Inn in New Galloway recently and everyone was from Cirencester apart from Oscar the pub dog who was from London. It was a very big shooting party. Someone made the usual joke about hunting peasants but as they chattered on, a weather beaten and worldly old man was scooping-up their 50 pound notes into a huge wad which reminded me of Willie Neill's poem, 'The Marksman':

> I never saw him waste a single shot.
> He wouldn't fire unless he knew a kill,
> Marksmanship guaranteed to fill the pot.

In memory I see him standing still
over the autumn moor. The swollen
  bags
of bowed-and-scraped-to gentry on
  a shoot,
wounding or blowing driven game
  to rags
or wasting cartridges without a hit
he sneered at, although sometimes
  paid to beat

their fostered game-birds on an
  autumn day.
'There goes some London glutton's
  annual treat...
and mostly killed by accident,' he'd
  say.

('The Marksman', William Neill)

See **Ghost Landscape**

Shuggie MacDiarmid (Big Shuggie)

Big Shuggie, as he appears in his pictures and cartoons, that giant head full of Lallans and dialectic surmounted by a vitrified shocking crop of hair. Unlike some of my contemporaries who, even as boy poets, were career-minded enough to be beating a path to the door of the likes of MacDiarmid and McCaig, I never met the man, but his influence is great and it is satisfying that the poet some describe as Scotland's greatest in the last hundred years came from Dumfries and Galloway. I find some of his poetry strong and beautiful but I suppose his role in putting Scottish poetry and putting the Scots language, synthetic though much of his was, on the map is his most important legacy.

You can't avoid his ideas. As Philip Larkin snootily said when he was editing the *Oxford Book of 20th Century English Verse*:

> I am so averse to his work my eyes can scarcely bear to look at it on the page but I agree many people will expect to see it there.

Larkin was averse to writers who saw poetry as a weapon in the class struggle. Others nearer home were equally exercised:

As an outspoken communist and nationalist, Big Shuggie didn't go down particularly well among many in his home town. Ruth Cockburn, a young dramatist and comedienne from Langholm, is organising a MacDiarmid Festival in the town: 'Local feeling about

MacDiarmid is mixed,' she told me. 'The younger generation I think are more interested than the old as they don't carry with them the feeling that he was "just a communist that got too big for his boots". They see a man that was a great artist who asked questions that others were afraid to, and with the referendum coming up these questions are being asked again about who is best to run Scotland.'

She sees Langholm as a town uncomfortable with the idea of creative genius:

Langholm is a creative place that sometimes lacks confidence. That's how I see it. I grew up in Blackpool, a far cry from the leafy riverside town I now find myself in, and I marvel at how much people here take for granted, but also how little they believe in themselves to a certain degree. People here have created some great art but only a few people see themselves as being worthy of attention.

As in the way of all wee conservative towns. However, Shuggie made enemies not by his politics but by casting aspersions in his own backyard. In his autobiography *Lucky Poet* he alleges inappropriate sexual relationships between teachers and pupils in the local school, demonstrating that:

> Deep suroondin' darkness
> Is aye the price o' licht.

(From *Lucky Poet*, Hugh Macdiarmid)

When he was buried his friend Norman MacCaig said MacDiarmid's death should be celebrated by 'three minutes of pandemonium'. His widow, more quietly, said 'They'll have to live with him now'.

See Makar, Deafness, Oily Fish and Hugh MacDiarmid

Siller Guns

The Siller Guns of Kirkcudbright and Dumfries were trophies presented by King James VI of

Scotland to try and encourage skill and marksmanship using the new technology of musketry, at the 'wappenshaws'. The idea, as ever, was to have the locals able to defend themselves properly against the English when they attacked. The Dumfries Siller Gun was presented at a banquet by the King himself to the Trades of Dumfries in Queensberry Square, not that it was called that then, on 3 August 1617, as the Dumfries poet John Mayne described in his poem of 1780:

And may this day, whate'er befa',
The King's birthday, our Waponshaw
Be hailed wi' joy by great and sma',
And through the land
May Concord, Liberty and Law
Gae hand in hand.

('The Siller Gun', John Mayne)

The Dumfries gun was originally a miniature cannon mounted on a wheeled carriage, but in the early 19th century it was vandalised and remade by the silversmith David Gray as a lintlock musket. The Kirkcudbright gun was a model of an early firearm called a hagbut, and has the date 1587 engraved, and the initials T Mc for Thomas MacLellan, Provost of Kirkcudbright. It is the oldest surviving sporting trophy in Britain.

The Kirkcudbright gun was older than the Dumfries one, but the contest for the Siller Gun in Dumfries is the one still regularly held, annually on or before the town's Guid Neighbours Celebrations in June. The shoot was held at Kingholm in the old days, but for health and safety reasons moved to the gun club in the old aerodrome at Heathall. Competing either as individuals or as teams, the participants are often from the gun club itself or from one of the cadet forces, or the Territorial Army. The rivalry is intense, and the punch bowl which is awarded these days is a much coveted prize.

In 2004, a weel kent ex-chef, let's call him Theo, heard some talk of the contest in a pub, and decided, for a laugh, to enter the Siller Gun with his mate, an ex-cabinet maker. It would be fair to say that at that time the pair had drifted from life's mainstream and were full-time ageing hippies and herbalists. Having signed up under the influence, and never fired a gun in his life, Theo sought advice from his drinking cronies, some of whom had past military experience. 'Breathe the bullet out,' intoned the artist Hugh MacIntyre, mysteriously, 'breathe it to the target.'

Having completely disregarded or forgotten any advice, the pair spent the morning of the competition relaxing in their usual fashion then reeled up to shoot, among the last of more than three hundred competitors. Said Theo later, 'We were like Butch Cassidy and the Sundance Kid, Drew was blazing away in the booth next door and giggling like a madman, his cartridges kept falling onto my back, burning me.'

Later on at the Hole in the Wa, a bemused Theo was sought out by one of the contest officials and told he'd scored ten perfect bulls-eyes, the best pattern since 1932 and had, much to his own and everyone else's astonishment, romped the Siller Gun.
*See **Munitions, Shooters***

Slow Tourism

Slow was once a derogatory term but is now a desirable ethic informing any enterprise or process, like slow food, or slow tourism. I am meeting with Darren Flint and Donald Greig, the two people currently researching and producing the *Slow Travellers' Guide to Dumfries and Galloway*. I go with the definite aim of picking their brains and stealing any stuff I think interesting, but it turns out they are trying to do the same thing and do it slower and therefore probably better. Slow tourism is about:

slowing down the rate of tourism and a guarantee of rediscovering oneself (the physiological and the psychological); it is about low greenhouse gas emissions and it is a synonym of patience, peace of mind, deeper experiences, improved cultural understanding and knowledge (Babou and Callot, 2009). Slow tourism means moving at a pace that allows rediscovery. It is to tourism what slow food is to the restaurant business; it is doing away with the stress and speed of travelling; it is accepting a slow pace as the norm for undertaking one's leisure activities. The illnesses that our contemporaries suffer from are for the major part linked to stress; based on this observation, slow tourism then appears as a therapeutic solution as well as one that deals out pleasure.

(Definition; Springer Reference)

Carl Honoré's 2004 book, *In Praise of Slowness*, explored how the slow philosophy might be applied in every field of human endeavour and thus coined the phrase 'slow movement'.

Slow tourism's been around for a while, of course, and has its roots in early adventurers or travellers who soaked in culture, geography and history by embedding themselves, for a while at least, in the societies in or through which they travelled. A great deal of the success of this would seem to be predicated on being quite rich, which is a sure stress buster anyway, but I suppose the backpacker was a slow traveller in the three decades before the term became trendy, and they were often skint, as I certainly was. Mind you, I'm not sure stumbling about being robbed on three continents actually does increase your appreciation of other cultures, so it helps to have

a four-by-four, or an air-conditioned coach, or a guidebook like Darren and Donald's to steer you to the best pottery studios and cheese makers.

My favourite slow traveller was Xavier De Maistre who in 1794 chronicled his experiences in a volume entitled *Journey Round my Bedroom* which he followed 30 years later after much research with a sequel *Nocturnal Expedition Round my Bedroom* which chronicled his travels as far as the window ledge. Xavier's journeys went two ways, one was an intimate examination of the landscape of the familiar, like his sofa, the other an internal journey through memory and random association a bit like the author Nicholson Baker achieves in *The Mezzanine*. I am currently urging a friend who seldom leaves his flat except to buy Tartan Special to chronicle his daily journey through the exquisite nuances of the predictable as far as the off licence.

Darren and Donald are fly enough to persuade me before I leave to write, for nothing, a little article for their *Slow Travellers' Guide* on the subject of literature in Dumfries and Galloway. I agree to do it, hoping to get slow revenge on some of the contemporary writers against whom I currently hold completely baseless grudges. Quite pleased with myself, I walk slowly down the road towards the bus stop where a knot of old ladies are raging about slow buses.

See Stagecoach – Not the Company, the Mode of Transport

Smugglers

My mother used to take in lodgers to make ends meet and her favourite was a fisherman, originally from Stranraer, called Michael, whose boat was based in Kirkcudbright. Michael's feats were much admired but one of them was, in the words of my mother, to 'smuggle Ulster Fry into Scotland' during the foot-and-mouth epidemic in the early '70s when the movement of animals was banned and bacon was in short supply. Our house ran on bacon, broth and mince and a shortage of any one of these was unthinkable. Ulster Fry was a kind of bacon mince formed into a loaf then sliced, and was a very unique taste. What joy there was in the house when the figure of Michael was seen carrying sacks of Ulster Fry in his sailor's bag – or so I imagine the scene, deep in retrospect. I have never clapped eyes on Ulster Fry since these halcyon days, but I remember the taste still. Good because it could be fried, but bacon it wasn't.

When I read about Galloway's great smugglers, and how for a time in its history the smugglers far outnumbered and out-resourced the paltry forces up against them – the revenue even recruited poets, how desperate they must have been – I can't help but think how Galloway was again, in a way, asserting its differentness and sense of independence from the authorities.

Because of the many wee coves, inlets, ports, and because of the proximity of that great illicit bonding warehouse , the Isle of Man, the Solway was ideal for smuggling. Smuggling was the hobby of choice and the profession of many in Galloway in the past. The minister of Anworth was sacked for it, Alexander Murray's autodidact itinerant book-selling friend McHarg was a smuggler. Even the excisemen were smugglers, or often sympathetic to them.

> We'll mak our maut, and we'll brew our drink,
> we'll laugh, sing, and rejoice, man,
> And monie braw thanks to the meikle black Deil,
> that danc'd awa wi' the Exciseman.

('The Deil's Awa wi the Exciseman', Robert Burns)

One of the most astonishing things when you read the sources is the sheer scale and size of the operation. How many times are the excisemen forced to sit twiddling their flintlocks on the shingle, not just outwitted by the smugglers but vastly outnumbered by entire communities energised by the reception and passage of contraband?

> One clash that was particularly humiliating for the preventive forces took place just off Philip and Mary point on the east side of the (Luce) bay. Local troops heard about a landing, and lined up on the beach, while the two smugglers' luggers, armed with a total of 36 guns, and with a complement of 100 men, hovered offshore. The smugglers shouted to the troops that they should retire a little, as a run was about to take place, and they did not care to be observed too closely. The alternative — a fight against far superior forces — was declined, and the dragoons retreated. When the excisemen returned, there was a reward waiting for them — a row of barrels on the shoreline.

(*Smuggling in the British Isles*, Richard Platt)

Wigtown and Creetown were both centres of smuggling. One account tells how in 1777, 100 or more smugglers led twice this number of horses within a mile of the town, despite the attentions of 30 soldiers who had been sent to stop them.

The most famous smuggler in Galloway was Captain Yawkins, or Dick Hattaraik, as Walter Scott called him in *Guy Mannering*, whose feats were so extraordinary some said he had sold his soul to the devil. I'm reminded of Jack

Sparrow, maybe because Yawkins' ship was called the Black Prince, named, they say, after his pal Satan. My favourite tale is when he kidnapped a revenue man and took him to Amsterdam for the weekend just for the hell of it. Billy Marshall, the King of the Gypsies, was Yawkins' mate, of course, and they used to meet often. Imagine the scene! I have:

> Dick Hattaraik and Billy Marshall
> are drinking at the bar.
> It's blue and carved from a boat
> and they are sharing some porky
>   scratchings
> smuggled over last night from
>   Holland.
> On the bay, the Black Pearl, no
>   Prince,
> rocks at anchor, carronades trained
> steadily up the Dumfries road.

('Auchencairn As It Should Be')

Everybody loves stories of individuals beating the system, making a fool of the authorities, whether it's a poacher, a smuggler or a reiver. I used to frequent a pub that was nicknamed The Smugglers because of the contraband booty that went through its doors. I distinctly remember someone shouting out 'for God's sake Sean I ordered an 8–10 months romper suit, this is 12–18!' Nonetheless in spite of the odd incidence of tobacco smuggling – 1.5 million counterfeit and smuggled cigarettes were discovered in December 2013 in the back of a 40-foot refrigerated unit on the A75 in Dumfries and Galloway – all seems much more subdued, and boring these days on this once libertarian front. Though I do believe you can still get the odd bit of reindeer smuggled in by Scandinavian lorries.

See Feisty, Travellers

Speugs

A speug is a sparrow, a very small bird, though not in its own estimation. In the writing workshops I do through the year, which involve all ages of school kids, there's always someone in the room who knows Scots words still commonly used in the area to describe birds, 'hoodie craws, an doos, an speugies, an heckil-breistit thrushis,' as Bill Herbert described in a poem.

Add to that throstles, whaups and corbies. And houlets, never forget the houlets who are always, according to the great William Soutar, 'houlity-hootin' in 'chittery weather.'

The massive definitive and scholarly book *The Birds of Dumfriesshire* was written by HS Gladstone in 1810, he himself named after a bird, the Red Kite or Gled, thriving again in the region since 2004.

Of course poets have waxed lyrically about birds in the region for centuries, but it's hard today to avoid thinking that the emblematic bird of Dumfries and Galloway is not the softly contoured barnacle goose of the Council logo but instead the combative, ugly, right in your face herring gull like the one that stole my tuna mayonnaise roll the other day, swooping from a rooftop seizing and swallowing in one perfect artful parabola. The regional authorities have wasted much sleep wondering how to get rid of gulls from town centres. They're not allowed to shoot, gas, or blow them up but many other things have been tried; real falcons, fake falcons, nets, short spikes, long spikes, nest removals and so on. Through all these attempts the gulls have retained a haughty and stubborn indifference. My favourite failure was the poor falcons who were chased ingloriously from the skies by, in the words of a regional council report, gulls who appeared to 'have become particularly agitated' by their presence, in fact downright enraged. They're so brazen and so beautifully barbaric, the herring gulls especially, that I can't help feeling that I'd have the folk who leave their kebabs or chips lying about the streets culled long before them. I've featured gulls many times in poems, as have others, but the piece of literature that perfectly encapsulates the cruel yellow beaked Viking gulls of the region has to be Brian McCabe.

We are the dawn marauders.
We prey on pizza. We kill kebabs.
We mug thrushes for bread crusts

with a snap of our big bent beaks.
We drum the worms from the
   ground
with the stamp of our wide webbed
   feet.
We spread out, cover the area –
like cops looking for the body
of a murdered fish-supper.
Here we go with our hooligan yells
loud with gluttony, sharp with
   starvation.

('Seagulls', Brian McCabe)

St Trinians and Kirkcudbright

Margaret Houliston was a formidable Victorian lady who carved a name for herself in the field of education in South Africa in the 1920s–30s.

Born in Kirkcudbright, she emigrated and became Principal of the Girls' High School, Somerset East, and then at Riebeek College, Uitenhage in Natal in South Africa. She was appointed organiser of the Woman's Christian Temperance Union of the Cape Province in 1923 and the Provincial Superintendent of Moral Hygiene in Cape Province. Moral hygiene is one of these dodgy terms. Was she a proto feminist into family planning or a proponent of the social eugenics supported by Marie Stopes and later famously Adolf Hitler? Or both? I'm shown a picture of her. She's dead serious and ramrod straight, one of the femmes of Empire. I can imagine her girls being pretty feart of her. I wonder if they rebelled?

Rebellious schoolgirls and Kirkcudbright brings us very easily to Ronald Searle and St Trinians. In 1941 Searle was in the Air Force and was posted to Kirkcudbright and became friends with the Johnstone family whose two daughters attended a school in Dalkeith called St Trinneans but who had been temporarily evacuated. As a joke he drew them a cartoon showing a group

of schoolgirls in gymslips and stockings looking at an official noticeboard which read, 'Owing to the international situation, the match with St Trinian's has been postponed.' It was the first of the famous St Trinians Cartoons, born in Kirkcudbright. Like Margaret Houliston, the girls that became the Belles of St Trinians are hard to figure. Do they reflect a male view of women as nymphomaniac sociopaths, who if they get mad enough, you can lock away in an institution? Or do they show empowered women, ready and willing to blow things up and triumph over their environment? Or both?
See Feisty

Stagecoaches – Not the Company, the mode of transport

Once a hugely expensive, uncomfortable, unending and unreliable way to travel between destinations, and sometimes still is. My ire while writing this is fuelled by standing in a bus shelter for three hours last week in sub-zero temperatures, my only company being a man with a huge slowly freezing drip coming from his nose and the electronic display, installed at massive expense by the Council, which instead of saying something useful like 'your bus is 40 minutes late/ been cancelled' or whatever, insisted instead on wishing me, repeatedly, a Merry Christmas.

Stagecoaches were once the only way to travel long distances if you didn't want to take your own horse and didn't want to do the proletarian thing and walk, which most ordinary people did. People walked tremendously long distances in the past but there were obvious dangers, not just the weather but the lawless state of the country. Andrew Fletcher of Saltoun, in a pamphlet of 1698, talked of 200,000 vagabonds roaming Scotland, 'both men and women, perpetually drunk, cursing, blaspheming, and fighting together'.

Another problem was the state of the roads. Before 1777 what roads there were followed the two main Roman routes, one through Longtown, another through

Gretna and snaking north and east to Lochmaben then through the Devil's Beef Tub to Crawford with a branching loop to Nithsdale, Thornhill and Durisdeer which also ended up in Crawford. There were also drovers' roads such as at the Enterkin Pass used by people on foot, pack horses and sledges. Some old tracks had also been established by smugglers, bringing home the booty from the Isle of Man. One route was from Portpatrick up to Clydesdale. Routes from several coves led to Kirkcowan and from there to Glasgow via Minnigaff and Dalmellington. Edinburgh was reached by Moniaive and Penpont then through the Dalveen Pass. All these were mostly beaten tracks though, unmaintained and impassable at certain points of the year. The one exception was a military road from Dumfries to Portpatrick constructed in the 1760s by William Caulfield to take troops to Ireland. It was far easier to travel round the coast by sea than stagecoach. One famous example proves just that. After the death of Grierson of Lagg, the great persecutor of the Covenanters,

in the winter of 1733, sailors in the Solway saw a light astern of them which seemed to be gaining at an unnatural pace. As it passed it revealed itself to be a great state coach drawn by six black horses, with driver, footmen, coachman, torchbearers and so on. The skipper had hailed it. 'Where bound, where from?' The answer came succinctly: 'To tryst wi Lagg! Dumfries! Frae Hell!'

Not everyone got to travel so fast and in style, but after the Turnpikes Act roads were built from Glasgow to Lochmaben, Annan and Carlisle, the forerunner of the A74, from Moffat to Nithsdale and from Carlisle to Dumfries and onward to Portpatrick. Bridges were also constructed.

By 1812 there were six bridges over the Nith, five over the Annan and five over the Esk. These new maintained roads meant passenger-carrying mail coaches could travel north to south. The Craigengillan coach ran through Carsphairn and Moniaive on the journey between Glasgow and Dumfries, taking 13 and three quarter hours for the journey. There were also other coaches, nicknamed roaring dillies, to Edinburgh and Glasgow. The relative safety of the stagecoach with its insurance and its armed guard was an attractive option, though it was pricey. It was still difficult to travel though, if not impossible, beyond the main roads:

> When the Marquis of Downshire attempted to make a journey through Galloway in his coach about the year 1760 a party of labourers attended him to lift the vehicle out of ruts and put on the wheels when it got dismounted... when within 3 miles of the village of Freetown near Wigtown he was obliged to ...pass the night in the coach with his family.
>
> (*The Life of Thomas Telford*: Samuel Smiles)

I've often sympathised with the Marquis of Downshire, especially when sitting at the side of the road in a bus after the alternator's packed up or the doors blown off, or a tree has tumbled across the road. I've never driven, as poets don't drive, everyone knows that, so I judge myself an expert in public transport. Why should everyone need to have a car to live in the countryside? Rural buses are a lifeline but the service is poor, though the drivers are often, though not always, men and women of great humanity and kindness. If you depended on the buses completely, however, you would evolve into a creature with no social life past quarter to five in the evening. I have thought this more keenly since my local pub shut down and often, at a bus stop, think of Henry Thoreau's words:

> It would be some advantage to live a primitive and frontier life, though in the midst of an outward civilization, if only to learn what are the gross necessaries of life and what methods have been taken to obtain them.
>
> (Henry Thoreau, *Walden*)

I have a theory that somehow in the centre of all our technological advance, some of the population are, through poverty or remoteness, living essentially a medieval life, or a medieval life with some mod cons. Some folk embrace this lifestyle, of course, and become reiki therapists and the like but most are just trying to have a decent life. Difficulties in rural transport encourage depopulation and add to the ghost landscape. Mind you there's another way of looking at it. I was having a conversation with a young man about to leave school in Newton Stewart, but who lives some miles from there, and the talk got to buses. I was saying what a shame it was that there weren't more services and he said, 'aye it's a conspiracy to keep us here, they don't want us to leave. Even the ones you get take you round in circles'.

It's true of course. I used to get a bus that took 50 minutes to travel the 13 miles to Dumfries, and half an hour into the journey we were further away than when we started. There's an implicit symbolism in the region's bus services which should not be underestimated.

We butt into the countryside.
Our bus is aggrieved:
it grinds through swamps and ruts,
between dykes and crippled hedges,
down miles of wet tarmac,
from one telegraph pole to another,
from one five bar gate to another,
from one muddy bunkered cottage
    to another,
criss-crossing land dank and
    paralysed
below an oatmeal sky.
There seem hundreds of miles,
thousands, but it is the same mean
    mile
circling, taking us back where we
    didn't want
to come from, where we didn't
    want to leave.

('Mean Mile')

See Ghost Landscape, Haunted, Walkers

Stanes

Christ Almighty no anither pile o stanes!

(S2 pupil on history trip)

Stanes are an intrinsic part of the Scottish landscape, and those of

Dumfries and Galloway, some would say, are one of its defining features.

People were erecting stanes for burial purposes here 4,000 years ago and have continued to hoik them up to the present day. Andy Goldsworthy's enigmatic pinecones or acorns or Matt Baker's sculptures in Cairnsmore are the modern versions of the lonely and lovely Laggangarn Stones, ways of imprinting and making sense of our relationship with the landscape. We may not have the sheer number of ancient stones that they have further north but typically we've got some of the weirdest and best. The Twelve Apostles at Holywood is one of the largest stone circles in mainland Britain. The Taxing Stone, in Little Laight Hill near Cairnryan, was a toll marker but before that was, according to legend, the grave of Alpin, father of the first Scottish King, Kenneth MacAlpin, who was killed in Glenapp in 741 while leading a Scottish invasion of Galloway.

Try as you might, though, you'll not find a stane with a better story to tell than the Lochmabenstone. This was a tribal meeting place and also, you can tell by the name, the religious centre for the Celtic Sun God, Mabon, our version of Apollo. It's mentioned in the famous *Ravenna Cosmography*, a kind of mad road map of the world written by a monk in Ravenna, North Italy in the 8th century AD. Later in history the Lochmabenstone was a parlay point for the reivers to talk and exchange prisoners and was regarded as marking the southern limit of Scots territory. The Battle of Lochmabenstone, or Sark, on 23 October 1448 even saw a Scottish army under the command of Hugh Douglas, Earl of Ormonde, win a rare victory over the invading English forces of Henry Percy, 2nd Earl of Northumberland, with 1,500 English soldiers killed to a mere 26 Scots. Those are facts, sort of, but the stone is also shrouded in romantic legend. A local story claims it to be the stone that held the sword Excalibur until Arthur pulled it out. Ridiculous? In *The Quest for Merlin*, published in 1985, Nikolai Tolstoy places Arthur's mentor and pet wizard Merlin in Lochmaben as a priest of the Sun God.

Our carved stones are international class. The Ruthwell Cross, a Northumbrian Christian cross carved in the 7th century

AD, suffered severe damage by Presbyterian art critics in the 1640s, but, partly restored, still stands near its original location, a monument to art and poetry too as it prefigures in its runic panelling the first real poem written in the English language, 'The Dream of the Rood'. Its distant cousin a few hundred years older lives, as I've referred to elsewhere, in a precarious state in a field on the A702 between Thornhill and Penpont. Galloway has the earliest Christian monuments in Scotland in and near Whithorn, centre of the cult of Scotland's native saint, St Ninian. Stones here date from the 5th and 6th centuries. Galloway saw the superseding in stone of the old Celtic Catholicism of St Ninian with Northumbrian Roman Catholicism which the Ruthwell Cross represents.

Most wonderful of all are the cup and ring stones, two thousand years old. EA Hornel's painting *The Druids* was inspired by a walk in which he discovered cup and ring marks, and imagined the rest. Galloway has more of these mysterious marks than any other part of Scotland apart from Argyll. They're concentrated in the Machars, the Cree estuary and the area between Dundrennan and the Dee. What do these strange modernistic punctures and sworls depict? Astronomical movements, sun worship, methods of metal smelting, someone with a Bronze Age bursary doing public art? Currently there are more than a hundred different theories, the recent favourite being that they are representations in stylised symbol writing of the rebirth of a god, in this case Tascio, the Phoenician Sun God brought by the Celts from Lebanon to the banks of the Cree. Death and rebirth, Tascio, Mabon, Mithras and Jesus, all a continuum in Dumfries and Galloway stone. What a legacy.

It's irresistible to think of your name carved in stone, or your name being associated forever with such an ageless and permanent feature as a big rock. Like Bruce's stone in Glentrool which marks the turning of the tide in the Scottish Wars of Independence, or the Steading

Stone, near Dalbeattie where Mary Queen of Scots took her last view of Scotland. In my most megalomaniacal moments I imagine kids of the future walking past, jerking their thumb in the direction of a big flat stone in Cookie's Wood saying in reverential whispers, 'that's where Hugh McMillan hid when he was making up all that stuff for that book.' Mactaggart talks about 'throwing a stone to the cairn',

adding a stone in remembrance, in the belief that human memory can prevail through our most useless, and most useful, resource, stone. People are still doing it. There's a little stretch of coastline near Colvend full of cairns, benches, marked with the name Stuart Mossman. Who's he? The locals don't have a clue, but they'll remember the name.

See Art, Badges, Nith Cross, Ritual Roads

Strong Old Men

They say the rocks scattered around Glentrool were missiles aimed at Scottish giants by their Irish equivalents in an epic battle the Irish won eventually by low trickery, when Finn MacCool realised he was outmatched and dressed himself as a baby so the Scots got scared in case he told his father on them. Galloway folk have long been reputed and feared for their strength, if not their ability to see through disguises.

A great pursuit in the area historically was stane putting, a bit like modern shot putting, where you would hurl a stone as

far as you could, for prizes, or just the kudos. No one knows how old this tradition was, but it was carried on even by poets. Burns had a putting stone at Ellisland Farm and would challenge visitors to see how far they could chuck it, a contest he invariably won, because poets are supermen.

Galloway men were not only reputed to be strong but to live long: there's a story quoted in various sources of the 'eighty-five year-old Galloway man' who was found in tears after his father had given him a skelp for hurling boulders at his granddad. Archibald

Nibloe recalled in 1930 how 70 years previously his grandmother of 110 had recalled her grandfather describing William of Orange's fleet leaving Lochryan en route to the battle of the Boyne in 1690. So are the centuries spanned. This regional reputation for strength and longevity is personified today by Stranraer power lifter Bill McFadyen.

Bill was the subject of a 12 minute film commissioned in 2009 by Dumfries and Galloway Council to celebrate the opening of the new leisure centre in the town. The film follows Bill's attempts to regain the World Power Bar Lifting Championship, and is called *Ma Bar*, the words Bill cried when he picks up the weights.

'There's no point tripping out like you're picking daisies,' he said, 'You've got to get the anger in you, real anger in you and just shout it out – "ma bar!"'

The film won a Scottish Bafta and was shown at the Sundance Film Festival in Utah. All very remarkable but made more so for the fact he was 73 years old at the time of filming.

Since then he's been on the road, still competing. In May 2011 Bill won Silver at the World Bench Press Championships in Denmark and the World Record of 150kg bench press in the 83kg bodyweight class. He also got Gold at the British Powerlifting Championships in Colchester. As of last week he was still going strong, providing, in the words of the Wigtownshire Sports Council, 'continuing experience and inspiration'.

T

Teachers: Class-War

I was earwigging on two old ladies on a bus near Newton Stewart and they were reminiscing about their old school near Sorbie. As an ex-teacher myself I was always sensitive to the idea that nowadays teachers get short shrift from parents, pupils, the community and so on, whereas in previous eras they were seen as pillars of the community and worthy of respect. This conversation, however, was not running that way: 'Remember when Mary Morrisson's mother cam in yon day? Whit did she say again, "you'll no ca my Mary names ye fat bitch!" Next thing ye know they were rolling roon the floor pu'ing each ithers hair while a' the weans, we were a cheering an clappin!'

One thing I've always thought unfair is that people revered teachers in spite of, or perhaps because of, the tawse, that leather strap made in Lochgelly which now fetches tidy sums on the S and M market. Good teachers now are good because of sheer personality and talent rather than their ability to break a desk in two with some specially treated piece of leather. Not that they needed belts of course. Well do I remember the fear, as a 12 year old, of the morning Physics test when 'Taff' Robertson, swinging a wooden metre stick, would go round the room asking revision questions of each member of the class. A wrong answer and Taff would sit down with a weary sigh and hold his metre stick in front of him, so he could talk confidentially to it. 'Metre stick,' he would say wistfully, 'we must be protected from this ignorance.' Then he would crack whoever it was over the head with it. Another teacher would creep behind you with a huge French dictionary and with a cry of 'Jemimah' smash you across the back of the head with it.

There was also psychological warfare. When I was at a teachers' training course a few years back they were talking about positive assessment or something like that – the idea that you pick out what the wean has done correctly and build on that, rather than rip them apart for what they haven't done. This brought to mind a cameo from my French o Grade class, which was presided over by a Mr Weir, who used to give us huge tracts to translate into French, taking a half mark off for every error. I remember my friend entering the classroom and being regaled by Mr Weir with the cry of 'Well done, MacDonald, only -20 out of 50 today! Work hard and one day you might get nothing!'

Such cruelty was nothing new but you wonder why it happened. Mactaggart, talking about teacher Anro Gemmell said:

He was of a crazed nature, like every old soldier who has seen much blood, and when any little thing curled his temper he became a madman complete.

Many servicemen came back from the war mentally damaged, of course, my father being one of them. It's only recently I've realised that the generation of teachers I hated at school were probably the same, and that it may not have been completely their fault they were psychopaths who felt the compulsion to hit children over the head with bits of wood or large French dictionaries. After all it must have been a bit of a change, one moment garrotting German soldiers with cheesewire and the next teaching irregular verbs. A teacher in Stranraer even wore his Paratrooper beret into work and 'when he smiled, and you saw the glint of his gold tooth, you knew you were in for it'.

In such paranoid dictatorships the heroic efforts of pupils to defy and subvert their teachers often reached legendary status, such as the time pupils at St Joseph's College removed all the screws from the desk of their English teacher, Hairy Nell, followed by his chair and blackboard. An ex-pupil told me:

The tension was unbearable, we went through the entire lesson just about. He even sat on the chair and nothing happened. Then right at the end someone began to laugh uncontrollably, it was nerves I think, just like one of these scenes in a prison camp when someone cracks under the strain, and he lost his temper, slammed a book down on the desk, then the desk collapsed, he fell off his chair and in the final crowning moment with a huge explosive crash the board fell off the wall.

In another regional school, a sixth year class took the opportunity of having an absent minded and short sighted man as their registration teacher to invent a member of their class. Someone would always say 'present' when his name was read out. Before the ruse was discovered the boy had been entered into the Chess Club, Sports Day and the school trip to France.

Some teachers were worthy of devotion though. Jim Laidlaw remembers, at Penpont School, the scenes of devastation and loss when the pupils were told that their headmaster, another Laidlaw, had been killed in the wartime RAF.

I'm always very taken by old pictures of teachers. The idea that people in years to come will examine these, wonder at the hair loss, weight gain and so on, has always prompted me to avoid being part of staff photographs, but they can be very evocative. There is a photograph hanging outside the staffroom of Dumfries Academy showing a group of teachers sitting with their mortarboards one summer's day just before World War One. I know nothing about them beyond their names inscribed below the picture. What's one of the themes of this book? Where history fails, the gap is filled by myth, or poetry: A black and white photograph.

> It would be a brave colour
> that would infiltrate this group,
> sat gowned and booted
> outside the school in 1913.
>
> Hugelshofer. Not even port
> in the Headmaster's study
> will cheer him up this year.
> He knows
> the strapping lads he coached this morning
> in Catullus
> are marked for death.

(From 'Hugelshofer, Jackson, Gilruth, Chinnock and Bain')

See **Geniuses, Insane, War**

Things that Go Blink in the Night

I came across a newspaper article from the *Dumfries and Galloway Standard*, November 1914:

> Last night about half past seven o clock persons resident along the road between Dumfries and New Abbey observed singular moving lights, associated it was suggested with an airship that seemed to be manoeuvring over Criffel... Later in the evening about eleven o clock, there was seen what seemed to be direct signalling...The appearance was that of a very large star, but it changed in colour, being by turns yellow, green, white, and red, and its movements clearly showed that it was not a planetary object.

As the war was only a few months old, and all sorts of scaremongering was going on, people automatically assumed that the lights they saw in the sky over Criffel that night were those of a German airship and the signals some fiendish collaborator with an Aldis lamp. Or was that a convenient explanation? In fact the big vessel and the little flashing lights fit into a long tradition of sightings in the sky which follow a similar kind of pattern, large objects or lights being followed by small faster moving ones. In the latest sighting reported on a Dumfries and Galloway website, in mid December 2013, 'Rachel' talks of '3 balls, grey and black in colour almost, in a triangular formation stationary then moving away fast'.

In Penpont on 16 March 1712, Agnes Fokert, the landlady of the Volunteer Arms, reported that she and many of her customers saw in the sky what she described as two grand fleets of ships which came together and 'fought'. They saw several of the vessels sink or disappear, before one fleet headed off south and the other to the west at speed. The noise and brightness was so loud that the farm beasts were 'maddened'. In spite of the fact that Fokert had some months earlier been accused of mixing her beer with pepper and pigs' urine, this does not appear to have been a drunken hallucination, and people continuing to swear by what they had seen til the end of their lives.

The sighting took place at the time of the War of the Spanish Succession in which British, French and Spanish squadrons had been fighting each other in the Atlantic and Caribbean. Like the Criffel sighting, it was described in terms of the tensions and wars of the time.

Scotland's most famous and well-documented UFO story was the West Freugh Incident. This started in Luce Bay, Scotland, on the morning of 4 April 1957. That day mobile radar unit had been set up to track a bomber from RAF Farnborough. The plane was delayed and the radar units were shut off apart from one at Balscalloch near Corsewall Point which had not been informed and stayed ready to track the plane. The radar operator of that unit then saw on his screen a large echo from an almost stationary object, located high above the Irish Sea.

This echo remained stationary at 50,000 feet for about ten minutes 20 miles north of Stranraer. At some time its height appeared to alter from about 50,000 to 70,000 feet.

The Balscalloch unit phoned West Freugh air traffic control and informed them that the crew were now tracking several targets moving at extraordinarily high speeds and that these objects' echoes were different from any the operators had seen before. They were advised to phone the radar unit at Ardwell to get confirmation of their readings. Ardwell confirmed that they were seeing the same objects at the same range and height. The original target began to move north east at about 70 mph and at a height of 54,000 feet. Then a third radar station 20 miles away was asked to search for the object too. This third radar station identified and locked onto the same target. After it had travelled a further 20 miles, it did an 'impossible' sharp turn and proceeded southeast whilst increasing speed.

This third radar station then tracked four objects at 14,000 feet altitude and these were confirmed by the first two stations. The operators noted that the profile of the echoes were much larger than those of normal planes, closer to the size of ships. Wing Commander Peter Whitworth who was the base commander at West Freugh at the time of the sighting, wrote:

> After remaining stationary for a short time, the UFO began to rise vertically with no forward movement, rising rapidly to approximately 60,000 feet in much less than a minute. The UFO then began to move in an easterly direction, slowly at first but later accelerating very fast and travelling towards Newton Stewart, losing height on the way. Suddenly the UFO turned to the southeast, picking up speed to 240 mph as it moved towards the Isle of Man. It was at this stage that the radar signals became contradictory. Balscalloch tracked a single 'object' at high altitude while Ardwell picked up what appeared to be four separate objects moving line astern behind each other at a height of 14,000 feet. As the echoes disappeared, all three radars fleetingly traced the four smaller UFOs 'trailing' behind the larger object. The UFO had been tracked for 36 minutes… the sharp turn made near Newton Stewart would be impossible for any aircraft travelling at similar speed.'

The incident leaked to the press because the radar operators were civilian and several talked openly about it. Several papers quoted a government source as saying the echoes might have been a Russian reconnaissance plane, but the performance of the targets, the speed of climb, angle of turn and acceleration, were all beyond any plane designed then and for that matter, now.

At such happenings we are left to scratch our heads and say there must be a logical explanation. Some folk say that is that Galloway is a magnet to UFOs because West Freugh is an experimental research facility like Roswell. Is there a Galloway equivalent to Hanger 18?

We maybe shouldn't be surprised that a land so mired in myth should continue to attract it, like more and more layers to a very rich cake.

See Away with the Fairies, Biplanes

Tides

Tides are the rhythmic rise and fall of sea levels caused by gravitation and the rotation of the earth. Tides and the waves they cause are very important to poets as they can listen to them at night and imagine they symbolise things. What did Walter Scott say in 'Lochinvar?'

> Love swells like the Solway, but ebbs like its tide.

> ('Lochinvar', Walter Scott)

Even the Solway, a runt of a sea, named for the fact it's not even a sea at all, but a muddy crossing, has tides and waves and therefore also poets, imagining feverishly through the night, bearing unasked and unrewarded the burdens of the sleeping world and turning them into worlds of wonder. Here Stuart Paterson looks at the tides from Douglas Hall:

Twice daily the tides are here, sometimes
Breenging shoreward like an army
Of small, mad angry locals,
At others, creeping in on tourist feet.
They are their own beginnings & endings,
Stories that tell themselves, borderline ballads
Of loss & finding, war cries or sobs
Or occasional lullabies, all midnight
And moonlight, tender vessels of tiny waves
Bringing shallow white words & drifting
Tributes ashore, washed up at
The very end & very start of it.

('Douglas Hall', Stuart Paterson)

Tides like these are not to be confused with the Solway Bore, a man who will tell you he once surfed several miles on the unnaturally high tide that sometimes develops at the head of the firth.

Beats: nomads, travellers and vagrants. In 1597 the Act for the Repression of Vagrancy defined these people as:

1   Wandering scholars seeking alms
2   Shipwrecked seamen
3   Idle persons using subtle craft in games or in fortune-telling
4   Pretended proctors, procurers or gatherers of alms for institutions
5   Fencers, bearwards, common players or minstrels
6   Jugglers, tinkers, pedlars and petty chapmen
7   Able-bodied wandering persons and labourers without means refusing to work for current rates of wages
8   Discharged prisoners
9   Wanderers pretending losses by fire
10 Egyptians or gypsies

Galloway was one of the great centres for tinkers or travelling people. And deepest Galloway, the northern rocky lands, was the centre for all sorts of dodgy or debatable activity. The law ran sometimes round the coast but not there. And the most characterful could play several roles at once: highwayman, smuggler, leveller, gypsy, and even in the case of Billy Marshall, soldier of the crown. To live so many lives in one is difficult but it helps to live to 120 years old, like he did.

Billy claimed to be the King of the Gypsies in Galloway, and was a bare knuckle boxer, a smuggler, a soldier who deserted seven times at the time of the Horse Fairs at Rhonehouse, a sailor who deserted three times at the times of the Horse Fairs at Rhonehouse, a husband 17 times, and the father of 68 children, four reputedly after his hundredth birthday.

He led a band of gypsies or 'randies' but like a true Godfather of Galloway he operated under a strict, if a little skewed, moral code. According to Walter Scott, Marshall visited the aristocracy as an equal: 'he visited regularly twice a year... and partook no doubt of their hospitality, but he made a grateful and ample return'.

He should be a poster boy for the alternative left. I can practically see Johnny Depp in the role. Marshall was an early radical at the time of the Levellers. With his military training and expertise he was able to organise the country people and demolish the tyrannical dykes the landowners were building to parcel up the land, one of the major causes of rural depopulation, emigration and the ghost landscape in the 18th and 19th centuries.

The coming of the workhouses in the 19th century, with their special blocks for vagrants, led to a decline in the numbers. Easier communications also meant a fall in the number of folk on the roads selling and trading, though salesmen like the Petitjeans or Onion Johnnies were a common sight for close to a century from the 1860s. One, an M Quemener, is still working in the eastern Borders at the time of writing but none as far as I know still trade in Dumfries and Galloway. Small numbers of travellers still can be seen in Dumfries and Galloway which has two permanent facilities for travellers in Glenluce and in Collin, though the numbers using these are extremely small.

Where's the modern equivalent of the wandering scholars, jugglers and fortune tellers? Are they dark sky watching or practising reiki therapy from rustic cottages in Moniaive or New Galloway or Wanlockhead? Do they just come out for Knockengorroch or the Wickerman then go home? Or are there any still on the road living out of a backpack?

I was talking to some auld heids the other night and they talked of another type of nomad. Thanks to free travel concessions there are wee old men and women jumping on buses and criss-crossing the region, the nation, just for the hell of it. Must invent a name for them.

See **Levellers, Wandering Poets**

Tune Carrying

I've just been watching three primary schools perform with Scottish Opera. It's a programme where they are taught by their teachers the words of the songs, then three opera singers are parachuted in to whip a half hour show together, dance moves and all, in just four hours. It was brilliant. I'm telling this tale later and a man called Bruce Halliday says how in his day the opportunities to learn music were limited. Apparently he brought in his father's chanter into his primary school one day and tried to carry a tune. His teacher grabbed it from him and cracked him over the head, shouting, 'Halliday, you couldnae even carry a tune in a bucket.'

U

Trawling the ether I was shocked to find the following event organised by the Scottish Environmental Protection Agency: '30th June 2014, Loch Ken drop-in event for North American Signal Crayfish, Cross Keys Hotel New Galloway.'

Is it not enough that these creatures, over-sexed, over-fed and over here, have invaded many of our waterways and threatened the livelihood of our plucky young Scottish fish, do we also have to provide drop-in centres for them? Presumably this will just give them the chance to shoot some pool, and flash their dollars to impress local crustaceans. In *The Present Time*, in 1921 Thomas Carlyle was talking, I think, about American crayfish when he said:

Enormous Megatherions, as ugly as were ever born of mud, loom huge and hideous out of the twilight Future on America.

An attempt to fill Loch Ken with euro-eels to kill the crayfish appears to have failed and only provided an impending European Eel threat to native species. When will it end? Obviously only when Scotland becomes independent and Michael Scott can be given a commission by SEPA to sort it all out, or the Great Solway Worm is enticed ashore once again and trained not to kill local settlers, just the crayfish, though some casualties might be inevitable.

*See **Bram Stoker and the A75**, **Pine Martens***

V

It wasn't me who said it, just someone at the bus stop. The Ellangowan Hotel in Creeton is famous for having been *The Green Man* and the pub in the film *The Wicker Man* where the saucy barmaid, Britt Eckland, attempts to seduce the puritanical policeman, Edward Woodward by wiggling her bare bottom on the other side of his bedroom wall. Well, film being film it wasn't really, because their bedrooms were situated thirty miles apart and the bottom wasn't even Britt's as she was two months pregnant and didn't want it to be seen. Neither did her boyfriend Rod Stewart who said he would buy up all the negatives of the film to prevent her bottom being seen, even though it wasn't hers. But there were no negatives to buy, as they had been accidentally disposed of after the film was made.

Such is the chaos and confusion of *The Wicker Man*. A great motif for the place, providing a wee stream of visitors to Creetown, the barman of the Ellangowan explained, coming from as far away as Japan and Australia to savour the ambience of the bar where Britt was the butt of a highly charged and erotic song 'The Landlord's Daughter'.

The Wicker Man aside, Creetown seems well and truly bypassed. And not just by the A75 to Stranraer. On my travels in the ancient kingdom I have found places that have a reason to exist and places that don't but where often, and passionately, people are trying to invent a new identity for communities whose demographic has changed utterly. But what is this new identity?

The Creetown initiative is a trail blazer in a sense, a community organisation working, in its own words, to adapt to the fact that young people are leaving and retiring couples from wherever are coming in. It's so effective at this that it's acting as a consultant to other communities where the same thing is happening.

Like some other places it has embraced art. Its project Inspire involved all ages. Creetown has many public art projects, five for the population of 600 people, that's one each for every 120 people. I asked the girl at the bus stop about them. 'A big snowball,' she said, about the work by Hideo Furuta in the town's Adamson Square, 'I like it fine, and the ceilidhs are good. We should get a ceilidh for each bit of art. Wish there were more of them.' Then she came out with that stuff about it being the village of the damned. 'Don't worry though, I can hear the buses on the road, I listen to the vibrating, I'm like a Red Indian me, one's coming to take you away soon.'

See **Bells, Emigration, Ghost Landscape, Palnackie**

Voices

'Be nice to your voice,' said Becky Davy, speech therapist from the Dumfries and Galloway Royal Infirmary on International Voice Day, 16 April 2014, 'Rotate your head all the way around, stretching the neck... Tuck your chin in... pull your shoulders up to your ears and let them drop again... Gently hum a few notes, feeling the vibration in your throat and enjoying the wide open feeling in the throat. Lastly do some vowels... aaaahhhh eeeeeee oooooooohhhh.'

I think if anyone was sitting next to me with their shoulders up to their ears groaning in that manner, I might take flight. It got me thinking about voices though and their role in the landscape where, as the brochures say, people come 'seeking solitude', 'deserted beaches', 'peace and quiet' or 'to be alone'.

It was not always that quiet. Take the case of the ghost of Galdenoch and the minister from Kirkcolm. Galdenoch Tower was roughly halfway between Lochnaw Castle and the North Channel, close to Kirkcolm. The story goes that one of the sons of Galdenoch had been a Covenanter and while in hiding had killed a man who was trying to hand him over for a bounty. When peace was restored he moved back to Galdenoch but so did the ghost of the dead man who set out to make his life a misery, in spite of many attempts to exorcise it. The ghost was said to have an extremely loud voice.

The family at Galdenoch recruited the Reverend Marshall from Kirkcolm, a man with an equally loud voice of whom it was said, 'that his voice was so powerful on a quiet day when preaching outside in Kirkcolm he could be heard in Cairnryan on the other side of Loch Ryan.'

The pair of them set to roaring at each other, the minister using scripture, the ghost the kind of noises that Becky Davy might approve of if used *sotto voce*. When the Rev Marshall took to singing terrifyingly loud psalms to drown out the ghost, it conceded defeat and left Galdenoch for good. Considering the ghost was the aggrieved party, this is not a very moral tale but it shows the power of vocal chords even against the ranks of the supernatural. No such tasks

hopefully for eight year old Evie Croy from Creetown, recently chosen as Britain's youngest town crier in a competition organised by the Stove Artists' Collective. Judge Allan Lowden said, 'Evie might have been the smallest contestant but she definitely had the biggest voice'. 'There hasn't been a town crier in Creetown for 51 years, so I love my new job,' said Evie.

I can imagine her strident tones ringing out over the Machars, a loud sound of young hope, for a while anyway. I'm looking at Evie's picture in the paper and I'm reminded of that eerie and powerful statue by Epstein, *The Visitation*, situated til recently in the sculpture park at Glenkiln, a small lonely figure with plaits, a girl's face leaning forward from the clasp of a copse of trees, her hands folded, bent forward as if to listen.

*See **Bells, Ghost Landscape, Haunted***

Examining one of the panels of the ancient Knockhill Cross, it is clear that the figure near the Archangel Gabriel depicted with long hair and a microphone, is Neil Oliver, the historian with the best hair on television, even more beautiful than Helen of Kirkconnell.

O Helen fair! beyond compare,
A ringlet of thy flowing hair,
I'll wear it still for evermair
Until the day I die.

('Helen of Kirkconnell', Walter Scott)

Neil is an ex-pupil of my old school Dumfries Academy where, so we are told by his agent, 'his love of history was born'. As well as having hair, Neil is a great walker and has starred on TV tramping coastal paths round many countries that have a coast, like Scotland, Ireland and now Australia. My coastal walking is not as good as Neil's, and in fact only consists of a 22 mile hike done in the dead of night while completely drunk in Mull after my glasses had been buried in a landslide, but even that small experience has filled me with admiration for Neil's achievements as well as those of the TV crew who will have to trek the 35,846 kilometres round the variable coastline of Australia with heavy equipment and products to maintain Neil's hair in its good condition. Going at the pace they were in the programme I saw, they should be finished when Neil is 107 years old, in the year 2074, the year which is, coincidentally, the 250th anniversary of the publication of Mactaggart's *Gallovidian Encyclopedia*. What an achievement that will be.

Of course walking long distances without thought to fatigue is a well-established tradition in Dumfries and Galloway. The old Well Path north from Durisdeer in Nithsdale is thought to be the pilgrimage route that linked the south, ultimately Whithorn, with Edinburgh, Dunfermline and other royal centres. It's also where 'men of pairts' would think nothing of walking to university in Edinburgh or St Andrews from their homes. Alexander Murray for instance walked to Edinburgh from Minigaff to become, eventually, Professor of Oriental Languages in St Andrews. Joseph Thomson, explorer, was famous for his pedestrian activities. His brother noted in 1882:

On the hottest day of summer he walked from Gatelawbridge to the top of Criffel and back, a distance of 55 miles... indulging cheerfully in a dance on his return.
And not a hair out of place.

See **Love, and Death, Ritual Roads**

Wandering Poets

In the midst of a manhunt for the Sandyhills poet Stuart Paterson I am reminded of other wandering bards or makars from the area who have laid their heads on a street or a park bench, made a virtue, in fact, of their mission to stravaig through the world, delivering their gift to anyone who would want to listen. The most famous of these must be Roger Quin, the so called 'Tramp Poet', born in Dumfries in 1850, a clerk by trade skilled on the flute and the concertina, who wandered through the borders singing, playing and reading poetry before ending back in Dumfries to die in a nursing home in 1925.

He is revered quite rightly as a proletarian poet and entertainer, and the Glasgow poet Tom Leonard has written well about him. It seems to me that this type of poetry as a popular entertainment is particularly valid, historical and relevant to the survival of the art. Some poetry, the poetry of the review pages, The TS Elliot shortlist, The Scottish Poetry Library Top Scottish Poets of 2014 etcetera, is retreating to treeless spaces where only academics or fellow poets, or the people who publish it (often the same people) – can understand it. It inhabits rarefied slopes, a modern Mount Olympus where ordinary folk can't breathe. All this is a terrible pity because poetry is in everybody's blood until some idiot tells them, usually about the age of twelve, they're not good enough to write it. I used to wander into pubs and give impromptu readings and I can honestly say the experience has nearly always been one of all-round benefit and enjoyment. I remember at one of these 'guerrilla readings' I was half way through one poem and a man got up to leave and I said 'where do you think you're going?' to which he replied 'I'm going to cancel our table at the steakhouse.' This ranks among the greatest praise I've ever been given. Wandering poets are few and far between, however, unless they're wandering about intoxicated, which is a rarer and rarer sight too.

Where the poet once wandered, the busker or festival musician now goes, perfectly respected and rightly lauded. As I write the Eden Festival is on. 'I'm going down tonight,' said Eddie, who was serving me in Thornton's Sweet Shop yesterday. 'They want me to play. I maybe will or maybe won't. I'll take my guitar, maybe play maybe chill. Maybe both.' Seems an ideal existence, and the way art should be. Tommy is a busker, 'I'm self-taught, follow all the folk festivals, wander through all the towns, Dumfries and Galloway mostly, it's home territory. I play sea shanties, and Scottish and Irish stuff. If I make a pound or two I'm happy but to tell you the truth, sometimes I forget that's why I'm doing it. It pleases me that folk are wandering about their ordinary lives and whether they like it or not they're listening to "The Trip to Durrow" or "The Ale is Dear" and they're soaking in the culture of the country.'

My kids have just been taught some Gaelic songs by itinerant musicians in their school, members of Cherry Grove traditional music band. Two of their members, Grant and Marianne, have been working in primary schools through the region. They see themselves as part of a continuum, and Dumfries and Galloway as a stronghold of traditional music which is still in the blood of most people who live there. Even more hardcore is Scott Maxwell who wanders about with his guitar, playing where he can, sleeping where he can, 'I just think the land is ours, always has been. I like to go where I please, get a sing song going, play some of my stuff, their stuff. It's what folk have been doing for centuries and I like to think I'm keeping it going.'

In Dumfries, the louring Midsteeple
catches a tan from unseasonably
hot June sun, Simon & Garfunkel
songs are plaintively played & sung
    by an
earnest ponytail in torn breeks,
the town shimmers, wheechs in &
    out of early
summer, unsure, wary in that
    Scottish way,
fleeces topping shorts, jumpers
    round waists
tethering folk to all the seasons,
just in case. Guitar boy soars above
the frenzied yells of nesting gulls,
determined melody shall overcome
    us all,
the warm occasional sun, the
    cooling breeze,
the cautious chattering soundtrack
of unsure days such as these.

(*No Summer Yet:* Stuart Paterson)

It turns out that Stuart Paterson, in spite of leaving his belt, bag, phone and several pounds' worth of loose change in a series of separate locations, is completely safe and has been sleeping in the eaves of the Tam O Shanter pub, a wonderfully snug 17th century refuge for an itinerant poet. When found he says, 'I must go home, the moon is meant to be especially yellow tonight. A honey moon in fact. You can see it best in the country. The town is all very well but…'

These are sentiments that Roger Quin would have well understood.

The spell – the dream is over;
I awake but to discover
The city's rush – the jostling crowds
– the din on every hand;
But on my ear soft falling,
I can hear the curlew calling,
And I know that soon I'll see them
in the dear old Borderland.

('The Borderland', Roger Quin)

*See **Festivals, Makar***

When I think of war I think, as a broken-down history teacher, of the facts we know of invasion, defence and conquest: the Scots, the Picts, the Vikings, the 'Foreign Gaels', the Northumbrian Angles, Edward I, and so on. I think of the battles at Glengap, Glentrool, the Sark, flames over Annan, Dumfries, the Solway. Somewhere in my head I see pennants flying and hope my side won, whichever it was.

As for myself, though, I can't see past my parents, my direct experience of war. Both were in the RAF during World War Two, it's how they met. He had been a rear gunner in a Wellington Bomber and she was a driver, though she insisted on telling me that she had been in the SOE and had been dropped behind German lines to sabotage railways. I remember when I was about ten and expressed doubt on this she swooped huffily into the cupboard and produced a parachute, stunning me into silence for another four years. My father had been shot down in the desert, horribly injured. My mother, in the meantime, had met a fighter pilot, who my sister still claims was a Polish aristocrat, and had sent a letter chucking my father. This was intercepted by a nurse in the desert who returned it, snootily saying that he was too sick to receive such bad news. My mother, in a paroxysm of guilt, then shelved the fighter pilot and eventually married my father, with all the dubious results that then ensued.

My father was traumatised by the war, and often reverted to the day he was shot down, saying the same things he had said to his dead or dying comrades through his intercom as his bomber plunged to the sand that day in 1942. He was not an easy person to be with in any sense. Like a lot of people you see, he was still fighting his war.

My father left home when I was 11, going south then far north as deranged people do. He was remembered by my friends for his prodigious feats of athleticism, meanness and generosity. Our only contact was a monthly cheque from the Forestry Commission which we used to cash quite illegally in a strange little shop in Dumfries, long since swallowed by Tescos car park. Did we still cash it after he died? Surely not. I received one letter, shortly before his death.

War, I've always considered, is inexcusable and the effects go on like endless waves. It's what I always tried to say to my pupils, but the young are immortal, or think they are, and too many of them have gone out to Britain's recent wars and not come back.

Whenever I want to remind myself about war I go to Kingholm Quay and its tiny war memorial which lists almost an entire family dead, the MacFarlanes, three sons killed on the Western Front and the father killed while on railway guard duty for the Home Defence Force. A fourth son was wounded and taken prisoner but was eventually returned to his mother.

I want to talk of a forgotten poet, a subject always close to my heart. In this case Dumfries and Galloway's war poet, 2nd Lieutenant William Hamilton, born in Dumfries before emigrating in his teens to South Africa, enlisting in the Coldstream Guards and dying at the Third Battle of Ypres, Passchendaele, in 1917 aged 26. In the poem 'Song of an Exile' published just before his death he dreams of the home he would never see again:

I sigh for the heat of the veld, and
the cool-flowing river;
For the crack of the trek-whip, the
shimmer of dust-laden noon:
For the day sudden dying; the croak
of the frogs, and the shiver
Of tropical night, and the stars, and
the low-hanging moon.

War brings out the best and worst in us they say. What are we to make of Robert Burns being buried in St Michael's graveyard in the uniform of the Dumfries Militia just a few hundred yards away from the window of the Globe where he'd inscribed one of the world's most effective and concise pacifist manifestos in verse?

The deities that I adore
Are social Peace and Plenty;
I'm better pleased to make one more,
Than be the death of twenty.

('I Murder Hate', Robert Burns)

Of all the war stories I've heard, it's the quirky wee ones that tell of the cunning, resilience and triumph of the human spirit that I find most appealing. How humanity transcends whatever temporary enemy we happen to have in the search for a common goal. In Mike Craig from Kirkcudbright's story, the common goal is drink. He told me of a group of six volunteers in the Stewartry in World War Two who were supposed, in the event of a German invasion, to operate a campaign of sabotage behind enemy lines. They were given responsibility for a secret bunker with ammunition and other equipment including a sealed barrel labelled 'Navy Rum – NOT to Be Opened before the Invasion.' Rather than crawling about the terrain at the dead of night and training for their terrible task, the group apparently spent three months plotting how to remove and drink the contents of the barrel without breaking the seals. When the invasion didn't transpire, the bunker was emptied and the equipment given back to the regular army, including the barrel of rum, seal unbroken but needless to say completely empty. There is war and the horror of war, but at the same time it is hard to imagine Hitler's paratroopers prevailing against men of such ingenuity and determination.

See Eddie P, Insane

War Machines: Supermarine Stranraer and HMS *Nith*

In the Second World War two war machines were made, proudly perpetuating the names of Stranraer and the Nith.

Stranraer was an important seaplane base in World War Two guarding important routes used by merchant ships against U Boats. Winston Churchill also flew in a seaplane from Stranraer on 21 June 1942, making his second visit to the USA.

Most famously in terms of the Second World War, Stranraer was also the name of an anti-submarine seaplane, the *Supermarine Stranraer* which was one of the most derided planes ever built, being variously called the Whistling Shithouse, the Flying Meccano Set, The Marpole Bridge, the Seymour Seine Net, the Strainer, the Flying Centre Section of the Lion's Gate Bridge and the Whistling Birdcage.

It never saw serious action in the RAF or in the Royal Canadian Air Force to which it was sold, but 13 Supermarine Stranraers went to Queen Charlotte Airlines in Canada for civilian use where they gained a good reputation and were well liked by their crews, though Queen Charlotte Airlines was an eccentric organisation, sometimes nicknamed the Queer Collection of Aircraft.

The inane naming of war equipment after parts of Dumfries and Galloway is somehow reinforced by the service record of HMS *Nith*, a frigate launched in 1943, which, having been sold to the Egyptians after the war, took part in the only naval engagement of the Suez Crisis of 1956, and so it got sunk by the British, yes, the same folk who built it.

See Munitions

Weans' Tales

Kids exist in their own bubbles, some say. I prefer to think they're simmering pots of creativity and influences, ready to explode in interesting ways in all directions, like a Sanquhar firework. Especially in that primary stage when no one's really tried to tell them the proper way to do things. Talk some drivel to them, give them a pen and whoooooooomph watch the result. Stand back though!

There have been several projects in the region trying to tie historical events and theories to this great sense of thoughtful wildness that is, when it comes down to it, the unabashed and raw white spirit of creativity. The poet Liz Niven and the ceramicist Andy Adair have worked on the Pictish enigma of Trusty's Hill in Gatehouse and produced some brilliant work from schools in Gatehouse and around. I told the weans of five primary schools what's known historically about the Iron Age fortress of Tynron

Doon between Moniaive and Penpont. I then read them a little-known Victorian ghost story written about it, 'Tynron Doon: A Story.'

After reading it with them asked them to do their own adventure story, tapping into the established roots and the imaginative stuff. What great results. Sarah Jones tells how she went into a tavern and heard the tale of a man's father who went up the Doon: 'No food, no water, no gear, just himself and what he had on.' The hero Rose and her friend Roman, full of bravado, go up. Rose disappears, Roman comes back down 'limping to the village, blood trailing behind'. She shouts, 'Everybody! I'm here! I'm back!' She finishes the story: 'No one was to be seen. I looked in all the buildings. Nobody.'

Danny Buckley, searching for clues to save the world from an apocalyptic plague comes to Tynron Doon because rumours have it that the ancient Egyptians hid parts of a time machine in the ground. It was thought they often travelled to the future… how else could they have built the pyramids?

John McKay goes back in time and is caught up in the hunt for a giant cat. 'Then all the shimmering was destroyed, but still the cats came, I was trapped in the past.'

The finest of all in terms of atmosphere detail and tension was by Rhu Mackenzie who reminded me of a young John Buchan:

Jamie's boots slugged in the boggy mud that surrounded the bitter heaths at the edge of the forest. 'C'mon wee Jamie, me and Krankie are waitin for you…' yelled MacDonald a scrawny old man with grey greasy hair and a bald patch. 'What's keeping ya?'… they both slung their bags higher onto their backs and set off while Jamie followed cocking his head to one side. Suddenly he stopped. Something unnatural was in the air, something strange… something old. Shrugging he carried on, admiring the temperature, the uniqueness of the forest, the bright orange pines with dew running off their ends, the sparrows chattering and flying from tree to tree.

Now what does this all add to the rich tapestry of Dumfries and Galloway you might say? Inspired by some fantastic flapdoodle, weans come back with even better, but what is history but layers of stories, the imagination taking solid form? When I first visited Knossos in Crete I thought the palace of Minos was sublime, the frescos, the colours mirroring the Aegean blue and the honey browns mimicking the soil. And I believed the bull-leapers and read my Mary Renault and that classical magic, because magic is what it is, stayed with me, infects still to a great extent all I do. And needless to say it was nearly all, in a strictly historical way, nonsense. Arthur Evans, the ruin builder, they snidely call him, piecing his palace together in the finest Art Deco manner. Good for him I say. Since history is always slipping through our fingers, mutating, changing, I like it best as a gateway to the imagination, not some dark text to conform to, for where does that dogma lead you?

Weather

Sitting here in January and watching the smooth dip of hills crowned in perpetual night, even during the day, and listening to the wind howling through the single street of the village, it's hard to escape the idea you're in some kind of graphic novel near the end of which you discover you've been in Hell, or a psychiatric ward, or both, all along. My youngest daughter is so small I fear she may one day be blown away over the horizon, but she's more upbeat about the situation than me. In fact she's extremely jealous of one of her acquaintances who had to be rescued by helicopter from her house two weeks ago. 'Why has that never happened to us?' she demands, tapping her small foot. My older daughter used to say the same thing about the safety card on aeroplanes, hugely disappointed because the oxygen masks never appeared or the plane didn't actually ditch in the Mediterranean even though she had removed her shoes especially for the safety slide.

Winter has always been with us but drabness never so much.

Mactaggart is full of weather references but many of them are about snow. Likewise the old tales are about snow and ice. The Seven Sons of Morrison who went curling lustily with some fairy girls near Dalbeattie did so after the 'frost held for week after week after week with brilliant days and black bitter starlit nights'. Of course the ice broke and they drowned, as did the 'Robber Baron' of Cardoness Castle with his son and nine daughters, when the ice on the Black Loch gave way under the weight of their feast. Many of the tales of one of my favourite and most underrated Galloway authors, John Herries McCulloch, take place in snowdrifts and involve plucky border collies. In *Galloway Heather*, the recently bereaved Alick Maclear, alone in the world apart from his dog Laddie, sits in his cottage in a blizzard, his thoughts turning to suicide, when he decides to go out and dig out his sheep, finding something he didn't bargain for:

Little did he realise, as he battled against the blinding snow on that bleak Galloway coast... that nature was applying her own peculiar balm to his wound, and that after that night on the blizzard swept hills, things would never be the same for him again. Yet so it was to be. The collie suddenly stopped in a hollow in the slope running down to the edge of the cliffs, and commenced to bark. Alick was soon by his side, and, bending down, saw, almost covered with snow, the form of a girl about his own age, benumbed and senseless. The dead form of a sailor lay a few yards further down the slope, and on the breast of his seaman's jersey was the name 'Navarre'.

You can see that kind of thing happening in a blizzard but I bet if I go out now in this monotone drabness, in this light to heavy drizzle, this smirr, I won't find some lassie lying in the heather, or fairies to play with. All I'll get is a chill and profound depression. Alick uses the blizzard to cure his psychological ailment, but surely you need some extreme weather event for that. I've spent part of the morning scanning Mactaggart for weather references and there are many for snow and not many to express my mood between

November and March, so I've had to invent my own.

In the language of this remote area there are many terms for the feeling you get when you see a grey mist creeping down a cold hill where some wet sheep are waiting stoically:

Drod (n) Dull indefinable feeling of being involved in a scene that prefigures one's own death, as in 'This morning my father woke to a peculiar sense of drod'

Sleugh (n) Psychosomatic, but terrifyingly real, sense of nausea, often experienced in natural surroundings

Drod an sleugh

Fister (verb) To creep sickeningly slowly like an injured beast, or a disease, as in 'Uncle Ansel is fistering down the road'

Fistering drod

Fistering drod an sleugh

Shommers (n) plural (colloquial) A group of things that might be imagined but are very real to the person that experiences them

Shommers o drod

Shommers o drod an fistering sleugh

Dwank (adj) (archaic) Black, sodden, wet, often in relation to a carcass, as in 'Last night I found a dwank horse's head under the duvet'.

Dwank shommers o drod

Dwank an fistering shommers o drod
Dwank shommers o fistering drod

Crombled (adj) Crippled, hunched, incapacitated as if by great age or boredom

Crombled wi drod

Flacking (adj) Too weak to move while simultaneously exasperated

Flacking crombled

Flacking crombled wi drod

Flacking crombled wi shommers o drod an fistering sleugh

('Flacking Crombled wi Shommers o Drod an Fistering Sleugh')

*See **Lauren in Snaw and Flood***

Willie McMeekin, Dyker

When I was trying to be a teacher in the late 1970s I worked in Newton Stewart for three months, lodging at a boarding house in the town. My intention was to keep my head down and become a half-decent professional. It was terrible luck therefore to fall, within the first half hour of arriving, under the influence of Galloway's greatest drystane dyker, raconteur and drunkard of modern times, Willie McMeekin. McMeekin, originally of New Luce, ranged through Dumfries and Galloway from the '50s to the '90s, building dykes and often engaging in a range of other activities of the sort that generally gets you recognised as a character by people, and sometimes by the police.

I had wandered into the bar of the Black Horse, a pub I was very pleased to see still in rollicking good shape recently by the way, during the Wigtown Book Festival, and there he was, drinking whisky. I don't think it was that day he told me of his theory about olive oil and whisky, or the supernatural story of his grandfather's pipe, or his adventures in the Eighth Army when, as a Scots Guard and 'D-Day Dodger' he'd fought his way through Italy, Monte Cassino and all. I think, excellent story-teller that he was, he drip fed me these tales over the next 20 years just to keep me interested, and of course to keep the whisky coming.

He died about ten years ago, but you still come across people who will talk about Willie at length, probably because he still owes them money or because they remember that boyish grin as he sat back on his seat or barstool and spun some impossible story.

My friend Tony, from Castle Douglas and now resident in Sandyhills, has good cause to remember him. Willie was an excellent fisherman though notoriously poor at having permits for it. One day Tony came into a pub in Dumfries and we got talking to Willie, who was obviously a bit depleted of funds, and Tony said he could do with a really good, big salmon and would be prepared to pay for it. He was expecting it the following weekend or something like that. Willie rubbed his grizzled chin and replied in his Galloway Irish lilt that it was a distinct possibility and could we just wait there? Within ten minutes he was back with a giant salmon in a bin bag, headless and gutted. My friend paid him the money and Willie scarpered to one of his other haunts, leaving us to deal, ten minutes afterwards with the chef of a nearby hotel who had been about to cook it for a wedding banquet when it had vanished from the kitchen table.

Willie's theory about drinking was that he made sure to swallow a dessert spoonful of olive oil before starting. This is a classic Mediterranean tactic which he claimed to have learned in Italy during the war, and it does work, they say, in that it slows down the body's absorption of alcohol as well as providing detoxins which help the hangover. However it was only in Willie's description that the science was properly explained. 'The oil maks a puddle in yer stomach and the fumes which mak ye intoxicated canna get through to the brain,' he intoned gravely. 'The whisky has tae work doonwards. It's why sometimes yer thinkin clear as a bell but yer legs dinna work.'

Willie carried various clippings around in his wallet. He had been a champion dyker, a judge in national competitions, and was pretty contemptuous of those who he thought didn't do a good job or didn't pay enough for it. 'I never met a farmer who said he couldnae dyke,' he used to say, 'and I never met a farmer who could.' He was proud of his army record too, always wearing his Scots Guards tie, and often recalling the day he and his comrades had been praised by General Montgomery. 'Taller men I have seen, but braver, never.'

In his weather-beaten countenance, in that lilting voice, in, above all, his mischievous rootlessness, he summed up a whole way of life in Galloway which was and is timeless.

Willie said his dykes would last hundreds of years and the Galloway landscape has many dykes of such age. Willie once took me with him, to watch him work, tell me some of the craft. As we sat in the hills above New Abbey I remember him leaning back on his handiwork, sipping the gruesome mix of whisky and strong tea he favoured in his flask. It was a good day, a broad blue sky and the country below filling with spring. 'The land is ours,' he said, softly, 'the land is ours.'

And somehow it was just possible the way he said it, to believe it was true.

> His face is a map
> and like all landscapes
> is variable.
> Willie hasn't always been good.
> I think he predates such concepts.
> He is both sides of a very old coin.
> The man is Galloway.
> ('Willie')

See Dykers, Levellers

Woodcutters

In *The Woodcutters*, a painting by Castle Douglas artist William Stewart MacGeorge of the Kirkcudbright School, woodsmen use a two-handed saw on a fallen tree-trunk. Behind them tall trees sway russet against a sun streaked autumn sky in meadow carpeted by grass and flowers. MacGeorge uses a similar tree trunk in another painting, *The See-Saw*, where six long haired girls are playing with a branch laid over a fallen tree. Three have just fallen off, onto long lush grass and bracken. Even given Hornel and Co's inclination to transplant and frantically paint pre-pubescent girls into woodland settings, these are bucolic scenes hard to reconcile with Badger and Scotty's workplace in a forest near Gatehouse, an industrial-scale operation of mud and fumes and noise. Scotty is driving the Forwarder, a tree-cutting machine, with which he, a skilled operative, can fell about 2,000 tons of wood per week. The Badger has the machine at weekends and is catching up fast. Badger has a twinkle in his eye and a white beard. He could be a fairy tale woodsman, in fact, but 'it's a' changed noo, specially ower the last 20 years, it's a' high tech'.

In woods like the one in which Scotty and Badger work, woodsmen used to live, building their own shacks or later using caravans. A local worthy from Newton Stewart told me of the lifestyle of some of them he knew, 'They used to get drunk and run about the woods naked, men and women. Must have thought they were nymphs. God knows whose kid was whose.'

I tell Badger this and he twinkles some more. 'Sounds guid to me boy, but I dinnae think the wife would like it.'

See Art

X

X-Factor

About 15 years ago the Scots papers were full of news about an organisation called Scottish Watch which set out to monitor people who had moved into Dumfries and Galloway, purportedly to point out how they deprived local inhabitants of housing, a living and so on. There was a military arm to this, it was feared. There had been various 'attacks'. This was sensationalism, of course, though there had been some incidents, mostly, peculiarly, taking the form of removing or cutting television aerials from holiday houses. The sinister organisation behind this was run, it was reported, from a secret location deep in the region, by a militant called 'Mister X'. The security services were bamboozled. I wasn't. I knew his wife, who often referred to herself openly, even at the hairdresser's, as 'Mrs X'. Her husband, needless to say, was a TV repair man, thus explaining the chosen method of direct action. In Galloway, a little militancy can always be combined with the entrepreneurial spirit.

*See **Bank Managers, SR Crockett** and the British Union of Fascist Lifeguards* *y*

Yes & No & Amy McFall

I was there with the Scots and Catalan flags waving in George Square on the 18 September 2014, the day of the Scottish Referendum, and then with the Loyalists expressing their culture on the 19th. I had a grandstand view of the joy and the tears and the throwback thuggery, and now, in the ruins of the Referendum, I am back in Dumfries and Galloway. The Yes vote was strong in the places that needed dynamic change, and the No vote strongest in places that were doing quite well, thank you very much, depopulating nicely.

On the train south I heard one young boy saying, 'next time it'll be a yes cos all these old fuckers will be dead', a sentiment that had crossed my mind, too, though I dismissed it selfishly on account of being an old fucker myself. It did make me think though about what effect the whole process was having on the young who were so fully engaged in the campaign. Would the disappointment make them more disillusioned with Scotland, especially the bit on the bottom left whose young people have always deserted in droves? I ask Amy McFall.

Amy McFall is bright, beautiful, motivated and talented, just the kind of person whose genes would be traditionally welcomed in Australia or New Zealand. She's for staying though:

'On the 19th I stayed in bed all day being thoroughly miserable. All the hours of intelligent radio debate and bitter Facebook slagging alike had been, then, wasted. I say 'then' because on that day I felt as close to pointless as I hope I'll ever feel, but that's changed. The country's changed. The unenlightened are being led by the obstinate; those people who still press their "Yes" stickers to the window every morning, or brush a bright little badge in their pocket when they fumble for change.'

Amy is at University and a Member of the Scottish Youth Parliament. And a poet, I bet:

'The Dumfries & Galloway vote didn't exactly disappoint me. The region has pheasants, an

English border and a smooth-
talking Tory MP; what else could
we have expected? People are
people no matter where you go,
it's the lifestyles that make the
difference. Our region is rich, it
didn't need any more than it had.
It's the poorest Scottish towns and
cities that voted Yes. So no, I'm
not disappointed. I'm just a little
morose. I do try to distance
myself from the 'No'-ness,
though, by considering my soul as
a Glasgow one.'

I wouldn't dream of leaving
Scotland, but Dumfries and
Galloway? I can't promise
anything, there.

Zeitgeist, Thomas Carlyle, Walter Scott, Frederick the Great, and Hitler

I am in Annan after a meeting of the Thomas Carlyle Society and now in The Shed, a pub popular because it has 28 different television screens. Watching three football matches, darts and a horse meeting in Australia is a pleasure after a hard hour thinking about Thomas Carlyle and how he might be made accessible to the public. I respect Thomas Carlyle because he overcame terrible bullying at school in Annan and developed, possibly as a result, the theory of 'The Great Man' which was highly popular in a Victorian Society that imagined itself full of such creatures. I respect him too because he is another literary giant from Dumfries and Galloway. However he has fallen from fashion and not just because his theory of history has been largely superseded by the zeitgeist, the idea that people are shaped by their times and society rather than the other way round, but also because his style is difficult and dense. Walter Scott's prose is

difficult and dense too but somehow you can vividly imagine the heaving bosoms and flashing claymores and admire the man for trying to reinvent a country that had wilfully abandoned its identity.

No such luck for Thomas Carlyle who had some baggage which is very hard to admire. He called Disraeli 'a cursed old Jew not worth his weight in bacon'. And whose reputation could recover from the knowledge that when the Russians at last broke into the Fuhrerbunker at nine o clock in the morning on the 2 May 1945, the book sitting on Hitler's bedside table was *The Life of Frederick the Great* by one Thomas Carlyle? Apparently, in the last few days before his suicide, the only way Hitler could get to sleep was if Goebbels would sit beside him and read from the great man's work. You wonder what the last passage was that Goebbels read before padding off to give his six children those cyanide pills?

Maybe it was a grudging acceptance that the Great Men Theory of History was at last dead, so Long Live the zeitgeist, or as Carlyle put it, 'Happy the people whose annals are blank in history books.' He could have been referring to the people in this book, and those in John Mactaggart's *Gallovidian Encyclopedia*, because, when I read it, I breathe-in a Galloway full of rich language, poetry, but most of all, ordinary people.

And finally, John Mactaggart

Mactaggart carefully and lovingly describes a rural population who were poor but whose spirits were anything but crushed. His times were exciting times, and people were not afraid to engage in direct action, whether it was ambushing policemen, tearing down dykes or tossing avaricious merchants into the Solway. It was a time when only 2 per cent of the population could vote, when the land was owned, as ever, by a tiny minority but when the ordinary sons of shepherds could dream of becoming professors, generals or engineers and sometimes make those dreams reality. When you breathe in that book, you breathe in the human spirit with all the failings, generosities, complexities and hopes of a living vibrant population. The same have been mentioned in this book too, including the person I saw emerging from a wigwam near New Galloway, early the other morning, and auld heids like Willie McMeekin and Bobby Dalrymple and a new generation of dreamers such as Rhu MacKenzie and Amy McFall, whose spirits may help Dumfries and Galloway retain its stubborn, time-honoured identity, and not simply become a playground for the rich and the retired.

Gazetteer

Some of the objects, places and people in this book are real. Selected locations, for the curious, are listed below:

Anwoth Kirk · NX582562
Iconic ruined chapel, where some raunchy scenes from the cult classic the Wicker Man were filmed. Not far from Trusty's Hill (NX589560) a vitrified iron age hill fort famous for its wacky and largely unexplained Pictish carvings, one of which appears to be a spaceman with droopy antennae.

JM Barrie, Traces Of
In Dumfries Barrie lived in a house in Dumfries with a rather beautiful inscription outside, **6 Victoria Terrace, DG1 1NL** but sooner or later everyone's going to think he lived in Moat Brae House, George Street, DG1 1EA, a beautiful Georgian house which is in the course of being renovated and transformed into a centre of children's literature, helped by Joanna Lumley et al. This was the house of wee Jim's pal Stuart Gordon, the garden of which is claimed to be where he first thought up that nefarious book (his words not mine), Peter Pan. The really cool thing to do if you're a Barrie Fan would be to blag your way into Dumfries Academy next door where, untouched by the Moat Brae Foundation, traces of the man still exist in a kind of dilapidated stasis, his name on the prize boards for instance, or even more exotic, the JM Barrie piece of wood.

Broughton House, 12 High St, Kirkcudbright, DG6 4JX
The pile of EA Hornell, Scottish colourist, and a museum which contains a lot of his artwork and his huge collection of folk history.

Burrowhead · NX 457 340
A place of joint significance, the last place the fairies left Scotland, and the place where in the film *The Wicker Man*, the eponymous structure was burned, with the Glasgow Polis and sundry chickens and waterfowl inside. Until recently you could see the base of this but someone's nicked it. Also the site of a WW2 army camp and two miles past some promontory forts

along the cliffs from St Ninian's Cave. Particularly atmospheric at dusk in November.

Carsethorne
Major emigration port though you wouldn't know it now. In one year 1850, 10,000 left from a single pier here to America, Australia and Canada. Stand on the shore and imagine the despair and the emptying land then go for a pint in the Steamboat Inn. Great Irish chef there, as I write.

Crawick Multiverse · NS775115
An art and landscape installation in reclaimed mining site designed by Charles Jenks. Lots of stone circles and spirals. Make sure you visit here at the same time as a performance of the dance troupe www.oceanallover. co.uk because no arts event is worthy of the name unless it is attended by people dressed as prawns.

Creetown
A village often lauded as a model of rural regeneration, the only open business or premises in which seems to be the regeneration office. Or at least that's what it was like when I was last there. It is however famous for having, when it's open, the pub featured in *The Wicker Man* and a series of large public art works including *The Ferry Bell*, and work by Hideo Furuta of which the citizens are I'm sure justly proud.

Galloway Dark Skies Park
The UK's first. You can see up to 7,000 stars because due to depopulation no-one really lives here anyway. The few that do are seriously inconvenienced by special lighting that enables folk to observe the skies but not properly find their way home. If they get lost they can always shelter under the many pieces of public art here.

German Air Base · NX 326422
Fascinating remains, testament to the subtlety and skill of German imperial engineers who managed to build and conceal such a significant installation in the hills of Galloway. Remains of two hangers of considerable size and an accommodation block. From these buildings zeppelins bombed Criffel and shot at Richard Hannay.

Hugh MacDiarmid's Book
NT 382857
Large rusting memorial above Langholm to Hugh MacDiarmid a communist Scottish nationalist who singlehandedly revived Scottish poetry in the 20th century, or so the story goes.

Kirkcudbright or Pistapolis

The Omphalos of Galloway, what hasn't happened here? The first St Trinian's cartoon, Lawrence of Arabia, Pink Floyd's Manager, loads of artists, the man who saved Robert Burns' Life, the list goes on and on. In a region that's trading more and more on its emptiness and desolation here's a town that's keeping its chin above water without simultaneously turning itself into an Experience or bourgeois freak show. See also for residual grittiness in the face of it, **Annan, Sanquhar, Dalbeattie.**

Michael Scott Wizard

Resident for the last 700 years in Glenluce Abbey (NX185587). He keeps the devil as a lodger so watch when you call. Still waiting to save Scotland from something, but, even though I've left him many suggestions, has shown no sign of recent activity. Glenluce Abbey is the scene of the Legendary Necromantic Library but lots of real history, too.

Monreith

Mystical area full of ancient sites, and stones akin to Kilmartin in Argyll. Lots of ruins and romance. Near here Gavin Maxwell walked his otter on the beach and St Medan pulled out her eyes rather than be seduced by a poet, silly girl.

Mull of Galloway · NX155165T

The southernmost part of Scotland, further south than Hartlepool in fact. A place of ancient significance, historical and religious. St Medan supposedly had a chapel here before she pulled her eyes out. The double ditches across the isthmus speak of last ditch defence if you'll excuse the pun and this is reputed to be where the last Picts jumped for it rather than give the Romans the secret of Heather Ale. Lighthouse open to the public. Nearest beer five miles away in Scotland's most southerly village, Drummore.

Nith Cross · NX 868 954

Beautiful but neglected Northumbrian cross, 1,500 years old. In a striking spot near a tragic ferry crossing and the grave of an elephant.

Stove Initiative in Dumfries 100 High Street, Dumfries DG1 2BJ

An Artists' co-operative seeking to inspire and regenerate the people of Dumfries through engagement in the arts. Premises open most days, regular exhibitions. There are also popular Arts Centres in **Sanquhar A, the Airts 8–12, High St,** DG4 6BL and New

Galloway **The CatStrand, High St, DG7 3RN** as well as a gallery and performance space in Gatehouse of Fleet **The Bakehouse, 44 The High Street, DG7 2HP.**

The Bench at Douglas Hall
NX832614
A seat with magical properties, where film stars are often spotted chatting together

The pub that wasn't in the Wickerman
The Steampacket Inn, St Cuthberts Place, Kirkcudbright, DH6 4DH a lively fishermans pub. Scenes were shot in the pub and in the alleyway outside but none made the cut.

The pub that was in the Wickerman
The Ellangowan Hotel, St John St, Creetown, DG8 7JF

The pub that should have been in the Wickerman
The Craigdarroch Hotel, High St, Moniaive, Thornhill, DG3 4HN. It's mad enough.

Whithorn
Would have been like Santiago del Compastella if only the Presbyterians hadn't smashed it to bits. A place of pilgrimage through the centuries. There's a plaque here to a native son who fought in the International Brigade. Birth place of Alasdair Reid one of Scotland's finest modern writers.

Wigtown Book Town
A small dilapidated port which some say has been transformed by the power of books. Scotland's booktown has a vibrant festival every year, run by energetic and committed staff, but has the town been saved by books or rather colonised by booksellers and occupied once a year by a strange, itinerant army of old women looking for Martin Bell? Well worth a visit whatever you think.

Selected References

Ascheron, Neil. *Stone Voices: The Search for Scotland*. Farrar, Strauss and Giroux, 2004.

Baker, Nicholson. *The Mezzanine*. Weidenfeld and Nicholson, 1988.

Barrie, J.M. *The Little White Bird*. Hodder and Stoughton, 1902.

Barrie, J.M. *Peter and Wendy*. Hodder and Stoughton, 1911.

Baldwin, Jayne. *West Over the Waves: The Final Flight of Elsie Mackay*. GC Books, 2009.

Blacklock, Thomas. 'Pistapolis, an Unpublished Poem.' *The Scottish Historical Review*, 1918.

Brader, Chris. *Timbertown Girls: Gretna Female Munitions Workers in World War I*. PhD Thesis, University of Warwick, 2001.

Brewster, Donna. *The House That Sugar Built*. MPG Books Ltd, 1999.

Brown, Allan. *Inside the Wicker Man: The Morbid Ingenuities*. Sidgwick and Jackson, 2000.

Buchan, John. *The Thirty-Nine Steps*. George H Doran Company, 1915.

Cunningham, Allan [Ed.] *The Complete Works of Robert Burns: Containing his Poems, Songs, and Correspondence*. Phillips, Sampson and Company, 1855.

Daniell, David. *The Interpreter's House: A Critical Assessment of John Buchan*. Nelson, 1975.

De Maistre, Xavier. *A Journey Round My Room*. Riverside Press, 1871.

Dumfries and Galloway Life.

Dick, Charles Hill. *Highways and Byways in Galloway and Carrick*. GC Book Publishers Ltd., 1938.

Douglas, George [Ed.] *Scottish Fairy and Folk Tales*. W. Scott, 1901.

Dudgeon, Piers. *Neverland: J.M. Barrie, the du Mauriers, and the Dark Side of Peter Pan*. Pegasus Books, 2011.

Frank, Jane. '*Making Something out of Nothing?': A Study of the Book Town Movement*. Ph.D. Thesis, Griffiths University, Australia, 2014. '*Slow Books: A Meeting of Landscape and Literature*'. Article University of Queensland Review 2015

The Gallovidian.

Gladstone, HS. *The Birds of Dumfriesshire*. Witherby and Co., 1910.

Galloway Gallimaufry: *An Anthology of Galloway Literature of the Past and Present*. Wigtownshire Local Development Group for English, 1978.

Grant, Alexander. *Royal and Magnate Bastards in the Later Middle Ages: The View from Scotland*. Lancaster University Working Paper, 2013.

Gray, Daniel. *Homage to Caledonia: Scotland and the Spanish Civil War*. Luath Press, 2008.

Hornel, E.A. *Archive and Letters*. Ewart Library, Dumfries.

Kirkwood, David. *Garlieston: Emergence of a Village. Stranraer and District Local History Trust*, 2007.

Leonard, Tom. 'Roger Quin.' Definite Articles: Prose 1973–2012. Etruscan Books, 2013.

Livingston, Alistair. GreenGalloway [Weblog]. http://greengalloway.blogspot.com/

McCullough, John Herries. *Galloway Heather*. Parry Jackman, 1955.

MacDiarmid, Hugh. *Lucky Poet: A Self-Study in Literature and Political Ideas*. Methuen and Co., Ltd, 1943.

A Conspiracy of Silence: Article in the Scottish Vanguard 1968

McDowall, William. *The History of Dumfries*. Adam and Charles Black, 1867.

McIlvanney, William. *A Gift from Nessus*. Eyre and Spottiswoode, 1968.

McMillan, Catriona. *The Whithorn Pilgrimage: A Report*. The Whithorn Trust, 2014.

Mactaggart, John. *The Scottish Gallovidian Encyclopedia*. Morison, 1876.

Maitland, Sara. *A Book of Silence: A Writer's Search for Silence in a Noisy World*. Granta, 2008.

Maxwell Wood, John. *Witchcraft and Superstitious Record in Southwest Scotland*. J Maxwell and Sons, 1911.

Mayne, John. 'The Siller Gun.' *Ruddiman's Magazine*, 1780.

On the Grass Cloud. Dumfries Academy, 2010.

Platt, Richard. *Smuggling in the British Isles: A History*. Tempus Publishing, 2007.

Scott, Walter. *Guy Mannering*. Longman, Hurst, Rees, Orme and Brown, 1815.

Smiles, Samuel. *The Life of Thomas Telford*. Kessinger Publishing, 2004.

Temperley, Alan. *Tales of Galloway*. Mainstream Publishing, 2005.

Tolstoy, Nikolai. *The Quest for Merlin*. Little Brown and Co., 1985.

Trotter, Maria and Robert De Bruce Trotter. *Galloway Gossip Sixty Years Ago: Being a Series of Articles Illustrative of the Manners, Customs and Peculiarities of the Aboriginal Picts of Galloway.* 1877.

Westwood, Jennifer and Sophia Kingshill. *The Lore of Scotland: A Guide to Scottish Legends.* Arrow, 2011.

Williams, Chris. *A Companion to Nineteenth Century Britain.* Blackwell, 2004.

Luath Press Limited

committed to publishing well written books worth reading

LUATH PRESS takes its name from Robert Burns, whose little collie Luath (*Gael.,* swift or nimble) tripped up Jean Armour at a wedding and gave him the chance to speak to the woman who was to be his wife and the abiding love of his life.

Burns called one of 'The Twa Dogs' Luath after Cuchullin's hunting dog in Ossian's *Fingal*. Luath Press was established in 1981 in the heart of Burns country, and now resides a few steps up the road from Burns' first lodgings on Edinburgh's Royal Mile.

Luath offers you distinctive writing with a hint of unexpected pleasures.

Most bookshops in the UK, the US, Canada, Australia, New Zealand and parts of Europe either carry our books in stock or can order them for you. To order direct from us, please send a £sterling cheque, postal order, international money order or your credit card details (number, address of cardholder and expiry date) to us at the address below. Please add post and packing as follows: UK – £1.00 per delivery address; overseas surface mail – £2.50 per delivery address; overseas airmail – £3.50 for the first book to each delivery address, plus £1.00 for each additional book by airmail to the same address. If your order is a gift, we will happily enclose your card or message at no extra charge.

Luath Press Limited
543/2 Castlehill
The Royal Mile
Edinburgh EH1 2ND
Scotland
Telephone: 0131 225 4326 (24 hours)
email: sales@luath.co.uk
Website: www.luath.co.uk